Employee Lifestyle and Off-Duty Conduct Regulation

Employee Lifestyle and Off-Duty Conduct Regulation

MARVIN F. HILL, JR.
Professor of Industrial Relations
Northern Illinois University

JAMES A. WRIGHT
Attorney at Law

The Bureau of National Affairs, Inc., Washington, D.C.

Copyright © 1993
The Bureau of National Affairs, Inc.

Library of Congress Cataloging-in-Publication Data

Hill, Marvin.
    Employee lifestyle and off-duty conduct regulation/Marvin F.
Hill, James A. Wright.
      p. cm.
      "BNA books."
      Includes index.
      ISBN 0-87179-778-X
      1. Labor law and legislation—United States. 2. Privacy, Right
of—United States. 3. Labor discipline—United States.
4. Employees—United States—Conduct of life. 5. Employees—
dismissal of—Law and legislation—United States. I. Wright,
James A. (James Allan), 1962– . II. Title.
KF3540.H55 1993
344.73'012598—dc20
[347.30412598]   93-24696
                                                    CIP

Authorization to photocopy items for internal or personal use, or
the internal or personal use of specific clients, is granted by BNA
Books for libraries and other users registered with the Copyright
Clearance Center (CCC) Transactional Reporting Service, pro-
vided that $1 per page is paid directly to CCC, 27 Congress St.,
Salem, MA 01970. 0-87179-778-X/93/$1.

Published by BNA Books
1250 23rd St., N.W., Washington, D.C. 20037
International Standard Book Number: 0-87179-778-X
Printed in the United States of America

Preface

The Immutable Law of Broadway (and its Immutable Corollary) is that flops outnumber hits and playwrights and producers keep trying to "get it right." Compounding the problem, hits don't always make money.[1] The Immutable Laws also apply to writing books, especially books for employment advocates and arbitrators where movie rights will never be sold and the book will never see the inside of a bookstore at an airport.

This text represents an examination of the problems that exist when employers attempt to condition employment decisions on the lifestyle or off-duty conduct of its employees. To a significant extent the law has laid traps of constraints for the unwary. We have tried to "get it right" by examining these traps under individual headings, although we recognize that there is often overlap between the categories. We make no claims that all employers will find the answer to questions involving the particular lifestyle that produces doubts in the employer's view. Still, we believe that most problems are treated extensively and to this end we offer the reader something to aid in decision making.

Marvin Hill
James Wright

---

[1] Bruce Weber, "Make Money on Broadway? Break a Leg," N.Y. Times, June 3, 1993, at A-1.

Acknowledgments

Special thanks go to Emily Delacenserie, John McCarthy, and Amy Evenson (a.k.a., "Little Orphan Iowa"), former law students at the College of Law, Northern Illinois University, for their fine research efforts. Marvin will miss all of you more than you will miss him!

Contents

Chapter 1

Introduction

Examples of situations where management effects discipline or discharge because management disapproves of an employee's off-duty conduct or lifestyle are numerous. A recent example follows.

In Greenburgh, New York, Paul Solomon, once a popular sixth-grade teacher, faced possible dismissal for his role in the "Fatal Attraction" case involving the shooting death of his wife, Betty Jeanne Solomon. Mr. Solomon, who was granted immunity from prosecution, admitted in open court to having numerous extramarital affairs, including an affair with a fellow teacher, Carolyn Warmus, convicted in a second trial for the murder of Mrs. Solomon after a hung jury in her first trial. Leon Leighton, an 88-year-old lawyer who has lived in the community for 47 years, sent a letter to 100 citizens asking them to press the school board for Solomon's dismissal. Leighton is quoted in the *New York Times* to have said that "what he has done is immoral" and returning Solomon to the classroom would be "an unforgivable outrage to the integrity of our school system and a body blow to our property values."[1] Others have echoed similar concerns with Solomon's ability to function as a role model for students.[2]

---

[1] *Some Ask if Husband in Love-Triangle Case Is Fit to Teach*, N.Y. TIMES, Aug. 17, 1991, §1, at 23, Col. 2.

[2] Nadine Brozan, *A Post-Trial Question: Should Adulterer Teach?*, N.Y. TIMES, Aug. 17, 1991, at 23. In September 1991, Paul Solomon was denied classroom duties although he still draws full pay.

What *should* management, in this case the board of education, do? Even more interesting, what *can* management do in response to the citizens' desire to terminate the contract of Mr. Solomon? Would it be constitutional for Paul Solomon to be held to a higher standard of behavior than other employees of the district (the janitor, for example)? To what extent can private and public sector employers regulate or control, under threat of discipline or discharge, an employee's personal off-duty conduct or lifestyle? Can management withhold a benefit or promotion because of the employee's unhealthy or bizarre lifestyle?

Additional instances where management concerns itself with the employee's off-duty conduct, lifestyle, or the results of that lifestyle, including the following examples, are numerous.

American Airlines, like most carriers, has promulgated weight standards for flight attendants. Those who are overweight according to standard height and weight tables are placed on leave. If the weight standard is not met within a designated period, dismissal follows.[3]

In Cranston, Rhode Island, a hospital attendant is refused employment with her former employer, the State of Rhode Island, because at 315 pounds she is considered fat. Management believes that its workers' compensation costs might rise if it rehires her.[4]

Sol Wachtler, Chief Justice of New York State's highest court, is charged with attempting to extort $20,000 and threatening to kidnap the 14-year-old daughter of the woman who broke off an affair with him. A federal judge orders him detained in his home, monitored by electronic surveillance and private security guards. His six associate judges, after a private meeting to consider Mr. Wachtler's fate, decide to do nothing, treating his incarceration as they would a temporary illness.[5]

A bus driver, who received extensive publicity for his off-duty activities as Acting Grand Dragon of the Ku Klux Klan, is discharged

---

[3]*In The Air, A New Battle Over Weight,* N.Y. TIMES, Apr. 2, 1990, at A12.

[4]The Providence chapter of the American Civil Liberties Union (ACLU), Lynette Labinger, of counsel, has filed a lawsuit against the State of Rhode Island in U.S. district court. *See* Cook v. State of Rhode Island, Dep't of Mental Health, Retardation and Hosps., C.A. No. 90-0560-T (D.R.I. 1991).

[5]Josh Barbanel, *Top Judge Quits New York Court Over a Scandal,* N.Y. TIMES, Nov. 11, 1992, at A1.

for his "political" activities. Management rejects outright the employee's constitutional arguments relating to free speech and association.[6]

The Omaha Girls Club dismisses an unmarried staff member because she conceived a child out of wedlock. According to management, her condition made her a negative role model to the children and, thus, unsuitable for continued employment.[7] Similarly, Phillips Exeter, a prestigious New Hampshire preparatory school concerned with its public image, terminates its drama teacher upon his arrest for possession and shipment of child pornography.[8] And in Illinois, the School District of Barrington, in response to student and parent inquiries, dismisses Gerald Eberhardt, an elementary school physical education teacher after a community newspaper reports his arrest for disorderly conduct after he left a restaurant "clad only in a white shirt and dark socks." When asked why he was not wearing underwear and pants, Eberhardt responded that he was "doing his own thing."[9]

Concluding that management had to take steps to help contain medical costs and that "there are certain lifestyle decisions that we are just not going to assure the results of,"[10] the Circle K Corporation, the nation's second-largest convenience store chain, announced that it would terminate the medical coverage of "employees who become sick or injured as a result of AIDS, alcohol, drug abuse or self-inflicted wounds."[11]

The Walt Disney Company, in the midst of hiring some 12,000 employees to maintain and populate its Euro Disneyland theme park in Marne-la-Vallee, 20 miles east of Paris, has spelled out a dress and appearance code that goes beyond height and weight requirements. The rules mandate strict guidelines on the length of men's hair, and prohibit facial hair and the display of tattoos. Women's hair must be one natural color, and women can use only limited amounts of makeup. Further, the length of women's fingernails is restricted and false

---

[6]Baltimore Transit Co., 47 LA 62 (1966) (Duff, Arb.).
[7]Chambers v. Omaha Girls Club, Inc., 834 F.2d 697, 45 FEP Cases 698 (8th Cir. 1987), *reh'g denied en banc,* 840 F.2d 583, 46 FEP Cases 117 (1988).
[8]*Pornography Jury Convicts Teacher,* N.Y. TIMES, Oct. 10, 1992, at 7.
[9]Board of Educ., Barrington, Ill. Dist. 220 v. Eberhardt (1980) (Maslanka, Arb.) (unpublished).
[10]Kenneth Noble, *Company Halting Health Plan On Some "Life Style" Illnesses,* N.Y. TIMES, Aug. 6, 1988, at A1.
[11]*Id.*

eyelashes and other eye makeup are completely disallowed. Women are allowed one earring in each ear with the earring's diameter no more than 2 centimeters. Neither men nor women can wear more than one ring on each hand. Further, women are required to wear "appropriate undergarments" and only transparent pantyhose (no black or anything with fancy designs).[12] Although a daily bath is not mentioned in the rules, employees are expected to appear for work "fresh and clean."[13] Similar rules are in force at Disney's other three theme parks. The French government has lodged a formal complaint against Disney.[14]

An executive is dismissed because he was accompanied by someone other than his spouse at a convention. The executive argues that nothing less than a public policy is at issue and that management should not be allowed to effect a dismissal simply because the employee's lifestyle is different than that of his superiors.[15]

Edward Eadie, described as a disgruntled postal worker and recently released from a New Jersey psychiatric facility, was found by Virginia police to have more than a dozen firearms and 1,000 rounds of ammunition at his home. Of passing interest to management, Mr. Eadie was also found to have a poster-sized picture of a top postal official on his living room wall. Police reported that cross hairs were drawn on the official's face.[16]

Other examples include the Turner Broadcasting System, which will not consider employees for employment if they are smokers,[17] and U-Haul International, where workers who smoke or are underweight or overweight pay for their health insurance.

Is there a remedy in the courts or through labor arbitration for any of these employees, including the Mr. Solomons of the world, if management elects to effect a dismissal because the employee does not fit the company's ideal of what a good employee is, both on and

---

[12]*A Disney Dress Code Chafes in the Land of Haute Couture*, N.Y. TIMES, Dec. 25, 1991, at A1.

[13]*Id.*

[14]*Id.*

[15]Staats v. Ohio Nat'l Life Ins. Co., 620 F. Supp. 118, 118 LRRM 3242 (W.D. Pa. 1985) (upholding dismissal and rejecting public policy argument).

[16]*Va. Police Confiscate Gun Cache*, WASHINGTON POST, Oct. 7, 1992, at D6.

[17]J. Ellison, *Busybodies: New Puritans*, TIME, Aug. 12, 1991, at 20; *cf.* Grusendorf v. City of Oklahoma City, 816 F.2d 539, 2 IER Cases 51 (10th Cir. 1987). *Grusendorf* is discussed *infra* Chapter 2 note 80 and accompanying text.

off the job? What are the limits of management's power to regulate the individual lifestyles and off-duty behavior of employees, even when those lifestyles have little or no relation to the job in question? Are the rules different for public sector employers, both in and outside of the arbitration forum, where constitutional standards are operative? If employees are covered under a collective bargaining agreement and have access to the grievance-arbitration procedure, what are their chances of a successful challenge in the arbitration forum? When is arbitration an effective remedy? Will arbitrators, deciding cases in the public sector, accord more deference to management than they would to private sector companies because of the applicability of the Constitution to public employees? Are the rules different for the protective services? Should a special exception be carved out for the Postal Service, with the largest civilian work force in the country, where workplace violence is not uncommon?

This book will review judicial, administrative, and arbitral case law, both in the private and public sectors, dealing with employer attempts to regulate the personal lifestyles and off-duty behavior of employees.[18] Remedies under common law and federal statutes will be reviewed with a special focus on Title VII of the Civil Rights Act of 1964,[19] as recently amended, the Federal Rehabilitation Act of

---

[18]*Lifestyle*, noun. Also *life-style, life style*. "An internally consistent way of life or style of living that reflects the attitudes and values of an individual or a culture." AMERICAN HERITAGE DICTIONARY 452 (3d ed. 1979).

"The consistent, integrated way of life of an individual as typified by his manner, attitudes, possessions, etc." WEBSTER'S NEW WORLD DICTIONARY 398 (2d ed. 1986) (which lists it as two words).

As used in this text, "lifestyle" refers to all areas in life where an employee could expect that an employer would not interfere, such as sexual practices and identity, credit and financial references, off-duty drug or alcohol use, and religious practices. Other areas include medical infirmities, grooming and dress requirements, speech, and political and personal associations, all of which can impact or reflect the individual's way of life. In limiting most of the analysis to these areas we do not suggest that there are not other facets of lifestyle that may impact an employment decision. We confess to some sins of commission (for example, a one-time drug conviction, sometimes sufficient for dismissal from employment, may not reflect an employee's lifestyle) and omission (we left out the parts that people would skip!). Limiting a discussion of off-duty conduct and lifestyle to these areas will not alter our analysis or conclusions.

[19]Pub. L. No. 88-352, 78 Stat. 241 (1964), discussed *infra* Chapter 3 notes 2–141 and accompanying text.

1973,[20] and the Americans with Disabilities Act.[21] Constitutional limitations on public employers are discussed in the analysis. Our investigation also includes a review of published and unpublished private and public sector arbitration decisions in those cases where management's employment decisions are challenged under a just cause standard through the grievance-arbitration procedure.[22] A synthesis and conclusion follow with guidelines recommending when employer interference with employee lifestyles or off-duty conduct is appropriate.

One theme that emerges from studying court, administrative, and arbitral rulings is that absent a relationship or nexus between the employee's off-duty conduct or lifestyle and his or her on-the-job performance, or a significant showing that the employee's conduct affects the employer's product or reputation, any regulation or inquiry impacting off-duty conduct or lifestyles is suspect. A presumption often operates, both in the judicial and the arbitral forums, in favor of the employee when management effects discipline because of off-duty conduct. While at common law no nexus between the conduct complained of and the employee's job need be shown, courts and arbitrators often afford some protection from arbitrary dismissal to public sector employees and individuals covered under collective bargaining agreements. Accordingly, a secondary thesis is that employers covered under a collective bargaining agreement should not rely on the common law, employment-at-will rule in disciplining or dismissing employees. Indeed, there are a number of federal and state statutes that significantly restrict management's ability to effect a termination because of lifestyle or off-duty infirmities. To this end, Chapter 2 discusses the rights of employers and employees at common law. Chapter 3 addresses major statutory restrictions impacting manage-

---

[20]29 U.S.C. §794 (1991), discussed *infra* Chapter 3 notes 149–208 and accompanying text.

[21]42 U.S.C. §§12101-12112 (Supp. 1990), discussed *infra* Chapter 3 notes 209–230 and accompanying text.

[22]Some challenges to regulations regarding an employee's lifestyle, such as a regulation involving an employee's grooming, weight, or sexual preference, may be cognizable under the Constitution, a federal or state fair employment or rehabilitation statute, and arbitration under a collective bargaining agreement. When expedient, such restrictions are discussed in more than one section. In general, specific restrictions will be addressed in those sections where most of the litigation has occurred or, alternatively, where management's limitations are severely restricted.

ment's ability to regulate the lifestyles and off-duty conduct of employees. Chapter 4 discusses the U.S. Constitution as a remedy for public sector employees. Chapter 5 analyzes decisions of arbitrators for those employees covered under a collective bargaining agreement with arbitration as a remedy. A conclusion and synthesis follow in Chapter 6.

Chapter 2

Employers and Workers at Common Law

During the eighteenth and nineteenth centuries, without regard to considerations of fairness to employees, employers effectively had total discretion in directing all phases of their business. Under an 1877 legal principle, the employer-employee relationship was "at will," meaning that employment could be terminated at the will of either party, although usually the employer's, for a good reason,[1] a bad

---

[1]The term "good cause" is "largely relative in [its] connotation depending upon the particular circumstances of each case.... Essentially [it] connotes a fair and honest cause or reason, regulated by good faith on the part of the party exercising the power." ... The employer does not have a right to make an arbitrary or unreasonable decision about terminating an employee when there is an agreement to terminate only for good cause. In deciding whether the employee's termination was for "a fair and honest cause or reason regulated by the good faith of the employer," the trier of fact does scrutinize the employer's business judgment and determines whether the discharge was justified under all the circumstances. If the reasons advanced by the employer for the discharge are trivial, capricious, unrelated to business needs or goals, or pretextual, the finder of fact may properly find that the stated reason for termination was not "a fair and honest cause or reason" regulated by good faith. The employer does not have an unfettered right to exercise discretion in the guise of business judgment.
Wood v. Loyola Marymount Univ., 218 Cal. App. 3d 661, 5 IER Cases 263, 267 (Cal. Ct. App. 1990) (quoting Pugh v. See's Candies, Inc., [Pugh II] 203 Cal. App. 3d 743, 769–70, 3 IER Cases 945 (1988)).

With respect to declarations by arbitrators, see *infra* Chapter 5, note 1, and accompanying text.

reason, or even for no reason without intervention from the courts.[2]

As a practical matter, however, the at-will principle meant that the terms and conditions of the employment relationship existed solely at the will of the employer because few employees possessed the bargaining power to compel the employer to enter into a true contract of employment for a specific duration or to otherwise treat employees fairly.

Today, with the passage of protective labor legislation—particularly Title VII of the Civil Rights Act, the Rehabilitation Act, the Americans with Disabilities Act, and the presence of unions and collective bargaining with labor arbitration available to most employees covered under a collective bargaining agreement—the at-will doctrine has been significantly modified. In many employment settings, however, the at-will doctrine still prevails. This chapter examines the common law at-will rule and the most significant development in the entire field of labor and employment law in the last decade—the growing willingness of courts to modify the traditional doctrine of employment-at-will when the employer's action is determined violative of some public policy.

I. REVIEW OF THE COMMON LAW AT-WILL RULE

Approximately 60 million U.S. employees are subject to the employment-at-will doctrine, and approximately 2 million of them are terminated each year without the right to a hearing before an administrative agency or an arbitrator. Further, about 150,000 of these

---

[2]The Arkansas Supreme Court stated the common law rule this way:

Our own cases have adhered to this principle, that either party has an absolute right to terminate the relationship. . . . Moreover, we have held firmly to this view even where a contract of employment provides the employee will not be discharged except for good cause. We have said that where an employer and an employee agree the employee shall not be discharged without cause, the contract is not enforceable where there is no agreement by the employee to serve for any specified time. Griffin v. Erickson, 642 S.W.2d 308, 310, 115 LRRM 4300 (Ark. 1982).

For an in-depth treatment of the common law at-will rule and a suggested statute, *see* Marvin Hill, Jr., *Arbitration as a Means of Protecting Employees from Unjust Dismissal: A Statutory Proposal*, 3 N. ILL. U. L. REV. 111 (1982).

employees would have been found to have been discharged without just cause and reinstated to their former positions had they been accorded a hearing.[3] The argument has been made that the most significant development in the entire labor law field during the past decade is the growing willingness of state courts to modify the traditional employment-at-will rule.[4] Using tort or contract theory, judges have overturned the traditional at-will rule and have placed significant limitations on management's right to dismiss employees at will. Some of the theories applied by the courts are applicable to the employee's unconventional lifestyle or off-duty conduct, and for this reason it is instructive to review recent developments in employment-at-will.

A. Judicial Limitations

Judicial or judge-made limitations to the employment-at-will rule may generally be categorized into three major divisions: (1) public policy (the most widely applied exception); (2) "whistleblowing"; and (3) "malice and bad faith" exceptions. While there is admittedly over-lap between and within the categories of cases in these divisions, it is conceptually useful to examine leading cases within these categories.

1. Public Policy Exceptions

A theory adopted by courts in those states that limit the employ-ment-at-will rule is that employers should not be permitted to disci-pline or discharge employees for reasons violative of an established "public policy."[5] A rule to the contrary would mean that public policy

---

[3]Jack Stieber, *Recent Developments in Employment-At-Will* in PROC. OF THE 1985 SPRING MEETING, INDUSTRIAL RELATIONS RESEARCH ASS'N (IRRA) 557 (1985).

[4]Theodore J. St. Antoine, *The Revision of Employment-At-Will Enters a New Phase*, in PROC. OF THE 1985 SPRING MEETING, IRRA 563 (1985).

[5]In Palmateer v. International Harvester Co., 421 N.E.2d 876, 115 LRRM 4165 (Ill. 1981) (discussed *infra* note 42 and accompanying text), the court, addressing the issue of public policy, stated as follows:

There is no precise definition of the term. In general, it can be said that public policy concerns what is right and just and what affects the citizens of the State collectively. It is to be found in the State's constitution and statutes and, when they are silent, in its judicial decisions. Although there is no precise line of

could easily be defeated by the threat of retaliatory conduct on the part of employers. Public policy cases fall into four broad and sometimes overlapping categories: (1) refusal to violate a criminal statute; (2) exercising a statutory right; (3) complying with a statutory duty; and (4) adhering to professional codes of ethics. The courts, applying a public policy analysis, have, however, accorded little relief to employees terminated because of a particular lifestyle or when management finds infirmities in the employee's off-duty conduct.

a. Discharge for Refusing to Violate a Criminal Law. The leading and most often-cited case in this category is *Petermann v. Teamsters Local 396.*[6] In that case, a union business agent was discharged for refusing to commit perjury for his employer (a labor union). In ruling for the employee, the California Court of Appeal stated that "the right to discharge an employee under such a contract may be limited by statute . . . or by considerations of public policy."[7] The court noted:

> The threat of criminal prosecution would, in many cases, be a sufficient deterrent upon both the employer and employee, the former from soliciting and the latter from committing perjury. However, in order to more fully effectuate the state's declared policy against perjury, the civil law, too, must deny the employer his generally unlimited right to discharge an employee whose employment is [at will], when the reason

---

> demarcation dividing matters purely personal . . . a survey of cases in other States involving retaliatory discharges shows that a matter must strike at the heart of a citizen's social rights, duties, and responsibilities before the tort will be allowed.

Id. at 878–79 (citation omitted).

In Lucas v. Brown & Root, 736 F.2d 1202, 1 IER Cases 388 (8th Cir. 1984), the Court of Appeals for the Eighth Circuit defined public policy this way:

> Public policy is usually defined by the political branches of government. Something "against public policy" is something that the Legislature has forbidden. But the Legislature is not the only source of such policy. In common-law jurisdictions the courts too have been sources of law, always subject to legislative correction, and with progressively less freedom as legislation occupies a given field. It is the courts, to give one example, that originated the whole doctrine that certain kinds of businesses—common carriers and innkeepers—must serve the public without discrimination or preference. In this sense, then, courts make law and they have done so for centuries.

Id. at 1205.

[6]344 P.2d 25, 1 IER Cases 5 (Cal. Ct. App. 1959).

[7]*Id.* at 27.

for the discharge is the employee's refusal to commit perjury. . . . To hold that one's continued employment could be made contingent upon his commission of a felonious act at the instance of his employer would be to encourage criminal conduct upon the part of both the employee and employer and would serve to contaminate the honest administration of public affairs. This is patently contrary to the public welfare.[8]

In another frequently cited case, *Tameny v. Atlantic Richfield Co.*,[9] the Supreme Court of California found a cause of action in tort for an employee who was discharged for refusing to participate in an illegal price-fixing scheme. In so holding, the court declared "an employer's authority over its employees does not include the right to demand that the employee commit a criminal act to further its interests and an employer may not coerce compliance with such unlawful directions by discharging an employee who refuses to follow such an order."[10]

In *Sargent v. Central National Bank & Trust*,[11] the Oklahoma Supreme Court determined that a cause of action for tortious discharge in violation of the state's public policy arises when an employee is discharged "either for refusing to violate, by act or omission, a well-defined public policy or for performing an act in compliance with a clear and compelling public policy."[12] In *Sargent*, the employee claimed that he was discharged for refusing to destroy or alter a report to the bank's audit committee. Several statutes prohibited such an act. Specifically, the court noted that "a demand to destroy or

---

[8]*Id.*

[9]610 P.2d 1330, 1 IER Cases 102 (Cal. 1980).

[10]*Id.* at 1336–37. The public policy exception was further defined in Foley v. Interactive Data Corp., 765 P.2d 373, 1 IER Cases 1729 (Cal. 1988), where an employee was dismissed after reporting to his employer that his newly hired supervisor was currently under investigation by the FBI for embezzlement from his supervisor's former employer. The court found that his conduct did not implicate basic public policy because the employee disclosed information only to his employer that did not serve any public interest. *Id.* at 380. The *Foley* court also held that there is no remedy in tort for a breach of the implied covenant of good faith and fair dealing in an employment contract. *Id.* at 396.

See also Kessler v. Equity Mgmt., Inc., 572 A.2d 1144, 5 IER Cases 545 (Md. 1990) (finding cause of action for employee who refused supervisor's orders to enter apartment while tenant was absent to snoop through papers for information that landlord could use to collect past rent).

[11]809 P.2d 1298, 6 IER Cases 360 (Okla. 1991).

[12]*Id.* at 361.

alter a bank auditor's report clearly runs counter to the principles which the federal [banking] code espouses.[13] The court concluded that federal banking law did not preempt wrongful-discharge claims by officers who refuse to violate federal law.

Similarly, in *Adams v. George W. Cochran & Co.*,[14] the Court of Appeals for the District of Columbia found that "[it] seems universally accepted that an employer's discharge of an employee for the employee's refusal to violate a statute is a wrongful discharge in violation of public policy."[15] Thus, when an employee is actually forced between violating the statute or keeping his job, even if the criminal liability for the violation is not very great, it is contrary to public policy to compel the choice.[16]

The public policy exception may be narrowly applied. In *Guthrie v. TIFCO Industries*,[17] the Fifth Circuit found that the plaintiff failed to raise a cause of action for wrongful discharge when he alleged that the employer terminated him for refusing to violate customs regulations. Under Texas law, the court noted that the narrow exception to the employment-at-will doctrine "covers only the discharge of an employee for the sole reason that the employee refused to perform an illegal act."[18] This exception, according to the Fifth Circuit, applies only to employees discharged for "refusing to perform acts that carry criminal penalties."[19] In *Guthrie,* the plaintiff failed to establish that the regulations in question carried criminal penalties. Therefore, the employee failed to establish that he was discharged for refusing to perform an illegal act.

In summary, courts frequently recognize causes of actions for an employer's retaliation against an employee who refuses to violate a criminal statute. These cases, however, usually arise as a result of an employer's direct order to the employee to violate a specific statutory

---

[13]*Id.* at 362.

[14]597 A.2d 28, 6 IER Cases 1392 (D.C. 1991).

[15]*Id.* 6 IER Cases at 1396.

[16]*Id.* at 1397; *See* Martin Marietta Corp. v. Lorenz, 823 P.2d 100, 7 IER Cases 77 (Colo. 1992) (engineer's refusal to report quality-control deficiencies stated a claim for wrongful discharge in violation of public policy, where failing to report such deficiencies would have violated federal criminal statutes).

[17]941 F.2d 374, 7 IER Cases 284 (5th Dist. 1991).

[18]*Id.* at 288.

[19]*Id.*

provision. Employees seeking protection from employer's interference with personal lifestyles or off-duty conduct may only place reliance upon this category of cases to the extent they wish to exercise their personal right not to violate the law. Absent a statutory basis for the public policy asserted, the employee is likely to be unprotected under common law. Even those courts that sweep broadly in their definition of public policy are unlikely to rule for the employee.

b. Discharge for Exercising a Statutory Right. While recognizing that generally "an employee at will may be discharged without cause," in 1973 the Indiana Supreme Court, in *Frampton v. Central Indiana Gas Co.*,[20] carved out an exception to the at-will doctrine for employees discharged for exercising a statutorily conferred right to receive a workman's compensation award. The Indiana court reasoned that it would be against public policy to prohibit a cause of action because the language of the Indiana compensation statute prohibited any "device" to circumvent the employer's liability. The court stated that the statute created a duty in the employer to compensate employees for work-related injuries and a right in the employee to receive such compensation, and in order for the goals of the act to be realized and for public policy to be effectuated, the employee must be able to exercise his right without being subject to management reprisal.[21]

Most worker's compensation statutes now contain antiretaliatory provisions. Other state and federal statutes protect employees from retaliation or discrimination in labor relations claims,[22] occupational

---

[20]297 N.E.2d 425, 115 LRRM 4611 (Ind. 1973).

[21]*Id.* at 427. While some states have passed specific legislation prohibiting discharge of employees for filing workmen's compensation claims, *see, e.g.,* Peabody Galion v. Dollar, 666 F.2d 1309, 109 LRRM 2068 (10th Cir. 1981), others have not and, accordingly, several courts since the *Frampton* decision have had to address the issue. *See, e.g.,* Hentzel v. Singer Co., 188 Cal. Rptr. 159, 115 LRRM 4036 (1982); Kelsay v. Motorola, Inc., 384 N.E.2d 353, 115 LRRM 4371 (Ill. 1971). Generally, those courts recognizing a cause of action have relied on the clear mandate of the law encouraging employees who sustain on-the-job injuries to seek disability benefits. Courts refusing to grant employees a cause of action under this type of claim insist that the legislature is best suited to create a new cause of action. Absent express legislative intent, these courts are reluctant to imply a cause of action for a retaliatory discharge. *See* Dockery v. Lampart Table Co., 244 S.E.2d 272, 115 LRRM 4307 (N.C. Ct. App. 1978).

[22]*See, e.g.,* Labor Management Relations Act (LMRA), 29 U.S.C. §158(a) (4).

health and safety claims,[23] employee welfare and benefits plans,[24] and minimum wage claims.[25] When a statute fails to provide an antidiscrimination provision, however, courts may apply a public policy exception to employee exercises of substantive rights. For instance, in *Bowman v. State Bank of Keysville*,[26] the employees, who were also shareholders of the bank, were fired because they voted against a merger which had already been approved by the bank's board of directors. The court found that the employees were punished for exercising their statutory rights to vote their shares, and therefore the employer violated state public policy. Thus, even if no expressed statutory provision prohibits retaliation for the exercise of statutorily conferred rights, courts are inclined to enforce statutory policy by implying tortious causes of action for retaliation.[27] Thus, employees selecting to exercise statutorily conferred rights may be protected from interference from management.

c. Discharge for Complying With a Statutory Duty. In the leading case in this area, *Nees v. Hocks*,[28] the Supreme Court of Oregon held that an at-will employee may recover in tort for wrongful discharge when complying with a statutory duty to sit on a jury, reasoning that the legislature and the courts regard the jury system high on the scale of American institutions and citizen obligations. It follows that if an employer were permitted with impunity to discharge an employee for fulfilling jury duty obligations, the jury system would be adversely affected.

Another example of an employee's right to be free from retaliation for exercising statutory duties is *Ludwick v. This Minute of Carolina*,[29]

---

[23]Occupational Safety and Health Act of 1970 (OSHA), 29 U.S.C. §660(c) (2).

[24]The Employee Retirement Income Security Act (ERISA), 29 U.S.C. §§1001-1461 (1988), discussed *infra* Chapter 3, notes 231–44 and accompanying text, prohibits employers from discharging or discriminating against employees for the purpose of interfering with employees' rights under ERISA or under an employee benefit plan established under the statute.

[25]*See, e.g.,* IND. CODE ANN. §2-2-11(1) (1991); ILL. REV. STAT. ch. 48, ¶1101(8) (c) (1986); ARIZ. REV. STAT. ANN. §23-329(A) (1983).

[26]331 S.E.2d 797, 1 IER Cases 437 (Va. 1985).

[27]But not always. The *Bowman* decision was not followed by the Oregon Supreme Court. In Campbell v. Ford Indus., Inc., 546 P.2d 141, 115 LRRM 4837 (Or. 1976), the Oregon Supreme Court held that an employee who was also a shareholder has no cause of action to contest a dismissal for wanting to inspect the company's books and records.

[28]536 P.2d 512, 516, 115 LRRM 4571 (Or. 1975).

[29]337 S.E.2d 213, 1 IER Cases 1099 (S.C. Sup. Ct. 1985).

where the South Carolina Supreme Court determined that an at-will employee who was fired for honoring an Employment Security Commission subpoena had stated a cause of action for wrongful discharge. The court noted that requiring an employee not to comply with the subpoena as a condition of retaining employment violated state public policy.[30]

Clearly, when an employee is obligated to comply with a statutory duty, employers may not intervene without facing possible liability. Conversely, employees conforming to such duties are protected to the extent that a duty exists.

d. Discharge for Adhering to Professional Codes of Ethics. In *Pierce v. Ortho Pharmaceutical Corp.*,[31] the Supreme Court of New Jersey considered whether a cause of action existed for an at-will physician and research scientist who was dismissed for refusing to continue a project she considered medically unethical (she opposed continued laboratory research, development, and testing of a drug containing saccharin, which Ortho intended to market for the treatment of diarrhea). What is interesting in this case is the court's focus on the special considerations arising out of the right to fire an at-will employee who is a member of a recognized profession. As stated by the court:

> Employees who are professionals owe a special duty to abide not only by federal and state law, but also by the recognized codes of ethics of their professions. That duty may oblige them to decline to perform acts required by their employers. However, an employee should not have the right to prevent his or her employer from pursuing its business because the employee perceives that a particular business decision violates the employee's personal morals, as distinguished from the recognized code of ethics of the employee's profession.[32]

While the court made it clear that a cause of action would lie where the discharge is contrary to a clearly mandated public policy, it cautioned that not all professional codes of ethics express such public policy.[33] Absent legislation, the court indicated that the judiciary must define the cause of action in a case-by-case determination.[34] This

---

[30]*See* Shaffer v. Frontrunner, Inc. 566 N.E.2d 193, 6 IER Cases 328 (Ohio App. 1990).

[31]417 A.2d 505, 1 IER Cases 109 (N.J. 1980).

[32]*Id.* at 512.

[33]*Id.*

[34]*Id.*

approach was taken in *Warthen v. Toms River Community Memorial Hospital*.[35] In that case a registered nurse employed in a hospital's kidney dialysis unit was assigned to dialyze a double amputee patient who suffered from a number of maladies. On two occasions she had to cease treatment because the patient suffered cardiac arrest and severe internal hemorrhaging during the dialysis procedure. When she was again scheduled to dialyze this patient, she informed management that "she had moral, medical, and philosophical objections" to performing this procedure because the patient was terminally ill and, according to the nurse, it was causing the patient additional complications. Her request for reassignment was initially granted but, approximately eight months later, she was again assigned to dialyze the patient. Once again she objected to the head nurse who told her that if she continued to refuse to dialyze the patient, she would be dismissed.

On a retrial, the court concluded that the nurses' code of ethics is a personal moral judgment and does not rise to a public policy. The court reasoned that "identifying the mandate of public policy is a question of law, analogous to interpreting a statute or defining a duty in a negligence case" and that the burden is on the employee "to identify a 'specific expression' or 'a clear mandate' of public policy which might bar his or her dismissal."[36] The court accordingly held that the considerations cited by the nurse involving her own personal morals did not rise to the level of a public policy mandate.[37]

Thus, professional employees governed by strict ethical codes may be afforded some protections from employer meddling. Employees who decide to follow such codes may not be discharged at the employer's whim, and thus, compliance provides the employee some right to make professional "lifestyle" choices.[38]

---

[35]488 A.2d 229, 118 LRRM 3179 (N.J. Super. Ct. App. Div. 1985).

[36]*Id.* at 232–33.

[37]*Id.* at 233–35; *see also* Lampe v. Presbyterian Medical Ctr., 590 P.2d 513, 115 LRRM 4313 (Colo. Ct. App. 1979), where the court rejected a nurse's contention that a cause of action should be allowed for a wrongful dismissal for refusing management's order to reduce the overtime assignments of her staff since she felt that the reduction of overtime would jeopardize the health of the patients. *Id.* at 514–15. The court pointed out that a statute containing general principles pertaining to the licensing of nurses did not create a cause of action. *Id.* at 515–16.

[38]A sample of cases where courts have denied the public policy exception include: Crocker v. Chamber of Commerce of the U.S., 115 LRRM 4067 (D.D.C. 1983)

2. Whistleblower Exception

Related to the public policy exception are disciplinary measures triggered by an employee's reporting of allegedly unlawful conduct. In some cases the employee may report a supervisor's conduct to upper management;[39] in other cases the employee may report the company's activities to a governmental authority. Whistleblowing cases are often factually similar: (1) the employee objects to work or conduct he believes violates state or federal law; (2) the employee expresses his intention not to perform the requested work or engages in "self-help" activity outside the workplace to halt the work (often by going to the media); and (3) the employee is dismissed.

(rejecting duty to adequately investigate charges of employee disloyalty before discharge as public policy); Kavanaugh v. KLM Royal Dutch Airlines, 566 F. Supp. 242, 115 LRRM 4266 (D. Ill. 1983) (rejecting claim for wrongful discharge on theory that discharge violated public policy favoring right to counsel and free access to courts); Hinrichs v. Tranquilaire Hosp., 352 So. 2d 1130, 115 LRRM 4385 (Ala. 1977) (denying cause of action for at-will nurse who refused to falsify medical records as directed by supervisor); Larsen v. Motor Supply Co., 573 P.2d 907, 115 LRRM 4298 (Ariz. Ct. App. 1977) (refusal to sign consent form to take psychological stress evaluation test required by company policy not protected by public policy to justify exception to at-will rule); Abrisz v. Pulley Freight Lines, Inc., 270 N.W.2d 454, 115 LRRM 4777 (Iowa 1978) (denying cause of action to at-will employee who wrote letter in support of co-employee's application for unemployment compensation); Scrogham v. Kraftco Corp., 551 S.W.2d 881, 115 LRRM 4769 (Ky. Ct. App. 1977) (denying public policy protection for employee desiring to attend law school at night); Gil v. Metal Serv. Corp., 412 So. 2d 706, 115 LRRM 4460 (La. Ct. App. 1982) (no cause of action for employee alleging dismissal for protesting employer's practice of shipping foreign steel to customers who specifically had ordered domestic steel); Ising v. Barnes Hosp., 674 S.W.2d 623, 116 LRRM 3140 (Mo. Ct. App. 1984) (rejecting cause of action for at-will employee who refused to sign release exonerating employer and polygrapher from negligent or intentional conduct arising out of polygraph examination); Howard v. Dorr Woolen Co., 414 A.2d 1273, 115 LRRM 4578 (N.H. 1980) (rejecting discharge for sickness as violative of public policy where sickness remedied by medical insurance); Cisco v. United Parcel Serv., Inc., 476 A.2d 1340, 116 LRRM 2514 (Pa. Super. Ct. 1984) (employer's refusal to rehire employee following acquittal not violative of public policy); Jones v. Keogh, 409 A.2d 581, 115 LRRM 4193 (Vt. 1979) (upholding dismissal for asserting rights with respect to vacation time and sick leave); Ward v. Frito-Lay Inc., 95 Wis. 2d 372, 115 LRRM 4320 (Wis. Ct. App. 1980) (denying public policy exception to at-will employee who was dismissed for living with another employee to whom he was not married).

[39]*See, e.g.,* Ludwig v. C & A Wallcoverings, Inc., 960 F.2d 40, 7 IER Cases 566 (7th Cir. 1992) (denying cause of action to employee demoted after internal investigation failed to substantiate allegations that supervisor misappropriated leather coats and had coded job applications to indicate race of applicants, reasoning that Illinois does not recognize cause of action for mere demotion).

The courts have had little trouble in affording a cause of action in tort to an employee who is urged by his or her employer to violate a criminal or civil statute as part of a company pattern or practice. The more difficult situation involves those cases where an employee *reports* conduct he or she thinks or believes is illegal or, because of professional considerations, unethical.

For example, the Supreme Court of West Virginia, in *Harless v. First National Bank in Fairmont*,[40] considered whether an employee, discharged in retaliation for his efforts to require his employer to comply with a state consumer credit and protection statute, stated a cause of action in tort. Finding the legislature intended to establish a policy protecting credit consumers, the court ruled the "policy should not be frustrated by a holding that an employee of a lending institution covered by the Act who seeks to ensure that compliance is being made with the Act, can be discharged without being furnished a cause of action for such discharge."[41]

A similar result was reached by the Illinois Supreme Court in *Palmateer v. International Harvester Co.*,[42] where the court found a cause of action in tort for an employee who was discharged for supplying local law enforcement agencies information indicating a fellow employee might be violating criminal statutes. Reasoning that public policy favors the exposure of crime by citizens possessing knowledge of criminal activity, the court concluded "[p]ersons acting in good faith who have probable cause to believe crimes have been committed should not be deterred from reporting them by the fear of unfounded suits by those accused."[43]

---

[40]246 S.E.2d 270, 115 LRRM 4380 (W. Va. 1978).

[41]*Id.* at 276.

[42]421 N.E.2d 876, 115 LRRM 4165 (Ill. 1981).

[43]*Id.* at 880 (citing Joiner v. Benton Community Bank, 411 N.E.2d 229 (Ill. 1980)).

Palmeteer may establish the envelope of protection for at-will employees in Illinois. Subsequent to *Palmeteer,* the Illinois Supreme Court has refused to provide protection to employees dismissed for filing health insurance claims, Price v. Carmack Datsun, Inc., 485 N.E.2d 359, 121 LRRM 3536 (Ill. 1985), or for protesting employer violations of a municipal ordinance, Gould v. Campbell's Ambulance Serv., Inc., 488 N.E.2d 993, 122 LRRM 2672 (Ill. 1986). *See also* Zaniecki v. P.A. Bergner & Co., 493 N.E.2d 419, 1 IER Cases 1476 (Ill. App. Ct. 1986) (denying a cause of action for employee dismissed for reporting suspected criminal activity of co-workers to management).

In *Flesner v. Technical Communications Corp.,*[44] a Massachusetts court found "redress is available for employees who are terminated for asserting a legally guaranteed right . . . , for doing what the law requires . . . , or for refusing to do that which the law forbids."[45] The employee was discharged for participating in a U.S. Customs Service investigation of his employer. The court found that, even though the law did not require the employee to cooperate, public policy encourages cooperation.

With few exceptions, before a court will allow a cause of action for whistleblowing, the conduct complained of must be clearly illegal. The employee bears the burden of proving illegality. A mere possibility of criminal activity will be insufficient to protect the employee who goes to the authorities. A review of the cases indicates that, in finding a cause of action, the courts balance the competing interests at issue. The principal employer's interest is the efficient operation of a business, and the principal employee's interest is security in earning a livelihood. At the same time, the judiciary has recognized society's interest in ensuring its civil and criminal statutes are not violated. Accordingly, where the conduct complained of clearly violates a criminal or civil statute, courts will allow a cause of action in tort for a retaliatory discharge. These situations involve conduct the legislature has clearly seen fit to address. Courts reason that to refuse a cause of action would effectively permit an employer to increase its chances of escaping liability for violating civil or criminal statutes. It is difficult to rationalize any public policy that could be served if an employer were permitted to dismiss an employee for acting as a "private attorney general," at least in those instances where a court determines that the employee's allegations are correct and the employee acts in good faith.

A more interesting and difficult problem arises in the case where an employee reasonably, but incorrectly, concludes that the employer's conduct is illegal or otherwise improper. Even though the disclosure is motivated by a good faith belief the conduct was illegal, few courts will allow a cause of action for the so-called "good faith" whistleblower. Moreover, while many states recognize a tort of retaliatory dismissal, protection may not be available to other types of job reprisals, such

---

[44] 575 N.E.2d 1107, 6 IER Cases 1530 (Mass. Sup. Ct. 1991).
[45] *Id.* 6 IER Cases at 1533.

as demotion, transfers, alterations in job duties, or other disciplinary proceedings.[46] At the same time, there should be no difficulty in refusing a cause of action to an employee who, for vexatious reasons, falsely accuses an employer of violating statutes. No policy is served by affording protection in this case; indeed, an employer would likely have a cause of action in tort against such an employee.

It is of note that some states have passed legislation which prohibits employer reprisals or disciplinary action against an employee who reports to a public body an employer's violation or suspected violation of any federal, state, or municipal law or regulation.[47] Thus, given the common law protections and available statutory rights, employees choosing to report criminal or unethical violations to governmental agencies are provided protection from the employer's retaliatory responses.

3. Malice and Bad Faith Exception

The malice and bad faith exception operates in tandem with the public policy exception. This exception provides the employee with a "disapproved" lifestyle the greatest opportunity for relief.

The predominant case in this area is *Monge v. Beebe Rubber Co.*[48] In that case a married woman was discharged by her foreman because of her refusal to go out on a date with him. The New Hampshire court held the discharge malicious and unlawful and concluded that a termination by the employer of a contract of employment which is motivated by bad faith or malice or based on retaliation is not in the best interest of the economic system or the public good.[49]

---

[46]*See, e.g.*, Ludwig v. C & A Wallcoverings, Inc., 960 F.2d 40, 7 IER Cases 566, 568 (7th Cir. 1992) ("Recognizing a retaliation tort for actions short of termination could subject employers to torrents of unwarranted and vexatious suits filed by disgruntled employees at every juncture in the employment process. And why stop at demotions?").

[47]*See, e.g.*, Parten v. Consolidated Freightways, 923 F.2d 580, 6 IER Cases 129 (8th Cir. 1991) (citing MINN. STAT. ANN. §181.932(c) (1990), making it illegal for employer to discharge because "(c) the employee refuses to participate in any activity that the employee, in good faith, believes violates any state or federal law or rule or regulation adopted pursuant to law").

[48]316 A.2d 549, 115 LRRM 4755 (N.H. 1974).

[49]*Id.* at 551.

In *Lucas Brown & Root, Inc.,*[50] an employee was dismissed when she refused to sleep with her supervisor. Although the time for filing a sexual harassment claim had run out under Title VII, the Eighth Circuit reasoned that the decisions of the Arkansas Supreme Court established exceptions to the at-will rule when the bases for the discharge are so extreme and outrageous as to render the discharge tortious for intentional infliction of emotional distress.[51] According to the court, "a woman invited to trade herself for a job is in effect being asked to become a prostitute," and "[p]laintiff should not be penalized for refusing to do what the law forbids."[52] The court, citing the decision in *Tameny,* declared that "it is an implied term of every employment contract that neither party be required to do what the law forbids," and that if the plaintiff can prove she was dismissed for refusing to sleep with her foreman, and her employer was responsible for it, she can recover damages for breach of contract.[53]

Underlying the malice and bad faith exception is the principle that an implied covenant of good faith and fair dealing (often termed an "implied-in-law contract") exists. The principle essentially states that there is, in every contract, an implied covenant that neither party will do anything which would have the effect of destroying or injuring the right of the other party to receive the fruits of the agreement. In *Pugh v. See's Candies, Inc.,*[54] a California appellate court found an employee stated a prima facie case of wrongful termination in violation of an implied promise by the employer that it would not act arbitrarily in dealing with the employee.[55] The court stated that "[i]n determining whether there exists an implied-in-fact promise for some form of continued employment . . . a variety of factors in addition to the existence of independent consideration" are relevant to such a finding.[56] These include "the personnel policies or practices of the employer, the employee's longevity of service, actions or communica-

---

[50]736 F.2d 1202, 1 IER Cases 388 (8th Cir. 1984).
[51]*Id.* at 1204–05.
[52]*Id.* at 1205.
[53]*Id.* at 1205 (citing Tameny v. Atlantic Richfield Co., 610 P.2d 1330, 1335, 1 IER Cases 102 (Cal. 1980)).
[54]171 Cal. Rptr. 917, 115 LRRM 4002 (1981).
[55]*Id.* at 927.
[56]*Id.* at 925.

tions by the employer reflecting assurances of continued employment, and the practices of the industry in which the employee is engaged."[57] Given Pugh's 32 years of employment, the commendations and promotions he received, the apparent absence of any criticism of his work, the assurances he was given "that if you are loyal to [See's] and do a good job, your future is secure," and the employer's acknowledged policy that administrative personnel would not be terminated except for good cause, the court concluded that a jury could find an implied promise of fair dealing with the employee.[58]

Most courts have adhered to the common law and have not adopted a general requirement of good faith and fair dealing where employment contracts are of indefinite duration.[59] Moreover, even in the select jurisdictions that have ruled that employment contracts are subject to an implied covenant that the parties carry out their obligations in good faith,[60] courts have declined the invitation to transform the requirement of good faith into an implied-in-fact condition that an employee may be discharged only for good cause. Although an employee handbook may modify an at-will relationship,[61] the employee is left with little recourse at common law, absent such a

---

[57]*Id.* at 925–26.

[58]*Id.* at 927.

[59]*See* Hew-Len v. F.W. Woolworth, 737 F. Supp. 1104, 5 IER Cases 270 (D. Haw. 1990); Fogel v. Trustees of Iowa College, 446 N.W.2d 451, 453, 6 IER Cases 313 (Iowa 1989) (noting that "[t]he majority of jurisdictions that have addressed the covenant [of good faith and fair dealing] have unequivocally rejected it"); Burk v. K-Mart Corp., 770 P.2d 24, 4 IER Cases 182 (Okla. 1989); Brehany v. Nordstrom Inc., 812 P.2d 49, 55, 6 IER Cases 881 (Utah 1991) ("The covenant of good faith . . . cannot be construed to change an indefinite term, at-will employment contract into a contract that requires an employer to have good cause to justify a discharge.").

[60]*See, e.g.,* the discussion of the court in Western States Minerals Corp. v. Jones, 807 P.2d 1392, 6 IER Cases 575 (Nev. 1991); *see also* Luedtke v. Nabors Alaska Drilling, Inc., 768 P.2d 1123, 4 IER Cases 129 (Alaska 1989) (stating that at-will employment contracts in Alaska contain an implied covenant of good faith and fair dealing).

[61]*See, e.g.,* Vaske v. DuCharme, McMillen & Assoc., 757 F. Supp. 1158, 6 IER Cases 164 (D. Colo. 1990) (holding that employment manual containing noninclusive list of actions that constitute "cause" for which employees may be dismissed may form implied just-cause standard); Shumaker v. Frito-Lay, 6 IER Cases 155 (D.N.D. 1991); Duldulao v. Saint Mary of Nazareth Hosp. Center, 505 N.E.2d 314, 318, 1 IER Cases 1428 (Ill. 1987) ("an employee handbook or other policy statement creates enforceable contractual rights if the traditional requirements for contract formation are present").

modification.[62] Thus, employees are provided with minimal protection from employers' actions that violate the notion of good faith and fair dealing. Without an implied or expressed contractual relationship, this area of case law is of little significance for the employee seeking protection for individual lifestyle or off-duty conduct decisions.

B. Judicial Limitations: Lifestyle and Off-Duty Conduct Cases

A review of court decisions in lifestyle and off-duty cases reveals that employees have limited opportunity under common law to challenge the restrictions imposed by employers regarding the kind of employee management desires. Indeed, at common law no nexus between the conduct complained of and the employee's job need be shown, although in selected cases courts, substituting their views for those of management, have ruled in favor of employees. Six areas of recurring interest involve (1) association, (2) health and appearance, (3) sexual propriety and privacy, (4) tortious invasion of privacy consideratons, (5) drug and drug testing, and (6) speech.

1. Association

A major consideration in the association area is whether at common law a private sector employer may dismiss an employee because of his or her membership in an organization which the employer finds distasteful. Another major area is the employee's association with employees of competitors.[63] Reflective of the majority view, the Fourth Circuit, in *Bellamy v. Mason's Stores, Inc.*,[64] ruled that a private sector employee's right of association is not protected and he may be discharged because he belongs to an "obnoxious organization,"[65] in this case the Ku Klux Klan. Holding the complaint stated

---

[62]Suter v. Harsco Corp., 403 S.E.2d 751, 6 IER Cases 756 (W. Va. 1991).

[63]Other types of associations often of interest to management—the sexual partners of employees—are discussed *infra* notes 84–90 and accompanying text.

[64]508 F.2d 504, 9 FEP Cases 1 (4th Cir. 1974).

[65]*Id.* at 505.

no cause of action under Title VII of the Civil Rights Act,[66] the court declined to decide whether "religious pomp and ceremony" is enough to make the Klan a religion for purposes of Title VII.[67]

Likewise, in *Bloom v. General Electric Supply Co.*,[68] the issue was raised as to whether it was a public policy exception to the employment-at-will doctrine to protect an employee's ability to associate with employees of competing firms. In *Bloom*, the employee's husband, who was an employee of the company himself, resigned his job to work with a competitor. The wife was terminated by the company due to a potential conflict of interest. The court dismissed the employee's claim, stating that public policy exceptions to the employment-at-will doctrine required a showing that the public policy is evidenced by constitutional or statutory provisions. The employee failed to establish such a provision. The court, however, did allow the employee's restraint of trade cause of action to proceed to trial. The court noted that Tennessee has a longstanding policy prohibiting arrangements that inhibit free competition.

It should be noted, however, some states have statutory protection for spousal relationships that create public policy. In *River Bend Community Unit School District No. 2 v. Illinois Human Rights Commission and Virginia Ray*,[69] an Illinois Court of Appeals was faced with an issue of whether the Illinois Human Rights Act prohibited the transfer of an employee whose husband had been assigned as her supervisor. The School District had a policy that prohibited one spouse from directly supervising the other spouse and attempted to transfer one spouse on that basis. The Illinois Human Rights Act prohibited unlawful discrimination based on a person's marital status. The court found the School District's policy imposed a direct burden on marriage. Thus, the state statute prohibited such a transfer.

The court did not address the issue of whether the District breached the public policy exception to the employment-at-will doctrine because the employee was not discharged. However, once such discrimination is found violative of state statute, a court could easily

---

[66]42 U.S.C. §2000e-2 (1988), discussed *infra* Chapter 3, notes 2–141 and accompanying text.
[67]Bellamy, 508 F.2d at 505.
[68]702 F. Supp. 1364, 3 IER Cases 1842 (M.D. Tenn. 1988).
[69]597 N.E.2d 842 (Ill. App. Ct. 1992).

conclude the state's public policy has been breached if a discharge occurs.

Contrary to the general rule that a private sector employee's right to association is not protected, a California state court sustained a $300,000 ($100,000 compensatory and $200,000 punitive) jury verdict in favor of an employee dismissed for dating a competitor's employee. In *Rulon-Miller v. IBM*,[70] an association case with inconsequent implications (at least in those situations where management has issued some declaration regarding the privacy rights of its employees), the court found IBM's declarations that employees have a right to privacy and the right to hold a job even though off-the-job behavior might not be approved by management resulted in a cause of action for wrongful termination and intentional infliction of emotional distress. According to the court, the covenant of good faith and fair dealing embraces a number of rights, including the right of an employee to the benefit of rules and regulations adopted for her protection and the requirement that like cases be treated alike.[71]

How arbitrary can a private sector employer be in dismissing or failing to hire an employee because of conduct which has no bearing on the job at issue? Does *Bellamy*, which appears to reflect the majority view in at-will cases, stand for the proposition that management can exclude an individual from employment because he or she is a member of a certain club or organization? As we read the cases, absent state action, at common law there is no legal infirmity in dismissing a complaint by an at-will employee who was terminated or not hired because of his or her preference in football teams or even for race.[72] Thus, even though little or no factual basis for management's decision may exist, and it may be irrational and capricious, excluding individuals from employment because of their associations or even their race, sex,[73] or national origin[74] has not been recognized as a

---

[70]208 Cal. Rptr. 524, 1 IER Cases 405 (1984).

[71]*Id.* at 529.

[72]*See* Eklof v. Bramalea Ltd., 733 F. Supp. 935, 5 IER Cases 594 (E.D. Pa. 1989) (black employee who failed to pursue administrative remedies under Human Relations statute precluded from bringing tort action for wrongful discharge; racial-discriminatory discharge does not qualify as exception to common law at-will rule).

[73]*See* Borden v. Johnson, 395 S.E.2d 628, 5 IER Cases 828 (Ga. 1990) (denying tort claim for dismissal because of pregnancy).

[74]Guevara v. K-Mart Corp., 629 F. Supp. 1189, 5 IER Cases 1838 (S.D. W. Va.

public policy exception to the at-will rule. Unless the dismissal violates a clearly stated public policy, the employee, unlike his public sector counterpart, has little recourse to rectify an irrational decision.[75] If the employee has any recourse, it is under a specific intent to harm theory,[76] or a theory that the information requested or acted upon constitutes an "unreasonable, substantial, or serious interference with [the employee's] privacy." Thus, in *Cort v. Bristol-Myers Co.*,[77] the Massachusetts Supreme Court considered whether management could force three long-term sales employees to answer certain questions on an employment "biographical summary," which sought information about serious illness, operations, accidents, nervous disorders, smoking and drinking habits, off-duty problems, worries, medication, age and health of parents, and other medical and business matters. While the court ruled that there was no invasion of privacy because the employees did not complete the questionnaires, the court went on to state:

> [I]f the questionnaires sought to obtain information in circumstances that constituted an "unreasonable, substantial, or serious interference with [the employee's] privacy in violation of the principles expressed in G.L. c.214, sect. 1B, the discharge of an employee for failure to provide such information could contravene public policy and warrant the imposition of liability on the employee for discharge.[78]

2. Health and Appearance

In an effort to hire "healthy" employees, management frequently is interested in knowing whether it can refuse to hire employees

---

1986) (exclusive remedy provision of West Virginia Human Rights Act bar to national origin claim).

[75]There may be a glimmer of hope under the common law, even when there is no statutory expression of public policy. *See, e.g.,* Payne v. Rozendaal, 520 A.2d 586, 588–98, 1 IER Cases 800 (Vt. 1986), where the court ruled that public policy prevents all employment-based decisions that are "cruel or shocking to the average man's conception of justice."

[76]McIsaac v. WZEW-FM Corp., 495 So. 2d 649, 1 IER Cases 1396 (Alaska 1986); Mudd v. Hoffman Homes for Youth, 543 A.2d 1092, 1096, 1 IER Cases 800 (Pa. Super. Ct. 1988); Darlington v. General Elec., 504 A.2d 306, 2 IER Cases 1666 (Pa. Super. Ct. 1986).

[77]431 N.E.2d 908, 115 LRRM 5127 (Mass. 1982).

[78]*Id.* at 912 (footnote omitted).

who are smokers, drug users, or "unattractive" because of weight or grooming preferences. There has been some argument for the proposition that public sector management should not be allowed to impose a no-smoking ban that applies to an employee's off-duty conduct,[79] however there is authority to the contrary.[80] At common law, management can dismiss an employee who is deemed medically unfit because of drug problems[81] or presents a grooming or appearance

---

[79]*See, e.g.,* Rossie v. State, 395 N.W.2d 801, 805, 1 IER Cases 1048 (Wis. Ct. App. 1986) (upholding Wisconsin Department of Revenue directive banning smoking in certain areas of state building, noting that regulation does not prevent smoking "in the lunchroom, at home, or on the street").

[80]*See, e.g.,* Grusendorf v. Oklahoma City, 816 F.2d 539, 2 IER Cases 51 (10th Cir. 1987) (finding rational basis between no-smoking regulation and promotion of health and safety of firefighter trainees).

We have found no private sector case at common law holding that management cannot impose a no-smoking rule, both on-and-off duty.

Numerous states have enacted statutes prohibiting employers from discriminating against employees because they are smokers. *See, e.g.,* IND. CODE §22-5-4-1 (1991) (prohibiting off-duty use of tobacco); KY. REV. STAT. ANN. §344.040 (Baldwin 1990); LA. REV. STAT. ANN. §762 (West 1991) (prohibiting discrimination by employer for use or nonuse of tobacco); MISS. CODE ANN. §71-7-33 (1991) (protecting smokers' privileges during nonworking hours); N.J. REV. STAT. §34:6B-1 (1991) ("No employer shall refuse to hire or employ any person or shall discharge from employment or take any adverse action against an employee with respect to compensation, terms, conditions or other privileges of employment because that person does or does not smoke or use other tobacco products, unless the employer has a rational basis for doing so which is reasonably related to the employment, including the responsibilities of the employee or prospective employee."); N.M. STAT. ANN. §50-11-3 (Michie 1991) (making it unlawful to refuse to hire, to discharge or to disadvantage because of use or nonuse of tobacco); R.I. GEN. LAWS §23-20.7.1-1 (1990) ("[n]o employer . . . shall require, as a condition of employment, that any employee or, prospective employee refrain from smoking or using tobacco products outside the course of his or her employment"); S.C. CODE ANN. §41-1-85 (Law Co-op. 1990) ("use of tobacco products outside the workplace must not be the basis of personnel action, including, but not limited to, employment, termination, demotion, or promotion of an employee"); S.D. CODIFIED LAWS ANN. §60-4-14 (1991) ("unfair employment practice for an employer to terminate the employment of an employee due to that employee's engaging in any use of tobacco products off the premises of the employer during nonworking hours unless such a restriction: (1) relates to a bona fide occupational requirement and is reasonably and rationally related to the employment activities and responsibilities of a particular employee . . . or (2) is necessary to avoid a conflict of interest with any responsibilities to the employer or the appearance of such a conflict of interest"); TENN. CODE ANN. §50-1-304 (1990) (prohibiting discrimination against employee for engaging in the use of agricultural products).

[81]*See, e.g.,* Greco v. Halliburton Co., 674 F. Supp. 1447, 2 IER Cases 1281 (D.

problem for a company.[82] Most weight and grooming challenges are litigated under Title VII, the Rehabilitation Act, the Americans with Disabilities Act, or before arbitrators.[83]

3. Sexual Propriety and Privacy

To what extent does the common law allow management to inquire into or otherwise regulate the sexual activities of its employees? While most reported cases in this area relate to privacy under the Constitution[84] or challenges under a collective bargaining agreement, a number of cases involve management's right to inquire into areas deemed private by the employee or the employer's right to engage in off-duty surveillance of an employee suspected of falsification of disability or sick-leave abuse.

In the few reported cases in this area, the courts are in agreement that an at-will private sector employee has no protection against dismissal for homosexuality,[85] adultery,[86] or shenanigans involving moral turpitude repugnant to the employer.[87] Thus, in *Staats v. Ohio*

Wyo. 1987) (upholding dismissal for refusal to submit to urinalysis test). Drug testing is discussed *infra* notes 161–73 and accompanying text.

[82]*See* Fogel v. Trustees of Iowa College, 446 N.W.2d 451, 6 IER Cases 313 (Iowa 1989) (terminating employee for head lice, reporting to work in dirty uniform, and urinating in mop bucket while on duty); *cf.* Wood v. Jim Walter Homes, Inc., 554 So. 2d 1028, 5 IER Cases 256 (Ala. 1989) (cancer); Wilson v. Weight Watchers, 474 N.W.2d 380, 6 IER Cases 1368 (Minn. Ct. App. 1991) (qualified privilege to inquire about employee's alcohol problem).

[83]Litigation under federal statutes is discussed *infra* Chapter 3; arbitral standards are discussed *infra* Chapter 5.

[84]See *infra* Chapter 4 notes 72–106 and accompanying text.

[85]*See, e.g.,* Joachim v. AT&T Info. Serv., 793 F.2d 113, 1 IER Cases 726 (5th Cir. 1986) (sustaining dismissal of homosexual employee).

[86]In those states prohibiting discrimination because of marital status, an employee may have a cause of action. *See, e.g.,* Slohoda v. UPS, 475 A.2d 618, 620 (N.J. Super. Ct. App. Div. 1984) (reversing summary judgment for employee allegedly dismissed for engaging in adultery with co-worker, reasoning that "if an employer's discharge policy is based in significant part on an employee's marital status, a discharge resulting from such policy violates N.J.S.A. 10:5-12"—prohibiting discharge based on marital status).

[87]*See* Meleen v. Hazelden Found., 928 F.2d 795, 6 IER Cases 959 (8th Cir. 1991) (sexual relationship with patient); Myles v. Delta Air Lines, 1990 U.S. Dist LEXIS 19087 6 IER Cases 123 (D. Utah 1990) (arrest on drug charges); Jevic v. Coca Cola Bottling Co., 1990 U.S. Dist. LEXIS 8821 5 IER Cases 765 (D.N.J. 1990) (no public policy violation for revocation of job offer after testing positive for

National Life Insurance Co.,[88] a federal court held that a life insurance agent could not bring an action for wrongful discharge either in tort or contract under a public policy theory when he was terminated for showing up at his employer's convention with a person not his wife.[89] Reflecting the majority view, the court reasoned that freedom of association may be an important right, but there was no right under Pennsylvania law to " 'associate with' a non-spouse at an employer's convention without fear of termination. . . ."[90]

4. Tortious Invasion of Privacy Considerations

Many states now recognize the tort of invasion of privacy and management, intent on effecting discipline or discharge because of lifestyle or off-duty conduct considerations, should have a basic understanding of privacy torts. Indeed, privacy considerations are prevalent in the drug-testing[91] and polygraph[92] areas and courts may even find a public policy in a common law privacy tort.

---

marijuana); Shull v. New Mexico Potash Corp., 802 P.2d 641, 6 IER Cases 184 (N.M. 1990) (layoff of alcoholic employee); Hershberger v. Jersey Shore Steel Co., 575 A.2d 944, 5 IER Cases 710 (Pa. Super. Ct. 1990) (sustaining discharge based on positive results of unconfirmed drug test).

[88]620 F. Supp. 118, 118 LRRM 3242 (W.D. Pa. 1985).

[89]*Id.* at 120.

[90]*Id.; see also* Morris v. Coleman Co., 738 P.2d 841, 2 IER Cases 844 (Kan. 1987) (affirming reversal of summary judgment on tortious interference claim of dismissed unmarried company secretary and married employee who accompanied each other on plane trip).

[91]*See, e.g.,* Borse v. Piece Goods Shop, Inc., 963 F.2d 611, 7 IER Cases 698 (3d Cir. 1992), discussed *infra* notes 104–06 and accompanying text. See also *infra* Chapter 4, notes 170–248 and accompanying text for a discussion of drug testing and constitutional infirmities.

[92]The interested practitioner should consult the Employee Polygraph Protection Act of 1988 (EPPA), 29 U.S.C. §§2001-2009 (1988), which prohibits the use of the polygraph by most private sector employers for preemployment screening or random testing. The EPPA also significantly restricts the use of the polygraph in workplace investigations. Public sector employers are excluded from the Act's coverage. *Id.* §2006(a). The law does not apply to tests given by the federal government to certain private individuals engaged in national security activities. *Id.* at §2006(b). There is also a security services exemption for firms whose primary business consists of providing armored car personnel, personnel engaged in the design, installation, and maintenance of security alarm systems, or other uniformed or plainclothes security personnel. *Id.* at §2006(e).

A major exemption is the "ongoing investigation" exception where an employer may request that a current employee submit to a polygraph if the employee meets

Courts usually divide privacy torts into four categories: (1) intrusion upon plaintiff's seclusion or solitude, or into his or her private affairs; (2) public disclosure of embarrassing private facts; (3) defamation and publicity which places the plaintiff in a false light in the public eye; and (4) appropriation for the defendant's advantages of the plaintiff's name or likeness.[93] While a private sector employee's so-called "right to privacy" is dependent upon the law in a particular jurisdiction, in determining whether a privacy tort exists courts engage in a balancing process involving the employer's legitimate need to run its business against the employee's expectation of privacy. The

---

four conditions: (1) the test must be administered in conjunction with an ongoing investigation involving economic loss or injury to the employer's business (*id.* at §2006(d) (1)); (2) the employee has access to property that is the subject to the investigation (*id.* at §2006(d) (2)); (3) the employer had reasonable suspicion that the subject was involved in the activity or incident under investigation (*id.* at §2006(d) (3)); and (4) the employer executes a statement setting forth the specific incident under investigation and provides it to the examinee 48 hours before the testing (*id.* at §2006(d) (4)).

The statute also mandates that additional supporting evidence, beyond the results of the test or refusal to take the test, is required before an employee can be discharged, disciplined, or denied promotion, or otherwise discriminated against in any manner. *Id.* at §2007(a) (1). Any employee affected by an employer violation may commence a private civil action, *id.* at §2005(c) (1), and is entitled to such legal or equitable relief as may be appropriate. *Id.* at §2005(c) (1). Administration of polygraph tests to determine whether an employee has used drugs is prohibited. 29 C.F.R. §801.12(d) (1988). *See also* City of Warrensville Heights v. Jennings, 569 N.E.2d 489, 6 IER Cases 597, 597–99 (Ohio 1991) (just cause existed to deny unemployment compensation and dismiss police officer for refusal to submit to polygraph to confirm that he was not involved in off-duty drug use); Jackson v. Hudspeth Center, 573 So. 2d 750, 6 IER Cases 108, 109 (Miss. 1990) (no due process violation by state facility for retardation for dismissal of employees refusing to take polygraph exam during investigation of resident's injury, reasoning "it was the duty of the appellants to cooperate with Hudspeth Center in the investigation of the incident"); Eshelman v. Blubaum, 560 P.2d 1283 (Ariz. Ct. App. 1977) (upholding dismissal of police officer for refusing to submit to polygraph stating, "[t]he criteria for determining such a test in the course of an internal investigation are that the officer must be informed (1) that the questions must relate specifically and narrowly to the performance of his official duties, (2) that the answers cannot be used against him in any subsequent criminal prosecution, and (3) that the penalty for refusal is dismissal").

Successful actions based on federal and state constitutional challenges include Thorne v. El Segundo, 726 F.2d 459, 1 IER Cases 299 (9th Cir. 1983), *cert. denied,* 469 U.S. 979, 1 IER Cases 1136 (1984), and Long Beach Employees Ass'n v. Long Beach, 719 P.2d 660, 1 IER Cases 465 (Cal. 1986).

[93]RESTATEMENT (SECOND) OF TORTS (1965) [hereinafter RESTATEMENT], William L. Prosser, *Privacy,* 48 CAL. L. REV. 383 (1960)

degree and nature of the intrusion are important considerations in determining the existence of cause of action.

a. Intrusion Upon the Employee's Seclusion or Solitude. For an employee to establish a cause of action in tort for an employer's "intrusion upon seclusion," the employee must demonstrate that the employer intruded into a matter which the employee has a right to keep private, and such an intrusion would be objectionable to the reasonable person. Causes of action may also be recognized when management searches an employee's desk, car, locker, home, or other areas where the employee has a reasonable expectation of privacy.[94] The *Restatement (Second) of Torts* addresses this tort as follows:

> One who intentionally intrudes, physically or otherwise, upon the solitude or seclusion of another or his private affairs or concerns, is subject to liability to the other for invasion of his privacy, if the intrusion would be highly offensive to a reasonable person.[95]

In *Phillips v. Smalley Maintenance Services, Inc.,*[96] an Alabama court sustained a claim that the employer invaded the employee's privacy by repeatedly interrogating her behind "locked doors" about "how often" she and her husband had sex and what "positions" they used. The interrogations occurred two or three times a week. The court noted that the "intrusive, and coercive sexual demands upon [the employee] were such an examination into her private concerns, that is, improper inquiries into her personal sexual proclivities and personality,"[97] that they supported an invasion of privacy claim. The same court, in *McIsaac v. WZEM-FM,*[98] held, however, that "the dire affront of inviting an unwilling woman to illicit intercourse has been held by most courts to be no such outrage as to lead to liability."[99]

In *Fayard v. Guardsmark, Inc.,*[100] the employee sought to hold the employer liable for invasion of privacy as a result of the employer's

---

[94]*See, e.g.,* Lewis v. Dayton Hudson Corp., 339 N.W.2d 857 (Mich. 1983); DiTomaso v. Electronic Data Sys., 1988 U.S. Dist. LEXIS 16803, 3 IER Cases 1700 (E.D. Mich. 1988).

[95]RESTATEMENT §652B.

[96]435 So. 2d 705 (Ala. 1983).

[97]*Id.* at 711.

[98]495 So. 2d 649, 1 IER Cases 1396 (Ala. 1986).

[99]*Id.* at 1398.

[100]1989 U.S. Dist. LEXIS 14211, 5 IER Cases 516 (E.D. La. 1989).

alleged surveillance by watching the employee's house and running license checks on cars at the employee's house. The court noted the alleged activities created no physical invasion, and the surveillance was the only activity clearly in the public view. Thus, according to the court, summary judgment was appropriate because the alleged activities were not an unreasonable intrusion on the employee's privacy.

A similar result was found by a Michigan Court of Appeals in *Saldana v. Kelsey-Hayes.*[101] In *Saldana,* the employee, who had allegedly sustained injuries in the course of his employment, had been investigated by a private investigator in the employer's attempt to determine the extent of the employee's injuries. The investigator observed the employee's home, telephoned the employee to determine if anyone was home, looked into the employee's windows, interrogated occupants of vehicles leaving the employee's home, and gained entrance to the employee's home by posing as a process server. Finally, the investigator contacted the employee's physician by mail seeking information about the employee's condition. The court concluded that "[w]hether the intrusion is objectionable to a reasonable person is a factual question best determined by a jury."[102] However, the employee must show the objectionable intrusions were into matters which he had a right to keep private. Thus, because the employer's surveillance of the employee's home involved matters which the employer had a legitimate right to investigate, the intrusion, even if objectionable, failed to state a cause of action for invasion into private matters.

Of special interest to employers is the application of this tort to drug testing.[103] The few reported decisions involving drug testing in the private sector indicate that in deciding whether to provide a cause of action most courts balance the employee's privacy interest against the employer's interest in maintaining a drug-free work force. The Third Circuit, in *Borse v. Piece Goods Shop Inc.,*[104] held that an at-will private sector clerk discharged for refusing to take a drug test could state a tort claim for violation of Pennsylvania public policy if

---

[101]443 N.W.2d 382, 4 IER Cases 1107 (Mich. App. 1989).
[102]*Id.* at 1109.
[103]*See infra* notes 161–73 and accompanying text.
[104]963 F.2d 611, 7 IER Cases 698 (3d Cir. 1992).

the testing tortiously invaded her privacy. The court ruled that a urinalysis program might intrude upon the employee's seclusion by the manner in which the sample is obtained[105] or by revealing personal matters unrelated to the workplace.[106]

Employers often conduct investigations of workplace wrongdoing, sometimes with unexpected liability. In *K-Mart v. Trotti*,[107] the Texas Court of Appeals upheld a $108,000 jury award ($8,000 actual and $100,000 exemplary) against an employer for unlawfully intruding upon the seclusion of an employee by breaking into the employee's locker and searching the contents of her purse (the locker was provided by management, but the employee used her own lock). Absent justifiable suspicion that the employee had stolen company property, the search of the locker and purse was wrongful. The court's analysis with respect to the locker and ownership of the lock is particularly instructive in ascertaining when a private search is reasonable:

> The lockers undisputedly were the appellants' [employer's] property, and in their unlocked state, a jury could reasonably infer that those lockers were subject to legitimate, reasonable searches by the appellants. This would also be true where the employees used a lock provided by the appellants, because in retaining the lock's combination or master key, it could be inferred that the appellants manifested an interest both in maintaining control over the locker and in conducting legitimate, reasonable searches. Where, as in the instant case, however, the employee purchases and uses his own lock on the lockers, with the employer's knowledge [as in the instant case], the fact finder is justified in concluding that the employee manifested, and the employer recog-

---

[105]In the words of the court:

The process of collecting the urine sample to be tested clearly implicates "expectations of privacy that society has long recognized as reasonable". . . . In addition, many urinalysis programs monitor the collection of the urine specimen to ensure that the employee does not adulterate it or substitute a sample from another person. . . . Monitoring collection of the urine sample appears to fall within the definition of an intrusion upon seclusion because it involves the use of one's senses to oversee the private activities of another.
Id. 7 IER Cases at 706.

[106]According to the court:

Second, urinalysis "can reveal a host of private medical facts about an employee, including whether she is epileptic, pregnant, or diabetic". . . . A reasonable person might well conclude that submitting urine samples to tests designed to ascertain these types of information constitutes a substantial and highly offensive intrusion from seclusion."
Id. 7 IER Cases at 707.

[107]677 S.W.2d 632 (Tex. App. 1984).

nized, an exception that the locker and its contents would be free from intrusion and interference.[108]

Management should refrain from reading employees' personal mail, even if that mail is sent to the employees where they work.[109] Employers are also advised to stay out of their employees' homes.[110]

b. Public Disclosure of Truthful but Private Facts. Courts have also found employers liable for the publication of private facts of an employee's life, even though the facts published were absolutely truthful. The *Restatement* provides for liability when one publicizes a private matter if the private matter is highly offensive to a reasonable person and not a legitimate concern to the public.[111] Thus, to sustain a cause of action for public disclosure of private facts, the employee must prove (1) the public disclosure of information, and (2) that such disclosure would be highly offensive to a reasonable person and of no legitimate concern to the public.[112] Illustrative is *Miller v. Motorola, Inc.,*[113] where an employer was found liable for disclosing to company employees the plaintiff's mastectomy and reconstructive surgery. The employee argued that her right to privacy was violated because it was a public disclosure of private facts and it constituted an unreasonable intrusion into her seclusion. The lower court granted summary judgment for management. In ruling for the employee on the public disclosure claim, the appellate court followed a Michigan Supreme Court decision which stated:

> An invasion of a plaintiff's right to privacy is important if it exposes private facts to a public whose knowledge of those facts would be embarrassing to the plaintiff. Such a public might be the general public, if the person were a public figure, or a particular public such as fellow employees, club members, church members, family, or neighbors, if the person were not a public figure.[114]

---

[108]*Id.* at 637.

[109]Vernars v. Young, 539 F.2d 966 (3d Cir. 1976) (holding employee had cause of action when employer read employee's personal mail, recognizing employee's reasonable expectation of privacy).

[110]Love v. Southern Bell Tel. & Tel. Co., 263 So. 2d 460 (La. Ct. App. 1972).

[111]RESTATEMENT §652E.

[112]Ledsinger v. Burmeister, 318 N.W.2d 558 (1982); DiTomaso v. Electronic Data Sys., 1988 U.S. Dist. LEXIS 16803, 3 IER Cases 1700 (E.D. Mich. 1988).

[113]560 N.E.2d 900, 5 IER Cases 885 (Ill. App. Ct., 1st Dist. 1990).

[114]Beaumont v. Brown, 257 N.W.2d 522, 531 (Mich. 1977).

With respect to the unreasonable intrusion claim, the court ruled for management. In the court's view, the dissemination of information *voluntarily* disclosed to the employer by the employee was not an intrusion into the employee's seclusion. The principle that an employee who is the source of the publicity waives the right to sue on an unreasonable intrusion claim is black letter law in this area.

Under certain circumstances, disclosure of an employee's personal medical history may be privileged. In *Young v. Jackson*,[115] a supervisor revealed that an employee had had a partial hysterectomy. The Supreme Court of Mississippi, upholding a lower court's grant of summary judgment, ruled that the disclosure was privileged when it was made to co-workers "having a legitimate and direct interest in the subject matter of the communication" because the employee fainted on the job at a nuclear power plant and the supervisor was simply trying to squelch rumors that the cause of her illness was from radiation poisoning. There was no evidence that management communicated the employee's private facts to persons having no legitimate interest in the matter or that management acted with any malice or ill will toward the employee.[116] However, in *Bratt v. International Business Machines*,[117] the First Circuit, sitting in diversity jurisdiction, ruled that a physician-patient relationship existed when an employee was examined by a company's doctor, at least in the situation where the employee believed that a physician-patient relationship existed and the doctor knew that the patient held such an expectation. Accordingly, the court of appeals, reversing a grant of summary judgment for the employer, allowed a cause of action when the physician, retained by the employer, disclosed to management that the employee was paranoid and in need of psychiatric help.

Where an employer disclosed an employee's attendance record to her husband, which led to the husband's suicide after he realized from that record that his wife was having an affair, a privacy claim was rejected. Aside from proximate cause issues, the court found that disclosure of an attendance record "can hardly be considered 'private, secluded or secret.' "[118] The court accordingly sustained the trial

---

[115]572 So. 2d 378 (Miss. 1990).

[116]The dissent found that the communication was excessive, unreasonable, and reckless. *Id.* at 385.

[117]785 F.2d 352 (1st Cir. 1986).

[118]Kobeck v. Nabisco, 305 S.E.2d 183, 184, IER Cases 200 (Ga. App. 1983).

court's grant of summary judgment. A similar result was reached in favor of management where the employer disclosed financial information (compensation, reimbursements, expenses) to the IRS about an employee.[119] The government's interest in pursuing a legitimate investigation outweighed the employee's privacy concerns.

c. Defamation and False Light (1) *Defamation.* The *Restatement (Second) of Torts* defines defamation as a communication that tends to harm the reputation of another so as to lower him in the estimation of the community or to deter third persons from associating or dealing with him.[120] The recognized elements of defamation include: (1) false and defamatory words concerning another person; (2) unprivileged communication to a third party; (3) fault amounting at least to negligence on the part of the publisher; and (4) either actionability of the statement irrespective of special harm or the existence of special harm caused by the publication.[121]

Thus, in order for a statement to amount to defamation, it must be communicated to someone other than the plaintiff, it must be false, and it must tend to harm the plaintiff's reputation and lower him or her in the estimation of the community. In the employee/employer relationship, the publication of the unprivileged communication may arise without a specific employer publication. Some states recognize that an employee may have a cause of action when the publication is made by the employee to a prospective employer. In *Lewis v. Equitable Life Assur. Soc'y,*[122] the plaintiffs, who were former employees of the Equitable Life Assurance Society, had been hired at-will, and were subsequently discharged for "gross insubordination." Plaintiffs claimed they were defamed because the company knew they would have repeated the reason for their discharges to prospective employers. The court phrased the issue as "whether a defendant can ever be held liable for defamation when the statement in question was published to a third person only by the plaintiff."[123] The *Lewis* court acknowledged that other jurisdictions that have faced the issue have recognized a narrow exception to the general rule that communi-

---

[119]Wells v. Premier Indus. Corp., 691 P.2d 765 (Colo. Ct. App. 1984).
[120]RESTATEMENT §577 (1977).
[121]*Id.* at §558.
[122]389 N.W.2d 876, 1 IER Cases 1269 (Minn. Sup. Ct. 1986).
[123]1 IER Cases at 1275.

cation of a defamatory statement to a third person by the person defamed is not actionable.[124] Thus, according to the court, "if a defamed person was in some way compelled to communicate the defamatory statement to a third person, and if it was foreseeable to the defendant that the defamed person would be so compelled, then the defendant could be held liable for the defamation."[125] Citing a Georgia case, the court found there "may be a publication when the sender intends or has reason to suppose that the communication will reach third persons, which happens, or which result naturally flows from the sending."[126]

The *Lewis* court went on to hold:

> the concept of compelled self-publication does no more than hold the originator of the defamatory statement liable for damages caused by the statement where the originator knows, or should know, of the circumstances whereby the defamed person has no reasonable means of avoiding publication of the statement or avoiding the resulting damages; in other words, in cases where the defamed person was compelled to publish the statement.[127]

Other states, however, refuse to recognize self-publication defamation. In *Gore v. Health-Tex, Inc*,[128] the Supreme Court of Alabama denied an employee's claim that she was required to self-publicize the reason for her termination, stating that "[w]e are not prepared to hold that a plaintiff's own reputation of allegedly defamatory statements can supply the element of publication essential in a slander action."[129]

Employers may be protected from defamatory actions when an employee agrees to have his or her work product reviewed. In such cases the employee consents to the judgment of the reviewer. This consent absolves the reviewer from any defamation action as long as the comments were not made with malicious intent. Thus, in *Caslin*

---

[124]Citing, McKinney v. County of Santa Clare, 110 Cal. App. 3d 787 (1980); Colonial Stores, Inc. v. Barrett, 38 S.E.2d 306 (Ga. 1949); Grist v. Upjohn Co., 168 N.W.2d 389 (Mich. 1969); Bretz v. Mayer, 203 N.E.2d 665 (Ohio 1963); First State Bank of Corpus Christi v. Ake, 606 S.W.2d 696 (Tex. Civ. App. 1980).

[125]1 IER Cases at 1276.

[126]*Id.* at 1276, citing Colonial Stores, Inc. v. Barrett, 38 S.E.2d (Ga. App. 1946) at 307 (quoting 36 Corpus Juris Section 172).

[127]*Id.* at 1277.

[128]567 So.2d 1307, 5 IER Cases 1643 (Ala. 1990)

[129]5 IER Cases at 1644.

v. General Electric Co.,[130] where the employee had been fully aware for years that he would periodically be reviewed as to efficiency, in spite of not obtaining the status he thought he deserved, the court concluded the reports were communications that were necessary to the company's functioning. Therefore, such reviews do not incur tort liability to the employer.[131] A similar attempt was rejected in *Bratt v. International Business Machines Corp.*[132] The *Bratt* court concluded that just because a review of past work is not favorable, or even fair, the statements are not actionable.

It should be noted, however, there can be liability for an employer although the defamation occurs between two or more employees. In *Loughry v. Lincoln First Bank, N.A.,*[133] a bank employee was present at a meeting with his immediate supervisor, a bank vice president, and a bank investigator. The meeting was held to discuss improprieties uncovered during an investigation. The investigator made comments to the effect that the plaintiff was a criminal. At trial, the jury determined the statements were uttered out of pure malice. At the appellate level, the court determined there is a qualified privilege to defame employees during the course of an internal investigation. However, the court found this privilege may be lost if the purpose of the statements were to derail the plaintiff's career or for some other malicious purpose.

Moreover, to satisfy an action for defamation, in addition to the publication, the information published must be false. In other words, if the facts being communicated to the third party are truthful, a defamation claim cannot prevail. The truthfulness of information, however, is often difficult to ascertain. In *Lewis v. Equitable Life Assur. Soc'y*, the court noted "[t]rue statements, however disparaging, are not actionable."[134] The truthfulness of the communication, however, must relate to the underlying implications of the statement and not merely to "verbal accuracy" of the statement.[135] It should be noted that even though the truth is a defense to defamation, the truth can

---

[130]608 S.W.2d 69 (Ky. Ct. App. 1980).
[131]*Id.* at 71.
[132]467 N.E.2d 126 (1984).
[133]494 N.E.2d 70 (N.Y. 1986).
[134]1 IER Cases at 1277.
[135]*Id. See also* RESTATEMENT §581A, comment e (1977).

subject the employer to an invasion of privacy action if the truth is a private fact.

To be actionable, the publication of false information must also amount to an unprivileged communication. Suppose an employee is fired because the employer has problems with the employee's off-duty lifestyle; say, for example, the employee is living with a female not his spouse. Alternatively, suppose the employee was discharged for an off-duty theft unrelated to the employee's job. Is management privileged to tell another employer the reasons for the dismissal?

Courts occasionally recognize an absolute privilege to defame. The defense of absolute privilege is well established in the common law of many states. Absolute privilege arises when an otherwise defamatory statement is made by a member of the executive, judicial, or legislative branch of government. Thus, in *Barr. v. Matteo*[136] the Supreme Court noted "officials of government should be free to exercise their duties without fear of potential civil liability." The Court reasoned that it is important that officials of government be free to exercise their duties unembarrassed by the fear of damage suits in respect of acts done in the course of those duties. Such suits would consume time and energies, and the threat of such suits might appreciably inhibit the administration of policies of government.

As such, when a public official is acting in his or her official capacity, courts may grant that individual an absolute privilege from defamation. In *McLaughlin v. Tilendis*[137] an Illinois State Court of Appeals found that a school superintendent had an absolute privilege from liability for slander and tortious interference with contractual relations when the superintendent appeared at a Board of Education meeting to speak out with respect to the qualifications of a school teacher. The court noted that the superintendent had an official duty to discuss the abilities of the teacher with the Board. Given this duty, the superintendent was absolutely privileged to make such comments and therefore could not be held liable for either slander or tortious interference.

It should also be noted that an absolute privilege cannot be overcome by a showing of improper motive or knowledge of falsity. This distinguishes an absolute privilege from one which is merely

---

[136]360 U.S. 564, *reh'g denied*, 361 U.S. 855 (1959).
[137]253 N.E.2d 85, 72 LRRM 2380 (Ill. App. 1969).

qualified.[138] Accordingly, assuming the relevant factors of an absolute privilege are present, the communication, even if performed with malice, does not preclude the absolute privilege.

It is also recognized that statements made during quasi-judicial proceedings may be absolutely privileged. In *Medina v. Spotnail, Inc.*[139] a discharged employee brought a suit against his former employer alleging the employer defamed the employee by publishing statements at an EEOC fact-finding conference held to deal with the employee's charges.[140] The court noted "[t]hese statements are privileged statements made in a quasi-judicial proceeding."[141] Similarly, in *Holland v. Marriott Corp.*[142] the plaintiff brought an action against the Marriott Corporation, his former employer, for employment discrimination, libel, slander, and infringement of common law copyright. The employee's libel claim was based on the employer's written communication to the District of Columbia Department of Employment Services. The written communication was in response to a Department inquiry concerning the employee's termination. The assistant personnel director of the employer filed a response that stated the employee was terminated because he removed company property from the hotel without authorization and had received three written disciplinary notices within one year. The court noted that "under the defamation law of the District of Columbia, defendant's written communications to the Department were absolutely privileged and, therefore, could not support a claim for libel."[143]

A leading case in this area is *Circus Circus Hotels, Inc. v. Witherspoon.*[144] Circus Circus gave defamatory information to the Nevada Employment Security Department when the Department was investigating the unemployment claim filed by Witherspoon.[145] The court concluded the statements were absolutely privileged as long as they were given pursuant to a judicial or quasi-judicial proceeding.

---

[138]*See* Blair v. Walker, 349 N.E.2d 385 (Ill. 1976).
[139]591 F.Supp. 190 40 FEP 1393 (N.D. Ill. 1984).
[140]*Id.* at 1396.
[141]*Id.*
[142]34 FEP 1763 (D.D.C. 1984).
[143]*Id.* at 1767.
[144]657 P.2d 101 (Nev. 1983).
[145]*Id.* at 103.

Fact finding and investigations involving state agencies are covered because they could lead to judicial or quasi-judicial proceedings. The courts reason that full and open disclosure of all facts without fear of liability is worth the risk of abuse by individuals making false and malicious statements.[146] The defamatory material only needs some relation to the subject matter of the proceeding.

In the employment setting, absolute privileges only arise in exceptional cases. A more typical defense in a defamation claim, however, is a "qualified" privilege. The elements of the qualified privilege are: (a) good faith by the defendant; (b) an interest or duty to be upheld; (c) a statement limited in its scope to the purpose; (d) a proper occasion; and (e) publication in a proper manner and to proper parties only, that is, only to those who "need to know."[147] In *Reynolds Metal Co. v. Mays*[148] the Supreme Court of Alabama stated:

> Where a party makes a communication, and such communication is prompted by duty owed either to the public or to a third party, or the communication is one in which the party has an interest, and it is made to another having a corresponding interest, the communication is privileged, if made in good faith and without actual malice. . . . The duty under which the party is privileged to make the communication need not be one having the force of legal obligation, but it is sufficient if it is social or moral in its nature and defendant in good faith believes he is acting in pursuance thereof, although in fact he is mistaken.[149]

In effect, the duty or interest to be upheld by a qualified privilege amounts to a showing of a nexus between the job qualifications and the individual's performance. Accordingly, the qualified privilege is limited to how well the employee did the job and the employee's work habits. If a nexus exists between off-duty lifestyle and the performance of the job, a sufficient duty or interest may arise and the employer acting in good faith may be qualifiedly privileged to make the communication, even if false. The general rule, therefore, is that the information must be limited to the employment concern, the statement is given in response to a request for a recommendation, and the statement is made only to the potential employer.

---

[146]*Id.* at 104.

[147]RESTATEMENT §593–96 (1977).

[148]547 So. 2d 518, 5 IER 1820 (Ala. 1989).

[149]*Id.* at 1824, quoting Berry v. City of New York Ins. Co., 98 So. 290, 292 (1923).

Finally, in discussing the availability of defamation actions for employees, it should be noted that state courts apply differing standards with respect to the employer's state of mind. Most jurisdictions retain a negligence standard in private defamation actions.[150] A negligence standard holds an employer liable as long as the employer was negligent when giving the information to the prospective employer. Some jurisdictions, however, have recognized an actual malice test for private figure cases involving speech of public or general interest.[151] This test holds that an employer must know or have reckless disregard for the truth of its allegations. New York, on the other hand, uses a gross irresponsibility standard. Under New York law, if an employer acts without due consideration for the standards of information gathering and dissemination ordinarily followed by responsible parties, a defamation action may stand.[152] Clearly, as a general principle because of the protections of the First Amendment's freedom of speech provisions, the applicable mental state in a defamation action depends greatly on the individual defamed and the content of the publication.

(2) *False Light.* As opposed to the tort of public disclosure of private but truthful facts, false light privacy deals specifically with the publication of false information about an employee. "False light" exists when management publicly attributes to the employee characteristics, conduct, or beliefs that are false, so that the employee is placed in a "false light." In general, a cause of action requires that management place the employee in a highly offensive position and that the employer knows, or has reason to know, that it is placing the employee in an offensive position. Whereas defamation concerns the employee's reputation, false light deals with the employee's right to be left alone. In *Zechman v. Merrill Lynch,*[153] an employee of Merrill Lynch, Pierce, Fenner & Smith was discharged after agents made a

---

[150]*See* Stone v. Essex County Newspaper, Inc., 330 N.E.2d 161 (Mass. 1975); Troman v. Wood, 340 N.E.2d 292 (Ill. 1975); Caruso v. Local Union No. 690, 670 P.2d 240, 120 LRRM 2233 (Wash. 1983); Miami Herald Publishing Co. v. Ane, 458 So. 2d 239 (Fla. 1984).

[151]*See* Gay v. Williams, 486 F.Supp. 12 (D. Alaska 1979); Diversified Management, Inc. v. Denver Post, Inc., 653 P.2d 1103 (Colo. 1983); Aafco Heating and Air Conditioning Co. v. Northwest Publishing, Inc., 321 N.E.2d 580 (Ind. 1974), *cert. denied,* 424 U.S. 913 (1976); Dienes v. Associated Newspaper, Inc. 358 N.W.2d 562 (Mich. App. 1984).

[152]Chapadeau v. Utica Observer Dispatch, Inc., 341 N.E.2d 569, 571 (N.Y. 1975).

[153]742 F. Supp. 1359, 5 IER Cases 1665 (N.D. Ill. 1990).

surprise visit to his office. The agents informed him of the discharge and remained in his office while he prepared to leave. He was immediately escorted from the building, and he was not allowed to speak with fellow employees. No actual statements were made or alleged by the employer; however, the employee claimed the employer's conduct communicated a false assertion that serious criminal or ethical misconduct caused his discharge.

The court noted that for a "statement" to be actionable under a theory of false light "the statement must not merely be published to a third person, as in defamation, but publicized, which the *Restatement (Second)* has defined as making the matter public by communicating it to the public at large, or to so many persons that the matter must be regarded as substantially certain to become one of public knowledge."[154]

The court further stated that the tort of defamation is quite similar to false light invasion of privacy, noting that "some authorities have stated that all defamation cases can be analyzed as false light cases, but not all false light cases are defamation cases."[155] The court relied upon Section 565, comment b of the *Restatement*, which states that in actions for invasion of privacy it is not necessary for the employee to be defamed: "it is enough that he is given unreasonable and highly objectionable publicity that attributes to him characteristics, conduct or beliefs that are false, and so is placed before the public in a false position."[156] Further, the court found the publication causing the false light must be highly offensive to a reasonable person. Thus, even though the publication could be innocently perceived by co-employees, a cause of action for false light may prevail. This distinction is contrary to the defamation innocent construction rule which denies a defamation claim if the publication could be innocently construed. To state a cause of action for false light privacy, "[t]he court must consider only whether the statement is susceptible of a false meaning which is highly offensive to a reasonable person."[157] Thus, the court denied the employer's motion to dismiss the false light claim, concluding that the actions by Merrill Lynch, as alleged,

---

[154]*Id.* 5 IER Cases at 1674, citing RESTATEMENT §652D, comment a.

[155]*Id.* at 2675, citing Lovgren v. Citizens First Nat'l Bank of Princeton, 534 N.E.2d 987, 16 Media L. Rep. 1214 (Ill. 1989).

[156]*Id.*, citing RESTATEMENT §652E, comment b.

[157]*Id.*

could be reasonably susceptible of an interpretation which should render them actionable under a false light theory.[158]

Where an employee had taken discarded nails worth less than $5.00, and his employer told co-workers that he had stolen company property, an appellate state court upheld a jury determination that the employee was placed in "false light."[159]

d. Appropriation of Name or Likeness. The *Restatement* provides that "[o]ne who appropriates to his own use or benefit the name or likeness of another is subject to liability to the other for invasion of privacy."[160] This tort has little applicability in the workplace.

5. Drugs and Drug Testing*

Drug use and drug testing have increasingly become concerns of both employees and employers. Management's plan may be directed at new hires (where organized resistance to testing is lowest), at employees in safety or security positions, or at the entire labor force, even management personnel. Employers may test any of the above groups under different circumstances, for any number of drugs, using various types of drug tests. Some employers limit drug testing to where there is reasonable suspicion or probable cause (a higher standard than reasonable suspicion) that an employee is under the influence of alcohol or drugs, although drug tests can only identify the presence of drugs, not the degree of impairment of a particular individual. Other employers schedule tests at set intervals. Random testing is more effective and more likely to yield a higher number of positives relative to scheduled tests. However, this method of testing is likely to cause more resistance from employees and thus cause labor and other administrative problems for management.

---

[158]*Id.*

[159]Diamond Shamrock Ref. v. Mendez, 809 S.W.2d 514, 7 IER Cases 531 (Tex. App. 1991).

[160]RESTATEMENT §652(C).

*See generally, MARVIN F. HILL & ANTHONY V. SINICROPI, EVIDENCE IN ARBITRATION, 181–95 (BNA Books, 1987), Chapter 11, *Alcohol and Drug-Related Evidence.* Alcohol and drug testing is also discussed in HILL & SINICROPI, MANAGEMENT RIGHTS: A LEGAL AND ARBITRAL ANALYSIS, 179–88 (BNA Books, 1986), Chapter 7, *Medical Screening.*

Rejection of applicants and employees who test positive is common, generating work for unions, labor lawyers, courts, and arbitrators.

Aside from challenging drug testing based on the inaccuracy of the test result, testing may be challenged (albeit not always successfully), either through litigation, arbitration, or negotiations, on the following bases:

1. it is an unreasonable search and seizure under the federal or a state constitution;
2. testing results in self-incrimination in violation of the Fifth Amendment and the absence of constitutional due process;
3. the establishment of a testing program is a failure to bargain in good faith (if management institutes a drug testing policy without consultation with the union);
4. testing is often discriminatory against the bargaining unit (in the case where management exempts itself or other groups from tests);
5. testing and acting on the results of tests are forms of racial discrimination under Title VII of the Civil Rights Act (to the extent that blacks and other protected minorities are disproportionally affected);
6. testing may result in discrimination against the handicapped;
7. drug testing is violative of the invididual's privacy as recognized at common law; and
8. effecting a dismissal for refusing to take a test is violative of due process and the just cause provision in a collective bargaining agreement.[161]

In the public sector employers are restricted by constitutional considerations.[162] Private employers, however, are not bound by such limitations. Without constitutional protection, and where state law does not prohibit such conduct,[163] private sector employees who seek to attack employers' disciplinary actions or testing procedures must

---

[161]For an example where plaintiffs asserted most of these theories in the same lawsuit, *see* DiTomaso v. Electronic Data Sys., 1988 U.S. Dist. LEXIS 16803, 3 IER Cases 1700 (E.D. Mich. 1988), discussed *infra* note 166 and accompanying text.

[162]See the discussion *infra* Chapter 4, notes 169–248 and accompanying text.

[163]*See generally* Morgan, et al. (eds.), *Drug Testing in the Work Place: State-By-State Drug and Alcohol Testing Survey*, 33 WM. & MARY L. REV. 189 (1991) (collecting statutes).

assert either a public policy or an invasion of privacy claim. Thus, a federal district court, sitting in diversity jurisdiction, ruled that a private sector employee had no constitutional right under the First and Fourth Amendments to be free of unreasonable searches regarding alcohol and drug testing.[164] On appeal to the Third Circuit, however, while not ruling on the constitutional question, the appellate court nevertheless found that a private sector clerk could state a claim in tort if the drug testing tortiously invaded her privacy. Reasoning that "there are few activities in our society more personal or private than the passing of urine,"[165] the Third Circuit concluded that the Pennsylvania courts, if presented the question, would hold that a private sector employee's discharge relating to a tortious invasion of privacy in connection with a urinalysis test violated public policy.

In *DiTomaso v. Electronic Data Systems,*[166] the federal court for the Eastern District of Michigan, rejecting the argument that off-duty drug use is a private matter unless it affects employees' work performance, noted that to state a cause of action for tortious invasion of privacy (in this case, disclosure of embarrassing private facts), the employees must demonstrate that disclosure of such facts (their off-duty marijuana use) was made available to the public or fellow employees. Without such a showing, no invasion of privacy occurred. The federal court also rejected an "intrusion" argument, reasoning that the right to be free from intrusion is not absolute and does not extend so far as to subvert those rights that spring from social conditions, including business relations.

In *Hennessey v. Coastal Eagle Point Oil Co.,*[167] the Supreme Court of New Jersey discussed the issue of whether a lead pumper at a refinery who handled combustible and toxic materials, discharged because he failed a mandatory random drug test, stated a cause of action for violation of a clear mandate of public policy. The New

---

[164]Borse v. Piece Goods Shop, Inc., 758 F. Supp. 263, 6 IER Cases 847 (E.D. Pa. 1991), *vacated and remanded,* 963 F.2d 611, 7 IER Cases 698 (3d Cir. 1992); *see also* Horne v. J.W. Gibson Well Serv., 894 F.2d 1194, 5 IER Cases 69 (10th Cir. 1990) (upholding discharge for employee who tested positive for drugs, rejecting argument that public policy protects employees from invasions of privacy due to unreasonable drug testing policy).

[165]*Borse,* 7 IER Cases at 706, quoting Skinner v. Railway Labor Executives Ass'n 489 U.S. 602, 4 IER Cases 224 (1989).

[166]3 IER Cases 1700 (E.D. Mich, 1988).

[167]609 A.2d 11, 7 IER Cases 1057 (N.J. 1992).

Jersey Constitution prohibited unreasonable search-and-seizure; however, the clause had not been interpreted to protect citizens from unreasonable searches by private parties.[168] The employee's argument that the state and federal Constitution created a right to privacy based upon public policy was rejected by the court.[169] However, assuming for the sake of argument that the right of privacy may serve as a source of public policy, the court went on to rule that "[the] public's interest in ensuring that workers in safety-sensitive positions are drug-free outweighs any individual right to privacy." Further, "one way to vindicate that interest is to permit employers to test those workers and discharge them for failing those tests."[170]

In general, aside from fair employment implications,[171] employees may only seek protection from drug testing where either state statutory law or a state constitution that applies to private action makes the protection available,[172] or the employee is able to demonstrate the elements of certain limited privacy torts.[173] When employees are in safety-sensitive jobs, courts that elect to provide a balancing approach to the problem are unlikely to provide protection against drug testing.

6. Speech

Black letter law in this area holds that at-will private sector employees have no First Amendment freedom of speech rights or, for that matter, any other constitutional rights, vis-a-vis their employers.[174] At common law when an employee's off-duty speech bothers management, the employee can be dismissed, whether or not a nexus to the job exists. As stated by one court: "[t]here is no public policy prohibiting an employer from discharging an ineffective at-will

---

[168]*Id.* at 1062.

[169]*Id.* at 1063.

[170]*Id.* at 1064.

[171]See *infra,* Chapter 3 notes 2–148 and accompanying text.

[172]As was the case in Luck v. Southern Pac. Transp. Co., 267 Cal. Rptr. 618, 627–28, 5 IER Cases 414 (1990).

[173]*But see* Twigg v. Hercules Corp., 406 S.E.2d 56, 6 IER Cases 819 (W. Va. 1990) (holding that dismissal of employee for refusing to submit to random urinalysis test violated public policy of West Virginia where employer had no individual suspicion of drug use).

[174]*See* Skinner v. Railway Labor Executives Ass'n, 489 U.S. 602, 4 IER Cases 224 (1989).

employee. The fact that [the employee's] job duties included public speaking does not alter that rule."[175]

The most expansive application of the public policy exception in the area of speech (and arguably other constitutional rights) is *Novosel v. Nationwide Insurance Co.*,[176] a decision by the Third Circuit. In *Novosel*, the employer was lobbying for a no-fault insurance law in Pennsylvania. Novosel, an employee of Nationwide from December 1966 until November 1981, was a district claims manager. When Novosel refused to lobby, and then in private said disparaging things about the campaign, his employment was terminated. Novosel sought damages, reinstatement, and declaratory relief. The district court granted Nationwide's motion to dismiss.[177]

On appeal, the Third Circuit ruled that Novosel's wrongful discharge claim was cognizable under Pennsylvania law because the "employment termination contravenes a significant and recognized public policy."[178] What is especially noteworthy is the appellate court's reliance on Novosel's First Amendment rights even though free speech protection had traditionally been interpreted as only applying to governmental interference.[179] The court found the concern for the rights of political expression and association of public employees was sufficient to state a public policy under Pennsylvania law.[180] Further, the court found no infirmity in the absence of a statutory declaration of a public policy.[181]

More typical of private employment speech claims is *Pagdilao v. Maui Intercontinental Hotel*.[182] Pagdilao was discharged from his employment as a bellman with the Maui Intercontinental Hotel after swearing at the company Director of Security during a company

---

[175]Korb v. Raytheon Corp., 574 N.E.2d 370, 6 IER Cases 1002 (Mass. 1991) (sustaining dismissal of company vice president, acting as liaison with Congress, after advocating decreased defense spending at press conference).

[176]721 F.2d 894, 1 IER Cases 286 (3d Cir. 1983).

[177]*Id.* at 896.

[178]*Id.* at 898.

[179]*Id.* at 899.

[180]*Id.*

[181]*Id.* Recent Pennsylvania decisions have limited the application of *Novosel* to First and Fourth Amendment claims. *See* Borse v. Piece Goods Shop, Inc., 758 F. Supp. 263, 6 IER Cases 847 (E.D. Pa. 1991); Herchberger v. Jersey Shore Steel Co., 575 A.2d 944, 5 IER Cases 710 (Pa. Super. Ct. 1990).

[182]703 F. Supp. 863, 3 IER Cases 1628 (D. Haw. 1988).

picnic. Pagdilao claimed he was wrongfully discharged under the public policy exception to the employment-at-will doctrine. He claimed his actions should be protected as "free speech." The court held that he "failed to present any arguments or authority to support his assertion that a barrage of profanities at a company picnic is for the 'public good' or in the 'interests of society.' "[183] To violate a clear public policy, according to the court, the values of freedom of speech should not include "that which has a tendency to be injurious to the public or against the public good and whatever contravenes good morals or any established interests of society."[184]

II. SUMMARY: HOW FAR CAN PRIVATE SECTOR EMPLOYERS EXTEND THEIR JURISDICTION OVER EMPLOYEES AT COMMON LAW?

The common law appears to present a window of opportunity for the at-will employee with a lifestyle or off-duty conduct repugnant to an employer, but the window is limited and, in most cases, is of little benefit to the dismissed employee. The common law employment-at-will rule has, in most jurisdictions, been modified by the principle that management motives may not be retaliatory in contravention of some substantial public policy. In some jurisdictions, employees who are discharged in retaliation either for having exercised a statutorily conferred personal right or for having fulfilled a statutorily imposed duty will have a cause of action in tort. The courts that have adopted the public policy exception, however, have focused on a specific policy consideration rather than the general equities of the particular fact situation. Matters that are the subject of personal preference, ethics, or morality which are not overlapped by specific legislative-type declarations have, as a general rule, little chance of finding protection by the courts. Courts talk of the balancing of interests in arriving at a decision, but unless an employee can point to a specific statutory

---

[183]*Id.* 3 IER Cases at 1632.
[184]*Id.* citing Parnar v. Americana Hotels, Inc. 65 Haw. 370, 115 LRRM 4817 (1982).

right or duty, the balancing will inevitably result in a resolution adverse to the employee. Thus, an employee who shows up at his employer's convention with a person not his wife, but presented as his wife, has no public policy defense to a wrongful termination.[185] If the employee worked for a public sector employer, he may or may not have a constitutional right to "associate" with a person not his spouse depending on his job and the agency he worked for,[186] but in most cases his claim to privacy or right to pursue a particular lifestyle will fall on deaf ears by a reviewing court. Only extreme and outrageous conduct, amounting to claims for outrage,[187] or intentional or reckless infliction of emotional distress,[188] may result in relief for the individual.

Courts have recognized claims arising in tort for invasion of privacy. These cases create an option for the employee, damaged as a result of the employer's invasion and publication of private truthful facts, publication of false facts, or likeness, or the invasion into the employee's seclusion. As the law in these privacy cases develops, an employer's ability to become actively involved in an employee's lifestyle choice and off-duty conduct will be curtailed.

Absent a cause of action in tort, an employee challenging a discharge must rely on a contract theory. Courts have rejected the principle that every contract of employment, whatever its duration, is subject to an implied covenant of good faith and fair dealing (thereby making every employment relationship subject to a de facto standard of "just cause").[189] Some courts have enforced promises of job security

---

[185]*See* Staats v. Ohio Nat'l Life Ins. Co., 620 F. Supp. 118, 120 118 LRRM 3242 (W.D. Pa. 1985).

[186]See *infra* Chapter 4 notes 44–166 and accompanying text.

[187]Eserhut v. Heister, 812 P.2d 902, 6 IER Cases 1135 (Wash. 1991).

[188]*See* RESTATEMENT §46 (1965) (requires that the conduct be "extreme and outrageous"); White v. Monsanto Co., 585 So. 2d 1205, 1208, 6 IER Cases 1340 (La. 1991) (noting that "[m]ost states now recognize intentional infliction of emotional distress as an independent tort, not 'parasitic' to a physical injury or a traditional tort such as assault, battery, false imprisonment or the like"); *see also* Boggs v. Avon Prods., 564 N.E.2d 1128, 1134, 6 IER Cases 1128 (Ohio Ct. App. 1990) (discussion of §46); Madani v. Kendall Ford, 794 P.2d 1250, 5 IER Cases 937 (Or. Ct. App. 1990) (allowing cause of action for intentional infliction of emotional distress for employee dismissed for refusal to pull down pants and expose himself to co-workers in portion of workplace open to public view, but disallowing claim for wrongful discharge under public policy exception to at-will rule); *cf.* Wagenseller v. Scottsdale Memorial Hosp., 710 P.2d 1025, 1 IER Cases 526 (Ariz. 1985) (refusing to participate in activities such as "mooning" constitute public policy exception to at-will rule).

[189]*See, e.g.,* Therrien v. United Air Lines, 670 F. Supp. 1517, 2 IER Cases 1572

in contracts of indefinite duration, but these decisions appear limited to extreme cases where legitimate expectations were created by the employer that dismissal would be for just cause only. Similarly, courts have rejected employee handbooks and personnel manuals as a basis per se for implying a just cause standard for all at-will employees. As stated by one federal court, an employment manual is only a unilateral expression of company policy and is not bargained for and, accordingly, it cannot be the basis of an employment contract.[190] Similar reasoning may even be applied to oral representations that are not mutually negotiated.[191] Courts finding a cause of action in contract have determined that a just cause provision is contained in a handbook or manual, or that the employer has orally promised not to dismiss except for cause.[192]

What results, then, is that management has significant discretion at common law to regulate the lifestyles and off-duty conduct of

---

(D. Colo. 1987) (rejecting implied covenant of good faith and fair dealing); Salazar v. Furr's, Inc., 629 F. Supp. 1403, 1409, 2 IER Cases 696 (D.N.M. 1986) (holding that discharged at-will employee has no cause of action for tort of wrongful discharge for marriage to employee of company's competitors, rejecting implied covenant of fair dealing contractual approach); Holmes v. Union Oil Co., 760 P.2d 1189, 1193–94, 3 IER Cases 1219 (Idaho Ct. App. 1987) ("the Idaho courts have not deemed it appropriate to articulate a covenant so broad that it would go beyond the public policy exception to the at-will doctrine creating liability for termination of employees whose activities were not otherwise worthy of judicial protection"); Martin v. Federal Life Ins. Co., 440 N.E.2d 998, 1001–02, 115 LRRM 4524 (Ill. App. Ct. 1982) ("[c]are must be taken to prevent the transformation of every breach of contract into an independent tort action through the bootstrapping of the general contract principle of good faith and fair dealing"); Morris v. Coleman Co., 738 P.2d 841, 848, 2 IER Cases 844 (Kan. 1987) ("principle of law . . . that every contract imposes upon each party a duty of good faith and fair dealing in its performance and its enforcement, is overly broad and should not be applicable to employment-at-will contracts").

[190]Rouse v. Peoples Natural Gas Co., 605 F. Supp. 230, 119 LRRM 2220 (D. Kan. 1985); *see also* Joachim v. AT&T Info. Serv., 793 F.2d 113, 1 IER Cases 726 (5th Cir. 1986) (sustaining dismissal of homosexual employee notwithstanding employee handbook provision that sexual preference would not be basis for job discrimination or termination); Tohline v. Central Trust, 549 N.E.2d 1223, 5 IER Cases 521 (Ohio Ct. App. 1988) ("[a]bsent mutual assent, a handbook becomes merely a unilateral statement of rules and policy which creates no obligations and rights").

[191]*See* Cederstrand v. Lutheran Bhd., 117 N.W.2d 213, 218–19 (Minn. 1962).

[192]*See, e.g.,* Toussaint v. Blue Cross & Blue Shield, 292 N.W.2d 880, 892, 115 LRRM 4708 (Mich. 1980) (oral statement to employee); *cf.* Mers v. Dispatch Printing Co., 483 N.E.2d 150, 154, 2 IER Cases 1031 (Ohio 1985) ("An additional limit on an employer's right to discharge occurs where representations or promises have been made to the employee which fall within the doctrine of promissory estoppel.").

its employees. Barring narrow privacy torts, virtually all courts are unwilling to incorporate constitutional-type rights into private employment relationships. The reason for not expanding public policy exceptions to the common law at-will rule, as articulated by one court, is that "application of constitutional values such as individual privacy to private relationships carries the danger that those values will 'expand like a gas to fill up the available space.' "[193] Private sector employees, desiring protection from employers, must look to statutes[194] or labor arbitrators[195] for protection. In addition to the above protections, the public sector employee may find protection in the Constitution.[196]

---

[193]*See* Hennessey v. Coastal Eagle Point Oil Co., 589 A.2d 170, 176, 6 IER Cases 513 (N.J. Super. Ct. App. Div. 1991) (quoting Luedtke v. Nabors Alaska Drilling, Inc., 768 P.2d 1123, 1128, 4 IER Cases 129 (Alaska 1989)).

[194]See *infra* Chapter 3.

[195]See *infra* Chapter 5.

[196]See *infra* Chapter 4.

Chapter 3

Statutory Restrictions

The once inflexible common law rule allowing an employer to discharge a worker at any time and for any reason is no longer universally controlling. Numerous statutes now limit an employer's right to terminate employees to such an extent that employers clearly have less freedom to terminate an employment relationship, perhaps even less than employees. Unlike the employer, a disgruntled employee can terminate the employment relationship whatever the reason.

Specifically, since 1964, managerial discretion has been significantly limited with respect to employees' civil rights. Management can no longer discriminate against employees (or applicants for employment) because of race, color, religion, sex, national origin, or age. These federally imposed restrictions are supplemented by numerous state statutes. At the state level, management's discretion may be limited in the areas of marital or sexual preference, handicap or physical disability, and creed or political affiliation.[1] This chapter discusses major civil rights and employment-related legislation, court interpretations, and federal guidelines affecting management's ability to discharge employees because of off-duty conduct, or unhealthy or unusual lifestyles.

---

[1]*See infra* this chapter, part II, State Statutes.

I. FEDERAL STATUTES

A. Title VII of the Civil Rights Act of 1964, as Amended

Title VII of the Civil Rights Act of 1964, as amended in 1972 and 1978,[2] is an all-encompassing federal statute regulating virtually every facet of personnel management. The Act explicitly prohibits discrimination in employment as to hiring, firing, compensation, terms, conditions, or privileges of employment on the basis of race, color, religion, sex, or national origin. Since 1972, the Act has applied to employers engaged in an industry affecting commerce who have 15 or more employees each working day in 20 or more calendar weeks of the current calendar year.[3] It also applies to employment agencies procuring employees for such an employer,[4] and to almost all labor organizations.[5] The 1972 amendments also extended coverage to all state and local governments; government agencies; political subdivisions, excluding elected officials, their personal assistants, and immediate advisors; and the District of Columbia departments and agencies, except where subject by law to the federal competitive service.[6]

Any person claiming to be aggrieved by a violation of the statute may file a complaint with the Equal Employment Opportunity Commission (EEOC). The EEOC is vested with the authority to investigate individual charges of discrimination, to promote voluntary compliance with the statute, and to institute civil actions against parties named in a discrimination charge.[7] The EEOC cannot adjudicate claims or impose administrative sanctions. Rather, the EEOC can (if it so elects) prosecute violations in the federal courts, which are authorized to

---

[2]42 U.S.C.§§2000e to 2000e-17 (1988).

[3]*Id.* at §§2000e(b), 2000e-2(a).

[4]*Id.* at §§2000e(c), 2000e-2(b).

[5]*Id.* at §§2000e(d), 2000e-2(c).

[6]Equal Employment Opportunity Act of 1972, Pub. L. No. 92-261,§2, 92 Stat. 103 (1972) (amending 42 U.S.C.§2000e(a)). As originally enacted in 1964, Title VII did not cover employees of the federal government. In 1972, however, the statute was amended to include most federal employees. *Id.* at §11 (amending 42 U.S.C.§2000e-16).

[7]42 U.S.C.§2000e-5(b), (f) (1) (1988).

issue injunctive relief and to order such affirmative action as may be appropriate.[8]

To effectuate the purposes and policies of the statute, Congress prohibited employers from retaliating against employees who initiate complaints under Title VII. The retaliation provision has been held to afford protection to employees even though the conditions and conduct complained of do not constitute a violation of Title VII.[9] Moreover, even relatives of persons who exercise rights under the statute are protected from employer retaliation.[10]

Under Title VII, discrimination based on religion, sex, or national origin is regulated by a different statutory standard than that applied to race or color. Employment discrimination with respect to religion, sex, or national origin is tolerated only where religion, sex, or national origin is a bona fide occupational qualification (BFOQ) reasonably necessary to the normal operation of a particular business.[11] There is no statutory BFOQ for race or color.

Accordingly, the statute mandates a two-step analysis in employment discrimination cases. First, the EEOC or a court must find that the defendant (usually an employer) has discriminated against an employee or applicant on a basis prohibited by the Act.[12] Only after a determination that a prohibited form of discrimination has occurred will the second step be considered. Thus, if discrimination other than race or color is found, the employer has the opportunity to

---

[8]*Id.* at §2000e-5(f), (g).

[9]See Novotny v. Great Am. Fed. Sav. & Loan Ass'n, 584 F.2d 1235, 1259, 17 FEP Cases 1482 (3d Cir. 1978), *cert. granted,* 439 U.S. 1066, *rev'd on other grounds,* 442 U.S. 366, 19 FEP Cases 1482 (1979).

[10]Kornbluh v. Stearns & Foster Co., 73 F.R.D. 307, 14 FEP Cases 847 (S.D. Ohio 1976).

[11]Section 703(e) provides:

Notwithstanding any other provision of this subchapter, (1) it shall not be an unlawful employment practice for an employer to hire and employ employees, for an employment agency to classify, or refer for employment any individual, for a labor organization to classify its membership or to classify or refer for employment any individual, . . . on the basis of his religion, sex, or national origin in those certain instances where religion, sex, or national origin is a bona fide occupational qualification [BFOQ] reasonably necessary to the normal operation of that particular enterprise. . . .

Civil Rights Act of 1964, Pub. L. No. 88-352, §703(e), 88 Stat. 255 (1964) (codified as amended at 42 U.S.C.§2000e-2(e) (1988)).

[12]42 U.S.C. §2000e-2e (1988).

demonstrate that the discrimination was justified as a BFOQ.[13] The reach of Title VII's prohibitions against employment discrimination has been expanded by the courts to include even neutrally stated and indiscriminately administered employment practices (in the absence of demonstrable business necessity) if the practice operates to favor an identifiable group of white employees over a protected class.[14]

The statute has also been used to protect traditional nonminorities. In *McDonald v. Santa Fe Trail Transportation Co.*,[15] the Supreme Court held that the terms of Title VII are not limited to discrimination against members of any particular race.[16] To rule otherwise, the Court said, would "constitute·a derogation of the Congressional mandate to eliminate all practices which operate to disadvantage the employment opportunities of any group protected by Title VII."[17]

1. Structure of Title VII

Title VII forbids discrimination only under specific circumstances. Under Title VII, "discrimination" is an unlawful employment practice only if: (1) committed by someone covered by the Act; (2) on a prohibited "basis" or consideration (race, color, religion, sex, national origin) cognizable under Title VII; (3) with regard to an "issue" (hiring, discharging, compensation, terms and conditions of employment, and so on) cognizable under the statute; and (4) with a causal connection or "nexus" between the prohibited basis or consideration and the issue.[18] Simply stated, not all discrimination is prohibited by Title VII. A person not covered by the Act (for example, an employer with less than 15 employees) can discriminate on the basis of race, color, religion, sex, or national origin and not violate Title VII, although such an employer would likely violate a state antidiscrimination statute. Similarly, discrimination by an employer with

---

[13]*Id.*

[14]*See Griggs v. Duke Power*, 401 U.S. 424, 3 FEP Cases 175 (1971), discussed *infra* notes 27–33 and accompanying text.

[15]427 U.S. 273, 12 FEP Cases 1577 (1976).

[16]*Id.* at 280.

[17]*Id.* at 279–80 (quoting EEOC Decision No. 74-31, 7 FEP Cases 1326, 1328 (1973)).

[18]*See* BARBARA LINDEMANN SCHLEI & PAUL GROSSMAN, EMPLOYMENT DISCRIMINATION LAW 1 (BNA Books, 1983).

3,000 employees on the basis the applicant is a Green Bay Packer fan does not violate the Act. It is only discrimination based on race, color, religion, sex, and national origin which the federal statute addresses. If race, color, religion, sex, or national origin is not involved, the federal statute is simply inapplicable to the conduct at issue.

Further, the discrimination must be linked in some way to employment or terms and conditions of employment. For example, it is not a violation of the statute for a city government (an entity otherwise covered by the statute) to exclude girls from playing Little League hardball because no employment is involved. Such conduct may violate a state statute prohibiting sex discrimination in public accommodations, but Title VII is not violated.

Finally, there must be a causal connection between the "basis" (race, sex, and so on) and the "issue" (terms and conditions of employment) before Title VII is violated. Thus, it is not a violation of Title VII for an employer to simply fail to hire a black or a female or a Catholic if there is no causal connection or "nexus" between the "basis" (race, sex, or religion) and the "issue" (the decision to hire).

2. The Concept of "Discrimination" Under Title VII

Title VII was not designed to right all wrongs in an employment setting, nor was it designed to mandate that employers act reasonably toward employees. The touchstone of the Act is "discrimination." If there is no discrimination, the statute does not apply.

The two theories by which an act of discrimination may be proved are disparate treatment and disparate impact. The most easily understood type of discrimination is disparate treatment, which involves treating an individual less favorably than others similarly situated because of race, color, religion, sex, or national origin.[19] *Proof* of a discriminatory motive is required in disparate treatment cases, although it may be *inferred* from the mere fact of a difference in treatment.[20] The plaintiff has the initial burden of proving, by a preponderance of the evidence, a prima facie case of discrimination.[21]

---

[19]Teamsters v. United States, 431 U.S. 324, 335–36 n.15, 14 FEP Cases 1514 (1977).

[20]*Id.* at 335–36 n.15.

[21]Texas Dep't of Community Affairs v. Burdine, 450 U.S. 248, 252–56, 25 FEP Cases 113 (1981). The burden is not onerous. *Id.* at 253.

Disparate impact involves employment practices that are facially neutral but have a discriminatory effect when applied.[22] In *Chambers v. Omaha Girls Club, Inc.*[23] the court discussed three ways of establishing disparate impact:

> (1) whether blacks (or women or black women) as a class or at least blacks (or women or black women) in a specified geographical area are excluded by the suspect practice at a substantially higher rate than whites (or men); (2) the percentages of class member applicants [employees] that are actually excluded by the practice or policy, or (3) the level of employment of blacks (black women) by the employer in comparison with the percentage of blacks in the relevant labor market or geographic area.[24]

If such practice cannot be justified as a business necessity, its use violates Title VII.[25]

The issue of whether a test, or other selection device that excludes an employee with a particular lifestyle, is a valid predictor of job performance, or is otherwise necessary for the safe or efficient operation of the business, arises in employment discrimination cases only after the plaintiff has demonstrated the challenged criterion exerts a disparate impact on a protected class. In other words, under Title VII an employer defending a charge of disparate impact discrimination is not compelled to demonstrate business necessity unless the selection criterion is first found to have a discriminatory impact.

In the case of a test, once it is shown to have an adverse impact, the employer, in order to escape liability under Title VII, must demonstrate the test is valid. Validation merely shows the test or other device accurately predicts job performance. In this regard, the first step in the validation process is for the employer to formulate a proper definition of the job. While EEOC Guidelines do not provide specific procedures for conducting a job analysis, they do state that any professional method of job analysis is acceptable if it is comprehensive and

---

[22]*See, e.g.,* Nashville Gas Co. v. Satty, 434 U.S. 136, 16 FEP Cases 136 (1977) (effect of neutral policy denying seniority to women returning from pregnancy leave); Albermarle Paper Co. v. Moody, 422 U.S. 405, 10 FEP Cases 1181 (1975) (disparate impact on blacks).

[23]629 F. Supp. 925, 40 FEP Cases 362 (D. Neb. 1986).

[24]*Id.* at 948 (citing Green v. Missouri Pac. R.R., 523 F.2d 1290, 1293–94, 10 FEP Cases 1409 (8th Cir. 1975)).

[25]*Id.*

otherwise appropriate for the specific validation strategy used. A validation-type study is then performed.

The Guidelines cite three validity strategies for showing that a test is job related: (1) Criterion-related validity—a statistical demonstration of a relationship (correlation) between scores on a test and actual job performance; (2) Content validity—a demonstration that the content of a test is representative of important aspects of the job. For example, a typing test given to an applicant for a secretarial position, or a driving test given an applicant for a fork-lift job. Content validity is present to the extent the actual content of a test contains samples of job performance; and (3) Construct validity—present where there is a relationship between a "construct" or a "trait," and that trait is important for successful job performance. Finally, it must be demonstrated that success on the test is a predictor or measure of success on the job. To validate a test through this method it is first necessary to determine through job analysis that a particular trait or construct (honesty, for example) is actually related to job performance (cashier). Second, it must be demonstrated the test used does, in fact, measure the specific trait.

The current Uniform Guidelines on Employee Selection Procedures define "adverse impact" as "a substantially different rate of selection in hiring, promotion or other employment decision which works to the disadvantage of members of a race, sex or ethnic group."[26] Although not a legal definition of discrimination, the Guidelines provide that an adverse impact exists when the selection rate for a particular group is less than four-fifths or 80 percent of the selection rate for other groups. For example, if 70 percent of the male applicants are selected and 60 percent of the female applicants are selected, no adverse effect exists because 60 percent, the female selection rate, is 86 percent of 70 percent, the male selection rate. However, if 60 percent of the male applicants and 40 percent of the female applicants are selected, an adverse impact exists because 40 percent is only 67 percent of 60 percent. Smaller differences in selection rates may still constitute adverse impact, where they are significant in both statistical and practical terms or where an employer's actions have discouraged applicants disproportionately.

---

[26]29 C.F.R. §1607 (1989).

If the number of candidates is small, the statistical results may not reflect the reality of the employment situation. Likewise, if the statistical universe is too small, the results achieved may be due to chance or random distribution.

3. Standards Limited by Law

The "granddad" of disparate impact cases is *Griggs v. Duke Power*.[27] Prior to the effective date of Title VII, Duke Power Company openly discriminated on the basis of race in the hiring and assignment of employees.[28] The plant was organized into five operating departments: (1) Labor, (2) Coal Handling, (3) Operations, (4) Maintenance, and (5) Laboratory and Testing.[29] Blacks were employed only in the Labor Department, where the highest paying jobs paid less than the lowest paying jobs in the other four operating departments in which whites were employed. Promotions were normally made within each department on the basis of seniority. Transferees into a department usually began in the lowest position.

In 1955 the Company instituted a policy of requiring a high school education for initial assignment to any department except Labor, and for transfer from Coal Handling to any inside department (Operations, Maintenance, or Laboratory). When the Company abandoned its policy of restricting blacks to the Labor Department in 1965, completion of high school was also made a prerequisite to transfer from Labor to any other department. Additionally, the Company required new employees to register satisfactory scores on two professionally developed aptitude tests, as well as to have a high school diploma. This was required of all applicants except in the Labor Department.[30] Completion of high school alone continued to render employees eligible for transfer to the four desirable departments from which blacks had been excluded if the incumbent had been employed prior to the time of the new requirement. Subsequently, the Company began to permit incumbent employees who lacked a high school education to qualify for transfer from Labor or

---

[27]401 U.S. 424, 3 FEP Cases 175 (1971).
[28]*Id.* at 426–27.
[29]*Id.* at 427.
[30]*Id.* at 427–28.

Coal to an "inside" job by passing two other tests—the Wonderlic Personnel Test and the Bennett Mechanical Aptitude Test. Since a smaller percentage of blacks relative to whites had received a high school degree (34 percent as opposed to 12 percent in North Carolina), and because whites fared better on the tests than blacks (58 percent vs. 6 percent), the court found the requirement had an adverse or disparate impact on blacks.[31]

More important, no relationship was shown between obtaining a high school diploma and successful job performance (it was found that a large percentage of whites without a high school diploma had performed successfully in the cited jobs). The *Griggs* Court made it clear that the statute proscribes not only overt discrimination, but also employment practices which are fair in form but discriminatory in operation. If a test that operates to exclude a protected class cannot be shown to be related to job performance, the practice is prohibited.[32] The Court stated that "any tests used must measure the person for the job and not the person in the abstract."[33]

After the *Griggs* decision, in a 1989 case, *Wards Cove Packing v. Antonio,*[34] the Supreme Court stated that once a plaintiff establishes a disparate impact resulting from an employment practice, he still has the burden of proving the employer's practice did not serve in a significant way legitimate employment goals.[35] However, in October 1991, Congress, with presidential backing, passed the Civil Rights Act of 1991.[36] The most significant provisions of the bill concern the Court-created business necessity test first announced in *Griggs*. The compromise legislation overturns the holding in *Wards Cove* and returns to the *Griggs* standard where the burden shifts to the employer to show a "manifest relationship to the employment in question." Under the 1991 Act, unlawful discrimination is demonstrated if the employer is unable to rebut a prima facie case by "demonstrat[ing] that the challenged practice is job related for the position in question

---

[31]*Id.* at 430 n.6.
[32]*Id.* at 436.
[33]*Id.*
[34]490 U.S. 642, 49 FEP Cases 1519 (1989).
[35]*Id.* at 659.
[36]Pub. L. No. 102–166, Nov. 21, 1991, 105 Stat. 1071 (Title 2, §§601, 1201 to 1224; Title 16, §1a-5 note; Title 29, §626; Title 42, §§1981, 1981 notes, 1981a, 1988, 2000e, 2000e note, 2000e-1, 2000e-2, 2000e-4, 2000e-4 note, 2000e-5, 2000e-16, 12111, 12112, 12209).

and consistent with business necessity." The 1991 statute identifies the following language as declaring the intent of Congress in referring to "practice" and "business necessity":

> When a decision-making process includes particular, functionally-integrated practices which are components of the same criterion, standard, method of administration, or test, such as the height and weight requirements designed to measure strength in Dothard v. Rawlinson, 433 U.S. 321 (1977), the particular, functionally-integrated practices may be analyzed as one employment practice.[37]

Business necessity is otherwise not defined.

Under the 1991 Act, management must now demonstrate that an employment practice shown to have a disparate impact is truly necessary, as opposed to simply being useful or convenient. Moreover, if disparate impact is established but not traced to any particular employment practice, the employer must demonstrate it needs the whole complex of employment practices from which the disparate impact flows.

Title VII was also amended to create the ability to sue for back pay, compensatory damages, and in extreme cases punitive damages. There are no limits on awards of back pay. All other damages (mental anguish, pain and suffering, and punitive damages) would be limited to $50,000 for employers of 16 to 100, $100,000 for employers of 101 to 200, $200,000 for employers of 201 to 500, and $300,000 for employers of 501 or more employees.

Based upon *Griggs* and the Civil Rights Act of 1991, any recruiting, hiring, promotion, or retention criterion that has a disparate impact on a protected class must be job-related to avoid liability under the statute. As noted, a disparate impact must be established before the employer's obligation to demonstrate job-relatedness comes into play. Title VII does not mandate that all selection criteria be job-related, but only those criteria that have an adverse impact on employment opportunities. A selection criterion may not be job-related, yet if the impact on both nonminorities and minorities is the same, Title VII is not violated. In other words, an employer is entitled to use a job criterion that does not predict performance on the job (weight, for example), so long as the criterion does not have a disparate impact on a member of a protected minority. One can, of course,

---

[37]137 CONG. REC. H9505-01, °H9534.

question why an employer would ever use a selection device that has no predictive utility whatsoever. Nevertheless, the law does not require rationality (making it difficult for employees with unconventional lifestyles), but only that the criteria used be nondiscriminatory in the statutorily understood sense.

4. Hiring Standards Applicable to Employee Lifestyle

Although management has much discretion in designating job qualifications, the courts' application of fair employment laws has limited an employer's consideration and use of factors that might otherwise be used in screening job applicants. Areas of special interest related to applicant's or employee's lifestyle include: (a) police or criminal history records; (b) garnishment, financial status, or credit references; (c) unwed mothers; (d) sexual preference and change of sex; (e) race association including interracial marriage; (f) weight and personal appearance; (g) drug or alcohol addiction; and (h) religion.

a. Police or Criminal History Records. Many employment applications ask applicants if they have prior arrest or conviction records. If the applicant's lifestyle has resulted in arrests or convictions,[38] there may be relief under Title VII or a state fair employment statute.

Both the EEOC and the courts have distinguished preemployment arrest inquiries from inquiries concerning convictions. Inquiries into applicant arrest records have been prohibited unless they are shown to be job-related.[39]

Courts have recognized that blacks are subject to arrest for serious crimes in disproportionate numbers. However, with few exceptions, conviction inquiries have been held to constitute a legitimate employer concern. Still, employers are advised not to adopt a blanket policy of excluding any applicant with a conviction record.

---

[38]*See, e.g., Glaz v. Ralston Purina Co.,* 509 N.E.2d 297, 2 IER Cases 497 (Mass. App. Ct. 1987) (holding no public policy exception to at-will rule in discharging employee who had been arrested, convicted, and imprisoned in Hungary for bribery, even though dismissal resulted from employer's policies).

[39]*Gregory v. Litton Sys., Inc.,* 316 F. Supp. 401, 2 FEP Cases 821 (C.D. Cal. 1970), *aff'd,* 472 F.2d 631, 5 FEP Cases 267 (9th Cir. 1972).

In *Green v. Missouri Pacific Railroad,*[40] the Eighth Circuit held that an employer violated Title VII by using a conviction as an absolute bar to employment. The court reasoned that because blacks are convicted at a higher rate than whites, the employer's practice of summarily rejecting all applicants with a conviction record (minor traffic offenses were excluded) had an adverse impact on a protected class under the statute.[41]

The EEOC consistently takes the position that reasonable cause exists to believe Title VII is violated when applicants are automatically eliminated from job consideration because of a conviction.[42] The reasoning of the Commission usually follows the same pattern: Because blacks are convicted at a rate significantly in excess of their percentage in the population, an employment practice of disqualifying persons for employment because of conviction records can be expected to have a discriminatory impact upon blacks and would, therefore, be unlawful under Title VII in the absence of a justifying business necessity.[43] To establish business necessity the employer must demonstrate the nature of a particular criminal conviction (retail theft, for example) disqualifies the individual job applicant from performing the particular job in an acceptable, business-like manner (cashier). The most important factor in this determination is the job-relatedness of the conviction. If the conviction is not job-related, to disqualify the individual because of the conviction is unlawful.[44]

Contrary to the position taken by the EEOC, however, most courts have concluded that a policy of rejecting applicants with a conviction record does not have a per se disparate impact on minorities.[45] Rather, to establish a prima facie case of discrimination, the rejected applicant is required to show the conviction rate for blacks is higher than for nonminorities in the relevant labor market. Again,

---

[40]523 F.2d 1290, 10 FEP Cases 1409 (8th Cir. 1975).

[41]*Id.* at 1298–99.

[42]*Id.* at 1295, 1298–99.

[43]*Id.* at 1298–99.

[44]EEOC Decision No. 80-12, 26 FEP Cases 1794, 1795 (1980) (citing Commission Decision No. 78-35, 26 FEP Cases 1755 (1978)).

[45]Hill v. United States Postal Serv., 522 F. Supp. 1283, 26 FEP Cases 1426 (S.D.N.Y. 1981); Craig v. HEW, 508 F. Supp. 1055, 25 FEP Cases 560 (W.D. Mo. 1981) (rejecting argument that courts should take judicial notice of probable disparate impact of rule against employing persons with felony convictions); Green v. Missouri Pac. R.R., 381 F. Supp. 992, 8 FEP Cases 1024 (E.D. Mo. 1974).

an employer need not demonstrate its policy is job-related absent a showing of discriminatory impact.

In addition to avoiding the exclusion of all applicants with conviction records, employers should also avoid applying discharge policies in a discriminatory manner. In *Ricks v. Riverwood International,*[46] a black employee brought a Title VII claim against his employer as a result of a discharge for a felony conviction of possession of marijuana. A fellow white employee, convicted of an offense described as "threatening a fourteen year old boy with a firearm and homosexual approaches toward a young man,"[47] was retained by the company. The issue, according to the court, was the "comparable seriousness" of the felonies in question. The court noted that because the evidence established a genuine issue upon which relief could be granted, the black employee raised a potential cause of action.

Failure to truthfully respond to conviction history questions on applications, however, may later be used by the employer to limit damages and other relief in a Title VII case.[48] In *Washington v. Lake County Sheriff's Department,*[49] the plaintiff was employed by the Lake County Sheriff's Department in September 1986 as a jailer. As part of his hiring process he completed an employment application which asked whether the applicant had ever been convicted of an offense other than minor traffic violations. In response, plaintiff indicated he had not been convicted on any such offense.

After being hired, he was terminated in July 1987 as a result of an arrest for criminal sexual assault. At the time of discharge, the employer had no knowledge plaintiff had lied on his job application. After the termination, the employer discovered the employee had lied on his application and had pleaded guilty to a criminal trespass charge in 1974 and was convicted for third degree assault in 1981. The employee pursued a cause of action under Title VII, claiming race discrimination. The Seventh Circuit stated the case presented two questions: first, whether the employer would have hired the employee had it known about his criminal convictions, and second, whether the employer would have fired the employee had it discov-

---

[46]782 F. Supp. 83, 57 FEP Cases 1524 (W. Ark. 1992).

[47]*Id.* 57 FEP Cases at 1526.

[48]Discharge for falsification of employment applications is discussed *infra* Chapter 5, notes 277–304 and accompanying text.

[49]969 F.2d 250, 59 FEP Cases 989 (7th Cir. 1992).

ered his false declarations about his convictions. Asserting that the employer would have been less likely to fire an employee after learning of the convictions, the court rejected the argument that the fraudulent conduct necessarily prevented relief for later acts of employment discrimination. Thus, the employer must show by a preponderance of evidence that, acting in a race-neutral manner, it would have made the same employment decision had it known of the "after-acquired evidence." The court found that management sufficiently set forth evidence to establish it would have fired the employee had it discovered the concealment of his convictions. Accordingly, the Seventh Circuit upheld the trial court's grant of summary judgment for the employer.

It is of note that numerous states have enacted legislation addressing the use and dissemination of information concerning an applicant's arrest or conviction record in an employment setting.[50] The effect of this legislation is, in most cases, a mandate that management cannot consider arrests not resulting in convictions or, alternatively, convictions which have been expunged from the employee's record.

---

[50]CAL. LAB. CODE §432-7 (West Supp. 1991) (allows limited exceptions for employers providing health care); *see also* CAL. PENAL CODE §11105 (West Supp. 1991); COL. REV. STAT. ANN. §24-72-308(1) (f) (I) (West 1990); CONN. GEN. STAT. ANN. §31.51i (West 1987) (arrest information not available to any member of firm interviewing applicant except the job personnel department or the person in charge of employment); MASS. GEN. LAWS ANN. ch. 276, §100A (West Supp. 1991) (an applicant for employment with a sealed record on file may answer "no record" with respect to an inquiry related to prior arrests); MICH. COMP. LAWS ANN. §37.2205(a) (West 1985) ("An employer . . . shall not in connection with an application for employment . . . make or maintain a record of information regarding an arrest, detention, or disposition of a violation of law in which a conviction did not result."); MINN. STAT. ANN. §364.03 (West 1991) (public employer limitation); N.Y. EXEC. LAW §296.16 (McKinney 1991) (unlawful discriminatory practice to make any inquiry about any arrest or criminal accusation in which a conviction did not result); PA. STAT. ANN. tit. 18, §9125 (1983) ("Felony and misdemeanor convictions may be considered by the employer only to the extent to which they relate to the applicant's suitability for employment in the position for which he has applied. The employer shall notify in writing the applicant if the decision not to hire the applicant is based in whole or part on criminal history record information."); R.I. GEN. LAWS §28-5-7(7) (Supp. 1991) ("unlawful employment practice" to "inquire either whether the applicant has ever been arrested or charged with any crime; provided, however, that nothing herein shall prevent an employer from inquiring whether the applicant has ever been convicted of any crime"); TEX. EDUC. CODE ANN. §51.215 (West Supp. 1991) (allowing institution of higher education to obtain from any law enforcement agency "criminal history information" to evaluate applicants for security-sensitive positions); VA. CODE. ANN. §19.2-392.4 (Michie 1990).

b. Garnishment, Financial Status, and Credit References. Some lifestyles result in bankruptcy or other financial problems. While at common law an individual could be dismissed for credit history problems,[51] both the courts and the EEOC have taken the position that since minorities are more frequently garnished than nonminorities, a policy of discharging employees after several garnishments violates Title VII. Some courts, however, require that the plaintiff use the debt-paying characteristics of the employer's work force rather than the population at large in establishing disparate impact.

Also of note is the Consumer Credit Protection Act,[52] which provides that an employer may not discharge an employee because the employee's earnings have been subjected to garnishment for any one indebtedness.[53] Further, under the Fair Credit Act,[54] any employer who denies a job to an applicant based on information contained in a "consumer report"[55] must advise the applicant of this fact and provide the name and address of the consumer reporting agency that compiled the report.[56] The antidiscrimination provisions of the Federal Bankruptcy Code may also provide relief to employees who are debtors under Chapter 11.[57]

---

[51]*See Comeaux v. Brown & Williamson Tobacco, 915 F.2d 1264, 5 IER Cases 1387 (9th Cir. 1990).*

[52]15 U.S.C.§1674 (1988).

[53]*Id.* at §1674(a).

[54]15 U.S.C. §1681 (1970).

[55]A "consumer report" is defined in 15 U.S.C. §1681(a) (d) (1988) as "any written or oral information bearing on the person's credit history, character, reputation, or mode of living prepared by a reporting agency."

[56]*Id.* at §1681m(a).

[57]The Bankruptcy Amendments and Federal Judgeship Act of 1984, in relevant part provides:

> No private employer may terminate the employment, or discriminate with respect to employment against, an individual who is or has been a debtor under this title, a debtor or bankrupt under the Bankruptcy Act, or an individual associated with such debtor or bankrupt, solely because such debtor is bankrupt—
> (1) is or has been a debtor under this title or the Bankruptcy Act;
> (2) has been insolvent before the commencement of a case under this title or during the case but before the grant or denial of a discharge; or
> (3) has not paid a debt that is dischargeable in a case under this title or that was discharged under the Bankruptcy Act.

11 U.S.C.§525(b) (1988); *see, e.g.,Stockhouse v. Hines Motor Supply,* 75 B.R. 83, 2 IER Cases 487 (D. Wyo. 1987).

Finally, at the state level, employer discretion to use garnishments or credit history[58] as employment criterion may be limited in some respects but, more often than not, the statutes specifically permit employers to use credit information for employment purposes.

c. Unwed Mothers. Section 701(k) of Title VII prohibits employers from discriminating against an employee because she is pregnant. Suppose an employer seeks to remove or avoid hiring a woman because she is pregnant and unmarried. Is Title VII violated? An employer who applies a legitimacy rule to one sex and not the other discriminates on account of sex under Title VII. It makes no difference that the resulting discrimination is between all males and some females (non-unwed mothers) versus some females (unwed mothers). Discrimination between members of a protected class regardless of class-specific distinctions is nevertheless sex discrimination under Title VII.

The more interesting question is whether an unwed mother rule can be supported by a bona fide occupational qualification (BFOQ) or, in a disparate impact case, a business necessity defense. Courts have considered the argument by employers that they should be allowed to discriminate against unwed mothers because they are poor role models. In *Andrews v. Drew Municipal Separate School District*[59] two unwed mothers challenged under the Constitution (Title VII was never argued) a policy which prohibited the district from hiring any teachers or teachers' aides who were unmarried parents.[60] The Fifth Circuit rejected the school district's argument that unmarried pregnant employees were bad role models for students.[61] The court of appeals found unpersuasive the argument that the presence of unmarried teachers or teachers' aides would encourage teenage pregnancy.[62]

---

[58]All states have laws concerning garnishments. Arizona, California, Maine, Massachusetts, New Hampshire, New Mexico, and New York have specifically addressed the use of credit references. *See also* Greeley v. Miami Valley Maintenance, 551 N.E.2d 981, 5 IER Cases 257 (Ohio 1990) (holding that employee discharged solely because of court order that child-support payments be withheld from wages has civil cause of action for damages under Ohio statute prohibiting such retaliation).

[59]507 F.2d 611, 9 FEP Cases 235 (5th Cir.), *cert. granted,* 423 U.S. 820 (1975), *cert. dismissed,* 425 U.S. 559, 12 FEP Cases 1222 (1976).

[60]*Id.* at 612.

[61]*Id.* at 617.

[62]*Id.*

In *Harvey v. Young Women's Christian Ass'n,*[63] a federal court found an unwed female employee was fired because of her desire to offer herself, as an unwed mother, as an alternative lifestyle role model to the young females in her community.[64] The court found sex discrimination, but because her alternative lifestyle was in conflict with both the moral and religious philosophy of the YWCA, the court concluded a legitimate, nondiscriminatory reason for discharge existed.[65] Conversely, in *Dolter v. Wahlert High School,*[66] a federal court for the Northern District of Iowa, in denying defendant's motion to dismiss, held that a Catholic high school's asserted BFOQ defense for the discharge of an unwed mother who was a Catholic lay teacher of English appeared to relate more to religious and moral qualifications than to sexual qualifications.[67] The court noted a code of moral conduct regarding unwed parents could constitute a religious BFOQ. However, the code must apply equally to both male and female employees.[68] To the extent that the plaintiff could show other single teachers violated the code of conduct, management's BFOQ defense would be pretextual. The court found no infirmity in extending Title VII's prohibitions against sex discrimination to a sectarian school.

The federal court for the Northern District of Nebraska, in *Chambers v. Omaha Girls Club, Inc.,*[69] agreed with the employer that an unwed mother served as a bad role model for the youth the club served.[70] The court conceded while Chambers may be a good example of hard work and independence, it is just as likely that she will serve as a negative role model and may defeat the objective of the Girls Club, which was to reduce the number of teenage pregnancies.[71] Finding that the Girls Club may be seen as "tacitly" approving of teenage pregnancies, the court held that Chambers' discharge was "necessary and adequately related to the core purpose" of the club.[72]

---

[63]533 F. Supp. 949, 27 FEP Cases 1724 (W.D.N.C. 1982).
[64]*Id.* at 956.
[65]*Id.* at 957.
[66]483 F. Supp. 266, 21 FEP Cases 1413 (N.D. Iowa 1980).
[67]*Id.* at 267–68.
[68]*Id.* at 271.
[69]629 F. Supp. 925, 40 FEP Cases 362 (D. Neb. 1986).
[70]*Id.* at 926.
[71]*Id.* at 927–28.
[72]*Id.*

In one of the few arbitration cases we know of involving the dismissal of an unwed mother for immorality, Arbitrator Sidney Mogul, in *Hawthorn School Dist. No. 17, Marengo, Illinois v. Jeanne Eckman*,[73] ruled that a school board could not dismiss a former novitiate resident of a Catholic convent who became pregnant as a result of a rape. Citing *Andrews*, the arbitrator held the dismissal violated due process under the United States and the State of Illinois Constitutions. In the words of Mogul, "an individual's private life is no basis for dismissal where the teacher's teaching ability is not affected."[74] Arbitrator Richard Mittenthal, in *Allied Supermarkets, Inc.*,[75] reached a similar conclusion regarding an unwed mother in holding that Allied Supermarkets could not dismiss an unmarried cashier for "immoral character" after a second pregnancy. In Mittenthal's words, "I doubt that the public holds an employer answerable for the morals of his employees after working hours."[76]

In limited environments (sectarian schools) management may have a legitimate interest in endorsing a specific lifestyle or role model for its market. Outside of the narrow situations present in *Chambers* and *Harvey* (we are not asserting that *Chambers* is decided correctly), little justification exists, economic or otherwise, for unwed parent rules.

d. Sexual Preference and Change of Sex. Title VII's prohibitions against discrimination on account of sex does not include discrimination on the basis of sexual preference. The Ninth Circuit, in *De Santis v. Pacific Telephone & Telegraph Co.*,[77] rejecting both a disparate treatment and disparate impact theory of discrimination, held Title VII was meant to put women on equal footing with men in terms of employment activities, and the prohibition of sex discrimination found in Title VII applies only to discrimination on the basis of gender and should not be extended to include sexual preferences.

Similarly, in *Dillon v. Frank*,[78] the District Court for the Eastern District of Michigan found that an employee failed to state a cause

---

[73]An unpublished 1982 decision.
[74]The School Board of Marengo gives new meaning to the old adage that it is management that creates labor unions.
[75]41 LA 713 (1963).
[76]*Id.* at 714.
[77]608 F.2d 327, 19 FEP Cases 1493 (9th Cir. 1979).
[78]58 FEP Cases 90 (E.D. Mich. 1990).

of action under Title VII for injuries which were alleged to have arisen out of verbal taunts and threats made by co-workers who believed that the employee was a homosexual. The court ruled that the term "sex" is limited to its plain, unambiguous, and traditional meaning. As such, Title VII's prohibition of "sex" discrimination applies only to discrimination based upon a person's gender and not on discrimination based on sexual preference—such as homosexuality. By proscribing sex discrimination, Congress intended only to guarantee equal job opportunities for males and females.[79]

Title VII has also not been found to extend to transsexuals or those undergoing sex change operations. The Seventh Circuit, in *Ulane v. Eastern Airlines, Inc.*,[80] recognized that while there may be differences between homosexuals and transsexuals, the same reasons apply for not extending Title VII protection to both.[81] A public sector employee who is discriminated against because of sexual preference or transsexuality may fare better asserting a due process or equal protection claim.[82] Because sexual preference discrimination often stems from a perception that homosexuals are "sick," one commentator has suggested that gay and lesbian employees might attempt to challenge discriminatory practices under Section 504 of the Federal Rehabilitation Act.[83] No cases supporting this view have been decided.[84]

e. Race Association (Interracial Marriage and Association). Does Title VII prohibit the refusal to hire or the discharge of an employee because of the race of the people the employee associates with? Courts addressing the question have disagreed. In *Ripp v. Dobbs Houses, Inc.*[85] and *Adams v. Governor's Committee on Post-*

---

[79]*Id.* at 94 [citations omitted].

[80]742 F.2d 1081, 35 FEP Cases 1348 (7th Cir. 1984), *cert. denied,* 471 U.S. 1017, 37 FEP Cases 784 (1985).

[81]*See also* Sommers v. Budget Mktg., 667 F.2d 748, 27 FEP Cases 1217 (8th Cir. 1982) (upholding discharge of a male who claimed he was a female when he applied for the job); Holloway v. Arthur Andersen & Co., 566 F.2d 659, 16 FEP Cases 689 (9th Cir. 1977) (allowing dismissal of employee after learning that employee was preparing to have a sex change operation).

[82]See *infra* Chapter 4, notes 130–53 and accompanying text.

[83]*See Developments in the Law, Employment Law Issues Affecting Gay Men and Lesbians,* 102 HARV. L. REV. 1508, 1581 (1989).

[84]*See* Blackwell v. United States Dep't of Treasury, 830 F.2d 1183, 44 FEP Cases 1856 (D.C. Cir. 1987) (sexual orientation not handicap under Federal Rehabilitation Act).

[85]366 F. Supp. 205, 6 FEP Cases 566 (N.D. Ala. 1973).

Secondary Education,[86] the courts held that white persons who have been discharged because of their interracial marriages (*Adams*) or association (*Ripp*)[87] with other races do not have a cause of action under Title VII because the discrimination did not occur because of the white person's race. In *Adams*, although the plaintiff alleged he was dismissed because of his marriage to a black woman, the court found he was discharged because his employer lost confidence in him. In dictum, however, the court stated "neither the language of the statute [Title VII] nor its legislative history supports a cause of action against a person because of relationship to persons of another race."[88] Interestingly, the court stated Adams could state a claim under 42 U.S.C. section 1981, which proscribes racial discrimination in employment. According to the court, "[i]t is settled that the nature of the discrimination in this case—taking adverse action against a white person because of his association with blacks—falls under §1981."[89] Having decided the real reason for Adams' discharge was his relationship to his superiors, and not his relationship to his wife, no violation of section 1981 was found.

Other courts, however, have held that employment decisions on the basis of interracial association or marriage are prohibited by Title VII. Relying on *Whitney v. Greater New York Corporation of Seventh Day Adventists*,[90] and quoting from *Reiter v. Center Consolidated School District*, No. 26-JT,[91] the court of appeals in *Parr v. Woodmen*

---

[86]26 FEP Cases 1348 (N.D. Ga. 1981).

[87]The holding in *Ripp* is an aberration. The better rule for employers is articulated by the Eleventh Circuit in Parr v. Woodmen of the World Life Ins. Co., 791 F.2d 888, 41 FEP Cases 22 (11th Cir. 1986), as follows: "When a plaintiff claims discrimination based upon an interracial marriage or association, he alleges, by definition, that he has been discriminated against because of his race" (791 F.2d at 891). Employers intent on discriminating against their employees or applicants for employment because management is displeased with their off-duty associations face liability under Title VII.

[88]*Adams*, 26 FEP Cases at 1351.

[89]*Id.* (quoting Fiedler v. Marumsco Christian School, 631 F.2d 1144, 1150 (4th Cir. 1980) (white female student expelled for dating black male denied right to contract because of racial association in violation of §1981), *cert. denied*, 422 U.S. 1006, 10 FEP Cases 1177 (1975)).

[90]401 F. Supp. 1363, 13 FEP Cases 1194 (S.D.N.Y. 1975) (where a white female employee was dismissed because she had a relationship with a black male).

[91]618 F. Supp. 1458, 39 FEP Cases 833 (D. Colo. 1985) (where the employee alleged she had not been hired because of her involvement with the Hispanic community).

of the World Life Insurance Co.[92] held the employer could not refuse to hire Parr because of his interracial marriage. The court concluded that the plaintiff's allegation of discrimination because of an interracial marriage or interracial association was, in essence, an allegation of racial discrimination because he was denied employment opportunities because his race was different from his wife's.[93]

Similarly, in *Chacon v. Ochs*,[94] a California U.S. district court held the reasoning of *Ripp* and *Adams* is inconsistent with both the language and intent of Title VII. According to the court, "[a]pplying Title VII protections to discrimination based on an interracial relationship is consistent with the very purpose of Title VII; by necessity, the race of the plaintiff is a factor affecting the conduct of the defendant."[95]

f. Weight and Other Personal Appearance Restrictions. Management's preference for employees who have the appropriate dress, look, and weight frequently clashes with the employee's desire for a different lifestyle with respect to dress, grooming, and weight. In all three areas courts accord significant discretion to management. Courts have taken a "common sense" approach and have recognized management's right to formulate and enforce dress, grooming, and weight restrictions, even where the employer's only interest is in enhancing its image with the public. Thus, in *Fagan v. National Cash Register Co.*,[96] the appellate court declared:

> Perhaps no facet of business life is more important than a company's place in public estimation. That the image created by its employees dealing with the public when on company assignment affects its relations is so well known that we may take judicial notice of an employer's proper desire to achieve favorable acceptance. Good grooming regulations reflect a company's policy in our highly competitive business

---

[92]791 F.2d 888, 41 FEP Cases 22 (11th Cir. 1986), *on remand*, 657 F. Supp. 1022, 43 FEP Cases 715 (M.D. Ga. 1987).

[93]On remand, the trial court dismissed Parr's complaint because he was not genuinely interested in the job; he was only trying to create a basis for EEOC charges. To have a claim under Title VII, the plaintiff must have been a bona fide applicant for the job. Parr v. Woodmen of the World Life Ins. Co., 657 F. Supp. 1022, 1032, 43 FEP Cases 715 (M.D. Ga. 1987).

[94]780 F. Supp. 680, 57 FEP Cases 1271 (C.D. Cal. 1991).

[95]*Id.* 57 FEP Cases at 1273.

[96]481 F.2d 1115, 1120–21, 5 FEP Cases 13335 (D.C. Dir. 1973).

environment. Reasonable requirements in furtherance of that policy are an aspect of managerial responsibility.[97]

Therefore, Title VII may, under certain circumstances, provide some relief.

It is not a per se violation of Title VII for management to formulate a dress or grooming code. However, when an employer applies a dress or grooming code to members of one sex and not the other, management's rule is likely to be invalidated by a court under Title VII.[98] Further, when dress or grooming codes impose a more defined standard of uniformity on female employees than on male employees, a violation of Title VII may result.[99] Thus, when management requires female accountants to "walk more femininely, talk more femininely, dress more femininely, wear make-up, have [their] hair styled, and wear jewelry,"[100] and does not apply similar requirements to male employees, then "there is trouble in River City."[101] Still, courts, as well as arbitrators, have ruled that different standards of dress are not discriminatory so long as employment opportunities of one sex are not disadvantaged relative to the other sex. In *Fountain v. Safeway Stores, Inc.,*[102] the Ninth Circuit found Title VII was not violated when a man was dismissed for failing to wear a tie even though no such requirement existed for women.[103] Likewise, another federal

---

[97]*Id. See also* Lanigan v. Bartlett & Co. Grain, 466 F. Supp. 1388, 1392, 19 FEP Cases 1039 (W.D. Mo. 1979) ("The decision to project a certain image as one aspect of company policy is the employer's prerogative which employees may accept or reject. If they choose to reject the policy, they are subject to such sanctions as deemed appropriate by the company. An employer is simply not required to account for personal preferences with respect to dress and grooming standards.").

[98]Laffey v. Northwest Airlines, 366 F. Supp. 763, 6 FEP Cases 902 (D.C. 1973) (requirement forbidding only female cabin attendants to wear eyeglasses violative of Title VII).

[99]Carroll v. Talman Fed. Sav. & Loan Ass'n of Chicago, 604 F.2d 1028, 20 FEP Cases 764 (7th Cir. 1969), *cert. denied,* 445 U.S. 929, 22 FEP Cases 315 (1980) (requirement of "career ensemble" for females and business suits for males discriminatory under Title VII).

[100]Hopkins v. Price Waterhouse, 825 F.2d 458, 463, 44 FEP Cases 825 (D.C. Cir. 1987), *rev'd,* 490 U.S. 228, 49 FEP Cases 954 (1989).

[101]MEREDITH WILSON, *The Music Man* ("Ya Got Trouble").

[102]555 F.2d 753, 15 FEP Cases 96 (9th Cir. 1977).

[103]*See also* Baker v. Taft Broadcasting Co., 549 F.2d 400, 14 FEP Cases 697 (6th Cir. 1977) (grooming codes requiring different lengths of hair for men and women not violative of statute); Knott v. Missouri Pac. R.R., 527 F.2d 1249, 11 FEP Cases 1231 (8th Cir. 1975) (permitting employer's regulation of hair length for men

court determined no violation under Title VII when an employee was dismissed for wearing a "corn row" hairstyle in violation of hospital policy.[104] The employee's "lifestyle" regarding her hair was beyond the reach of Title VII proscriptions against race or sex discrimination. However, in *Drinkwater v. Union Carbide*,[105] the Third Circuit declared "undue preoccupation with what female employees look like is not permissible under antidiscrimination laws if the same kind of attention is not paid to male employees."[106] Further, the court noted "[t]raditional ideas about what a woman should look like are not legitimate criteria for evaluating women in the workplace."[107]

Another interesting question is whether management can insist that female employees wear makeup, or if such a rule reflects "an impermissibly cabined view of the proper behavior of women."[108] Although no cases have directly addressed this issue, the Eleventh Circuit came the closest in *Tamimi v. Howard Johnson Co.*[109] In *Tamimi* the court ruled that an employer who adopted a mandatory makeup rule for the purpose of discharging a pregnant employee violated Title VII's prohibitions against sex discrimination. Sondra Tamimi was the only woman who did not wear makeup. Management's discontent with her looks began the day the company became aware she was pregnant. The makeup rule was adopted two days later. According to the trial court, "[i]t was only when plaintiff became pregnant, which caused her face to 'break out,' that [management] implemented the rule which [it] knew plaintiff would not obey."[110] While the trial court indicated it "need not decide whether an

---

but not women employees); Baker v. California Land Title Co., 507 F.2d 895, 8 FEP Cases 1313 (9th Cir. 1974), *cert. denied*, 422 U.S. 1046, 10 FEP Cases 1177 (1975) (suit by male employee fired for violating hair length policy allowing women to wear their hair longer than men properly dismissed).

[104]Carswell v. Peachford Hosp., 27 FEP Cases 698 (N.D. Ga. 1981) (employee dismissed for wearing "corn row" hair style in violation of hospital policy not entitled to relief under Title VII's proscriptions against race and sex discrimination). *See also* Rogers v. American Airlines, 527 F. Supp. 229, 27 FEP Cases 694 (S.D.N.Y. 1981) (restriction on wearing "all braided" hairstyle not violative of prohibitions on the basis of sex or race).

[105]904 F.2d 853, 56 FEP Cases 483 (3d Cir. 1990).

[106]*Id.* 56 FEP Cases at 491.

[107]*Id.*

[108](To borrow a phrase from Price Waterhouse v. Hopkins, 490 U.S. 228, 236–37, 49 FEP Cases 954 (1989)).

[109]807 F.2d 1550, 42 FEP Cases 1289 (11th Cir. 1987).

[110]*Id.* at 1554.

employer under certain circumstances may require its female employ-ees to wear makeup,"[111] the court went on to declare:

> Based on [management's] testimony, there is no doubt that if plaintiff had not become pregnant, she would not have been dismissed from her job. To require that plaintiff wear makeup because she appears less attractive [sic] when pregnant, even though the employer had no such requirement of plaintiff or any other employee prior to plaintiff's pregnancy, is a form of sexual discrimination. Pregnancy is a "fundamen-tal sexual characteristic" that is a protected characteristic under Title VII. Accordingly, the Court finds that the mandatory makeup rule was conceived, implemented and applied to plaintiff in a discriminatory manner because of plaintiff's pregnancy, and further finds that, in dis-missing plaintiff from her job, defendant discriminated against plaintiff on the basis of her sex.[112]

While an employer cannot take gender into account in making employment decisions, except in those cases where gender is a BFOQ, it is unclear whether requiring makeup is, as Justice Brennan pointed out in *Price Waterhouse,* an impermissible sexual stereotype. According to Brennan:

> As for the legal relevance of sex stereotyping, we are beyond the day when an employer could evaluate employees by assuming or insisting that they matched the stereotype associated with their group, for " '[i]n forbidding employers to discriminate against individuals because of their sex, Congress intended to strike at the entire spectrum of disparate treatment of men and women resulting from sex stereotypes.' "[113]

In *Price Waterhouse,* Justice Brennan noted that "[w]e need not leave our common sense at the doorstep when we interpret a stat-ute."[114] Because the classes created by a makeup requirement are some women (those who wear it) versus some women (those who do not) and all (or virtually all) men, and because a makeup requirement does not significantly limit the employment opportunities of women nor impact a fundamental right, we see no infirmity under Title VII

---

[111]*Id.*

[112]*Id.* [citations omitted].

[113]*Price Waterhouse,* 490 U.S. at 250 (quoting Los Angeles Dep't of Water & Power v. Manhart, 435 U.S. 702, 707 n.13, 17 FEP Cases 395 (1978) (quoting Sprogis v. United Air Lines, 444 F.2d 1194, 1198, 3 FEP Cases 621 (7th Cir.), *cert. denied,* 404 U.S. 991, 404 FEP Cases 37 (1971), *on remand,* 56 F.R.D. 420, 4 FEP Cases 926 (N.D. Ill. 1972)).

[114]490 U.S. at 241.

when an employer requires women, as part of a grooming code, to wear makeup.

Other circuits reason that grooming and dress codes do not violate Title VII unless the requirements affect immutable characteristics or constitutionally protected activities, such as marriage or child-rearing, which present insurmountable obstacles to one gender.[115] Under this standard, it would not be impermissible for an employer to enforce a no-beard regulation, although the rule would clearly have a disparate impact upon males. A beard is not an immutable trait of being male, nor is it a constitutionally protected activity to grow a beard.[116]

No-beard policies, however, have undergone statutory challenges. In a recent case, following a remand from the Eighth Circuit, a federal judge in Nebraska sustained the employer's charge that its policy did not unlawfully discriminate against blacks.[117] The EEOC argued the no-beard policy had a disparate impact upon black males. The EEOC presented evidence claiming nearly one half of black men suffer from pseudofolliculitis barbae (PFB), a genetic skin disorder. The judge found the plaintiff, even though he had PFB, was able to shave, and thus was not disabled under the state's Fair Employment Practices Act. Under the EEOC's Title VII claim, the judge noted the employer had a business justification defense in maintaining a clean, positive corporate image. Conversely, in *University of Maryland at Baltimore v. Boyd*,[118] a Maryland state court reached an opposite conclusion. The court found that because the PFB condition prevented the plaintiff from shaving, the policy discriminated against the plaintiff based upon his race and handicap. The court concluded that PFB is predominately found in the African American male popu-

---

[115]*See, e.g.,* Earwood v. Continental South Eastern Lines, 539 F.2d 1349, 14 FEP Cases 694 (4th Cir. 1976); Willingham v. Macon Tel. Pub. Co., 507 F.2d 1084, 9 FEP Cases 189 (5th Cir. 1975) (grooming regulation applicable to males with long hair not sex-based discrimination because employer applied personal grooming code to all employees); Sprogis v. United Air Lines, 444 F.2d 1194, 3 FEP Cases 621 (7th Cir.), *cert. denied,* 404 U.S. 991, 4 FEP Cases 37 (1971), *on remand,* 56 F.R.D. 420, 4 FEP Cases 926 (N.D. Ill. 1972) (unlawful to restrict employment of married females but not married males, even though most flight attendants female).

[116]Kelly v. Johnson, 425 U.S. 238 (1976), *on remand sub nom.* Dwen v. Barry, 543 F.2d 465 (2d. Cir. 1976) (upholding hair-grooming regulation for police officers against constitutional challenge of deprivation of liberty interest).

[117]Bradley v. Pizzaco of Nebraska, Inc., No. CV86-0-753 (D. Neb. Aug. 19, 1992).

[118]Case No. 1751 (Md. Ct. Spec. App. 1992).

lation and that wearing a beard is the most common cure. In the court's view, this is adequate proof to establish a prima facie case that the University's grooming policy is discriminatory and adversely affects African American males.

Management is not precluded, however, from having height and weight requirements for its employees, although height and weight requirements that have a disproportionate effect upon women are impermissible under Title VII unless shown to be job-related.[119]

The more difficult case is where the pool of job applicants is limited to women and, at the same time, the employer maintains a height or weight restriction which eliminates some, but not all, women for consideration. In light of the Supreme Court's rejection of a "bottom line" defense to discrimination,[120] employers are advised to examine their height and weight requirements and discard those with an illegal discriminatory effect. Even though there appears to be no discrimination in the process of selecting women for positions when the "bottom line" or end result is examined, if the criterion has an impermissible disparate impact that cannot be justified under a business necessity test, it is violative of Title VII.

Title VII was never intended to interfere in the promulgation and enforcement of nondiscriminatory personal appearance regulations by employers.[121] Accordingly, an employer may require male employees to adhere to different modes of dress, grooming, and weight standards than those required of female employees and still not run afoul of the statute.

g. Drug and Alcohol Addiction. Employees whose lifestyles result in a drug or alcohol problem have little or no recourse under

---

[119]Gerdom v. Continental Airlines, 692 F.2d 602, 30 FEP Cases 235 (9th Cir. 1982) (policy of requiring only female flight attendants to comply with weight requirements violative of Title VII).

[120]Connecticut v. Teal, 457 U.S. 440, 29 FEP Cases 1 (1982). In *Teal,* a group of black employees challenged under a disparate impact theory of discrimination management's use of a facially neutral examination which a disproportionate number of blacks failed. The Court rejected the employer's bottom-line defense that it took corrective measures to ensure that the number of black employees reflected the relevant labor market.

[121]Craft v. Metromedia, 572 F. Supp. 868, 33 FEP Cases 153 (W.D. Mo. 1983), *aff'd in part,* 766 F.2d 1205, 38 FEP Cases 404 (8th Cir. 1985), *cert. denied,* 475 U.S. 1058, 40 FEP Cases 272 (1986).

Title VII. In *New York City Transit Authority v. Beazer*,[122] the Supreme Court considered the Transit Authority's blanket policy of not employing persons who use narcotic drugs.[123] The Supreme Court, reversing both the district court and the court of appeals, found that management's policy of refusing employment to any person (car cleaner, track repairman, bus driver) who was on a methadone-maintenance program was not violative of Title VII or the Equal Protection Clause of the Constitution. Justice Stevens' majority opinion stated that a prima facie violation of Title VII could be established by statistical evidence showing the practice had the effect of denying the members of one race equal access to employment opportunities. Even assuming the employees established the necessary disparate effect upon blacks, the Court ruled that the Authority rebutted the prima facie case by demonstrating its narcotics rule, and its application to methadone users, was job-related. The majority found that the Authority's rule bore a "manifest relationship to the employment in question."[124]

h. Religion. Sometimes an employee's lifestyle regarding his religious practices will disqualify him for employment. Illustrative is *State v. Sports & Health Club*,[125] where management asked prospective employees whether they attended church, read the Bible, were married or divorced, prayed, engaged in premarital or extramarital sex, believed in God, heaven, or hell.[126] Applicants were also asked whether they lived with a person of the opposite sex and whether they were antagonistic to the Bible regarding homosexuals and fornicators.[127] To what extent can management attempt to convert others to its own beliefs when management's beliefs conflict with the employee's

---

[122]440 U.S. 568, 19 FEP Cases 149 (1979).

[123]In relevant part, the Authority's rule provided: "Employees must not use, or have in their possession, narcotics, tranquilizers, drugs of the Amphetamine group or barbiturate derivatives or paraphernalia used to administer narcotics or barbiturate derivatives, except with the written permission of the Medical Director Chief–Surgeon of the System." *Id.* at 571.

[124]*Id.* 440 U.S. at 587 n.31 (quoting Griggs v. Duke Power Co., 401 U.S. 424, 3 FEP Cases 175 (1971)).

[125]370 N.W.2d 844, 37 FEP Cases 1463 (Minn. 1985), *appeal dismissed,* 478 U.S. 1015, 41 FEP Cases 272 (1986), *on remand sub nom.* State *ex rel* Johnson v. Sports & Health Club, 392 N.W.2d 329 (Minn. Ct. App. 1986).

[126]*Id.* at 847.

[127]*Id.*

religious lifestyle? Can an employee clothe a particular lifestyle in the garb of religion and preclude management from effecting a termination?

Section 703(a) (2) of Title VII prohibits employment discrimination on the basis of religion. The 1972 amendments to the Act define the term "religion" to include "all aspects of religious observance and practice, as well as belief" and provide that an employer cannot discriminate on the basis of religion unless the employer can demonstrate inability "to reasonably accommodate to an employee's or prospective employee's religious observance or practice without undue hardship on the conduct of the employer's business."[128] The difficulty comes in ascertaining whether conduct is a religious belief or practice. This is important because only true, bona fide religious beliefs and activities require employer accommodation.

Suppose an employee has a "religious" practice totally repugnant to management, perhaps Satanic worship, as an example? Must management accommodate this employee on October 31st—the eve of All Saints' Day or "All Hallow Even"—the holy day for Satanic believers? In *United States v. Seeger,*[129] and *Welsh v. United States,*[130] two conscientious objector cases, the Supreme Court broadly defined religious practices to include moral or ethical beliefs as to what is right and wrong, sincerely held with the strength of traditional religious views. The EEOC, adopting the Court's definition in *Seeger* and *Welsh,* has been liberal in its interpretation of what constitutes a religion. The absence of a workable definition of religion is particularly distressing for the practitioner. After *Seeger* and *Welsh,* one might define religion to include *anything* an individual decides is religious in his or her own scheme of things. Such a definition would avoid embroiling the courts in the constitutional problem of entanglement with religion, but would create havoc in the workplace and due process problems for employers who would have no way of implementing such a broad and vague scheme if charged with an affirmative duty to accommodate an employee's religious observances.

---

[128]42 U.S.C. §2000e(j) (1988).
[129]380 U.S. 163 (1965).
[130]398 U.S. 333, 339–40 (1970) (expanding *Seeger* to include moral or ethical beliefs which assume the role and function of a religion in the objector's life).

As an alternative, one might determine an individual's belief was not religious as a matter of law because it fell outside the protection intended by Title VII. This, however, would require a court to read the statute as protecting only certain established religious beliefs, and such a reading would have serious constitutional problems.

Noting the warning issued by the Supreme Court that "it is no business of the courts to say . . . what is a religious practice or activity,"[131] the courts, with few exceptions, have accorded great deference to the religious claims of individuals under Title VII. This does not mean management must accommodate an employee merely because an individual characterizes some form of conduct as religious and asserts it is sincerely held. As stated by one court, if one were an avid sports fan, one could not use that enthusiasm, however intense, to require permission to attend a sports event.[132] Dr. Timothy Leary once argued the use of marijuana was necessary to the free exercise of his religion,[133] yet no person would seriously contend his conduct, if the basis of an employment decision, was a religion under Title VII. Many claims by employees can be characterized as mere philosophies which are not entitled to protection. For example, membership in the Ku Klux Klan has been held not to be a protected religious belief.[134] As such, an individual who wants to attend a "religious" Klan rally need not be accommodated.

The paradox here is apparent. At one extreme, there is no obligation to relieve an employee who wants to play golf on Sunday, no matter how sincere the employee is and regardless of the position the religion of golf occupies in the employee's life; golf is not a religion under Title VII. At the other extreme, traditional, established tenets of religion, such as traditional Sabbath observance by Seventh Day Adventists, Orthodox Jews, or members of the Worldwide Church of God, are clearly religious for purposes of the statute, and thus, deserving of accommodation. The difficult cases are those where the employee claims a practice is religious, but where the practice does

---

[131]Fowler v. Rhode Island, 345 U.S. 67, 70 (1953).

[132]Gavin v. Peoples Natural Gas Co., 464 F. Supp. 622, 630, 18 FEP Cases 1431 (W.D. Pa. 1979).

[133]Leary v. United States, 383 F.2d 851, 857 (5th Cir. 1967), *cert. granted*, 392 U.S. 903 (1968), *rev'd*, 395 U.S. 6 (1969).

[134]Bellamy v. Mason's Stores, Inc., 508 F.2d 504, 9 FEP Cases 1 (4th Cir. 1974).

not have the "ring of religion." In *Wessling v. Kroger*,[135] a Sunday school teacher was not protected under the statute for leaving work early to assist her church in preparations for a Christmas play after being denied permission by management. Similarly, a federal employee, in *Marcus v. Veterans Administration*,[136] did not establish religious discrimination in the form of retaliation for failing to attend an office Christmas party.

Under Title VII an employee will not be able to take a particular facet of his or her lifestyle—sexual preference, political association, speech, hair length, drug use,[137] weight, or even prostitution[138]—and announce to management it is a protected religious practice and expect a safe harbor from discharge, although, in certain cases, an employee may be able to don some form of religious garb[139] or even maintain facial hair[140] because of a bona fide religion. Furthermore,

---

[135]554 F. Supp. 548, 552, 30 FEP Cases 1222 (E.D. Mich. 1982).

[136]692 F.2d 759 (7th Cir. 1982).

[137]*Cf.* Rushton v. Nebraska Pub. Power Dist., 653 F. Supp. 1510, 1518–19, 2 IER Cases 25 (D. Neb. 1987), *aff'd*, 844 F.2d 562, 3 IER Cases 257 (8th Cir. 1988) (mandatory drug alcohol testing program constitutional notwithstanding employees' allegation that program incorporates view of alcoholism as illness, rather than sin, and thus burdened employees' free exercise of religion).

[138]*See Judge Weighing Claims of a Religion Based on Sex*, N.Y. TIMES, May 2, 1990, at A4–A5 (discussing a First Amendment claim to rights to a religion based primarily on "absolution" through sex and "sacrifice" through a payment of money).

[139]Karriem v. Oliver T. Carr Co., 38 FEP Cases 882 (D.D.C. 1985) (prohibiting employer from preventing Muslim security guard from wearing Islamic pin where pin bore no resemblance to badge of local police); EEOC Dec. No. 81-20 (Apr. 8, 1981), 27 FEP Cases 1809 (1981) (finding reasonable cause that statute violated by common carrier's refusal to consider for employment female of Pentecostal faith, which forbids women to wear pants, where carrier rejected applicant's offer to wear uniform-color skirts which would not interfere with operation of bus, and applicant had driven bus three years while wearing skirt); EEOC Dec. No. 71-779 (Dec. 21, 1970), 3 FEP Cases 172 (1970) (reasonable cause found by discharge of nurse whose "Old Catholic" faith requires her head to be covered at all times).

But see Goldman v. Weinberger, 475 U.S. 503, 570, 40 FEP Cases 543 (1986) (First Amendment does not prevent Air Force from applying uniform dress requirement in forbidding Jewish rabbi from wearing yarmulke while on duty); Abdush-Shahid v. New York State Narcotics Addiction Control Comm'n, 430 U.S. 946 (1976) (upholding decision prohibiting rehabilitation officer from wearing 'Sunni Muslim dress' as part of religious garb).

[140]EEOC v. Electronic Data Sys., 31 FEP Cases 588 (W.D. Wash. 1983) (protecting employee who has bona fide belief that shaving beard contrary to Jewish faith); Sharif v. City of Chicago, 530 F. Supp. 667, 27 FEP Cases 1607 (N.D. Ill. 1982) (prohibiting suspension of detective who grew goatee in observance of Al-

an individual need not believe in any particular god to claim protection (atheism has been recognized as a religion),[141] but the belief, to be cognizable under Title VII, must be based on some deity or have some spiritual type of focus, a necessary requirement if golf and marijuana use are to be excluded as "religions."

B. Civil Rights Acts of 1870 and 1871

The Civil Rights Act of 1870[142] in relevant part provides that "[a]ll persons within the jurisdiction of the United States shall have the same right in every State . . . to make and enforce contracts . . . and to the full and equal benefit of all laws and proceedings . . . ." The significance of this statute is its application to claims of discrimination in private employment apart from the Title VII remedy.[143] Indeed, in some cases the Civil Rights Act of 1870 will cover certain forms of discrimination, such as alienage, which are not otherwise prohibited under Title VII.[144] Finally, this statute, unlike Title VII, contains no stated limitations period in which a complaint must be filed. And

---

Islamic religion, where department agreed not to enforce prohibition against beards for medical reasons).

But see Tamimi v. Howard Johnson Co., 807 F.2d 1550, 1555, 42 FEP Cases 1289 (11th Cir. 1987) (no religious bias in dismissing female who refused to wear makeup where employee did not communicate religious belief to management); EEOC v. Sambo's of Georgia, Inc., 530 F. Supp. 86, 91–92, 27 FEP Cases 1210 (N.D. Ga. 1981) (no violation in refusal to consider Sikh job applicant for position of restaurant manager because of religious-based refusal to shave facial hair; employer could not accommodate where exemption from clean-shaven rule would affect company image and would impose risk of noncompliance with sanitation regulations); EEOC Dec. No. 71-1529 (May 9, 1971), 3 FEP Cases 952 (1971) (reasonable cause did not exist to find violation of statute where employer refused to consider for employment male with shoulder-length hair, where employer did not know that applicant considered long hair to be incident of religion); Greyhound Lines, Inc. v. New York State Div. of Human Rights, 265 N.E.2d 745, 3 FEP Cases 7 (N.Y. 1970) (no violation of Act where employer refused to consider for employment job applicant who insisted on wearing beard in adherence to religion).

[141]Young v. Southwestern Sav. & Loan Ass'n, 509 F.2d 140, 10 FEP Cases 522 (5th Cir. 1975).

[142]42 U.S.C. §1981 (1988).

[143]Patterson v. McLean Credit Union, 491 U.S. 164, 175, 49 FEP Cases 1814 (1989).

[144]St. Francis College v. Al-Khazrajiu, 481 U.S. 604, 43 FEP Cases 1305 (1987).

unlike Title VII, back pay awards are not limited to two years. In view of the Supreme Court's decision in *Patterson v. McLean Credit Union,*[145] concluding the Act does not apply to claims of discriminatory discharge, the 1870 Act has little utility in lifestyle cases for current employees.[146]

The Civil Rights Act of 1871,[147] in relevant part, declares that

> [e]very person who, under color of any statute . . . subjects, or causes to be subjected, any citizen of the United States or other person within the jurisdiction thereof to the deprivation of any rights, privileges, or immunities secured by the Constitution and laws, shall be liable to the party injured in an action at law. . . .

This section, similar to the Civil Rights Act of 1866, has been held applicable to discrimination claims independent of Title VII. However, state action is required for a successful claim under the 1871 Act. Any claimed infringement of constitutional rights to free speech or association can be maintained against a governmental official who deprives an employee of a protected right.[148]

C. Vocational Rehabilitation Act of 1973

Individuals with a physical or mental handicap may be protected by the Vocational Rehabilitation Act of 1973, as amended,[149] or state law prohibitions against handicap discrimination applicable to private or public employers.[150]

---

[145]491 U.S. 164, 175, 49 FEP Cases 1814 (1989).

[146]The Civil Rights Act of 1991, discussed *supra* notes 36–37 and accompanying text, has reversed the Court's decision in *Patterson* by amending §1981 to provide that "the term 'make and enforce contracts' includes . . . the enjoyment of all benefits, privileges, terms and conditions of the contractual relationship." The 1991 Act is significant for plaintiffs interested in obtaining unlimited punitive damages, which are not available under Title VII of the Civil Rights Act. The 1991 Act may accordingly have some relevance to plaintiffs who are able to assert a cause of action under §1981.

[147]42 U.S.C. §1983 (1988).

[148]Epps v. Clarendon County, 405 S.E.2d 386, 387, 6 IER Cases 725 (S.C. 1991).

[149]29 U.S.C. §§701–96 (1982).

[150]All states prohibit discrimination against the handicapped. Puerto Rico and the Virgin Islands have no state statute. Alabama, Arkansas, and Mississippi prohibit handicap discrimination only by public employers. ALA. CODE §21-7-8 (1988); ARK. STAT. ANN. §20-14-301(b) (Michie 1988); MISS. CODE ANN. §25-9-149 (1989).

Section 503 of the Rehabilitation Act requires that any contract in excess of $2,500 entered into by any federal department or agency for the procurement of personal property and nonpersonal services (including construction) include a provision requiring contractors to seek to employ handicapped individuals.[151] Contractors with transactions in excess of $50,000 employing 50 or more employees must maintain a written affirmative action program within 120 days after receiving the contract, and must update the program annually.[152] Although section 503 requires affirmative action programs to hire and advance qualified handicapped employees, these programs do not require goals and timetables.[153] Section 503 does not outlaw discrimination but, rather, requires affirmative action covenants in government contracts. The current regulations specify that a complaint may be filed with the Director of the Labor Department's Office of Federal Contract Compliance Programs (OFFCP) and the Director is responsible for investigating the complaints.[154] Section 503 does not provide a private right of action for handicapped individuals against the federal government or federal contractors.[155]

Section 504 of the statute prohibits discrimination against any individual on the basis of handicap in any program receiving federal financial assistance. Specifically, the statute provides:

> No otherwise qualified individual with handicaps . . . shall, solely by reason of her or his handicap, be excluded from the participation in, be denied the benefits of, or be subjected to discrimination under any program or activity receiving Federal financial assistance or under any program or activity conducted by any Executive agency or by the United States Postal Service.[156]

A handicapped individual is defined as any person who: "(i) has a physical or mental impairment which substantially limits one or more of such person's major life activities, (ii) has a record of such an impairment, or (iii) is regarded as having such an impairment."[157] The applicable regulations define "major life activity" as "functions,

---

[151] 29 U.S.C. §793(a) (1988).
[152] *Id.*
[153] *Id.*
[154] *Id.*
[155] *Id.*
[156] 29 U.S.C. §794 (1988).
[157] 29 U.S.C. §706(7) (B) (1988).

such as caring for one's self, performing manual tasks, walking, seeing, hearing, speaking, breathing, learning, and working."[158] Having "a record of such impairment" is defined as "a history of, or has been classified (or misclassified) as having a . . . physical impairment that substantially limits one or more major life activities."[159] "Regarded as having such an impairment" is defined as:

> (1) has a physical . . . impairment that does not substantially limit major life activities but is treated by an employer as constituting such a limitation; (2) has a physical impairment that substantially limits major life activities only as a result of the attitude of an employer toward such an impairment; or (3) has none of the impairments defined in [29 C.F.R. §1613.702(b)] but is treated by an employer as having such an impairment.[160]

The term "handicap" does not include an individual who is an alcoholic or drug abuser whose current use of alcohol or drugs prevents such individual from performing the duties of the job in question, or whose employment, by reason of such alcohol or drug abuse, would constitute a direct threat to the property or the safety of others.[161] Employees or applicants who test positive for drug use are accordingly not handicapped under the Act.[162]

There is no affirmative action requirement in section 504. A handicapped individual may bring a court action on his own behalf where a violation of section 504 is claimed, regardless of whether the primary objective of the federal funds is to provide employment opportunities.[163] The burden of proof in Rehabilitation Act cases follows the scheme under Title VII case law.[164]

The significance of this statute for labor and management is illustrated by *Southeastern Community College v. Davis*,[165] a decision

---

[158]29 C.F.R. §1613.702(c) (1988).

[159]*Id.* at §1613.702(d).

[160]*Id.* at §1613.702(e).

[161]29 U.S.C. §706(8) (c) (1982).

[162]McCleod v. City of Detroit, 39 FEP Cases 225, 228 (E.D. Mich. 1985).

[163]*See* Consolidated Rail Corp. v. Darrone, 465 U.S. 624, 34 FEP Cases 79 (1984) (Supreme Court approved the availability of back pay recovery by a private plaintiff under §504 without affirmatively declaring the existence of a private cause of action).

[164]*See, e.g.,* Whiting v. Jackson State Univ., 616 F.2d 116, 120, 22 FEP Cases 1296 (5th Cir. 1980); Guinn v. Bolger, 598 F. Supp. 196, 36 FEP Cases 506 (D.D.C. 1984) (applying the scheme for allocating the burden of proof in a disparate treatment case in McDonnell Douglas Corp. v. Green, 411 U.S. 192 (1973)).

[165]442 U.S. 397 (1979).

involving a postsecondary institution. During an initial interview of a person seeking admission to a nursing program, it became apparent to the interviewer that Davis was having trouble hearing the questions being asked of her.[166] Upon further investigation, Davis was found to have a severe hearing impairment.[167] An adjustment of her hearing aid was made, but even this allowed only the hearing of "gross sound" occurrences.[168] Lip reading would be necessary for Davis' full understanding of what was being said.[169] The admission committee subsequently rejected Davis' application for admittance into the program reasoning it would be detrimental to patient safety to allow Davis to become a nurse.[170] Davis then filed a complaint in federal court alleging both a violation of section 504 and a denial of equal protection and due process.

The Supreme Court held "otherwise qualified" to mean "qualified in spite of the handicap" rather that "qualified except for the handicap." Therefore, "an otherwise qualified person is one who is able to meet all of a program's requirements in spite of his handicap."[171]

While the question whether an individual meets the statutory definition of handicapped must be considered on a case-by-case basis, the implications of *Davis* for employers is clear. Management may properly take into account the physical requirements of a job in all phases of employment. An employee facing an "insurmountable impairment barrier," i.e., where the handicap itself prevents the individual from fulfilling the essential requirements of the position, is not "otherwise qualified" for the job under section 504. Moreover, a fair reading of *Davis* is that an individual facing a "surmountable employment barrier," a barrier to job performance which can be overcome with accommodation, is not otherwise qualified if accommodation requires a substantial modification in the requirements of the job, or would result in an undue administrative and financial burden to the employer. The burden of proving inability to accommodate rests with the employer. Factors considered in assessing hardship include the size of the program, the type and duration of the program,

---

[166]*Id.* at 400.
[167]*Id.* at 401.
[168]*Id.*
[169]*Id.*
[170]*Id.* at 401–02.
[171]*Id.* at 405–06.

and the nature and cost of accommodation. A business necessity test is used in determining whether accommodation of a handicapped individual is required. Accordingly, a covered employer may not deny an employment or training opportunity to a qualified handicapped employee, applicant, or participant if the basis for the denial is the need to make reasonable accommodation to the physical or mental limitations of the employee.

1. AIDS as a Handicap Under the Rehabilitation Act

Suppose management wants only healthy employees? Can management exclude an AIDS victim or someone infected with HIV showing signs of AIDS-related disease from employment consideration?[172] The question of whether AIDS[173] is a handicap under the Rehabilitation Act has not been addressed by the Supreme Court. However, in view of the Court's 1987 opinion in *School Board of Nassau County v. Arline,*[174] there is every reason to believe that employers cannot take adverse employment action against an AIDS victim based simply upon an individual's ability to transmit the disease or fear of contagion (co-workers, customers, public). In *Arline,* an elementary school teacher was discharged after suffering a third relapse of tuberculosis within two years.[175] Arline sued the school district under section 504 of the Rehabilitation Act. The Court ruled that in defining a "handicapped individual" the contagious effects of the individual's disease upon others cannot be meaningfully distinguished from the disease's physical effects upon the individual.[176] Thus, it would be unfair, reasoned the Court, to allow an employer

---

[172]*See* Dennis Hevesi, *Aids Carriers Win a Court Ruling,* NEW YORK TIMES, July 9, 1988, at 6. *See generally* Arthur S. Leonard, *Employment Discrimination Against Persons With AIDS,* 10 U. DAYTON L. REV. 681 (1985); Judith S. Merrell, Note, *AIDS and Cancer: Critical Employment Discrimination Issues,* J. CORP. L. 849 (1990).

[173]"AIDS is a clinical definition developed in 1982 by the Public Health Service's Centers for Disease Control to allow monitoring of conditions typically associated with severe breakdown of immunologic defenses against viral, bacterial and parasitic infections, subsequently found to be caused by [the Human Immunodeficiency Virus (HIV)]." Local 1812, AFGE v. United States Dep't of State, 662 F. Supp. 50, 52 n.2 (D.D.C. 1987).

[174]480 U.S. 273, 43 FEP Cases 81 (1987).

[175]*Id.* at 276.

[176]*Id.* at 282.

to seize upon the distinction between the effects of the disease upon others and the effects of the disease upon the individual, at least where the contagiousness and the individual's physical impairment result from the same underlying condition.[177] According to the Court, the Act does not exclude individuals based upon fear of contagiousness.

According to the regulations promulgated by the Department of Health and Human Services (HHS), physical or mental impairments include: "(A) any psychological disorder or condition, cosmetic disfigurement, or anatomical loss affecting one or more of the following body systems: neurological; musculoskeletal; special sense organs; respiratory, including speech organs; cardiovascular; reproductive, digestive, genito-urinary; hemic and lymphatic; skin; and endocrine."[178]

In addition, the Civil Rights Restoration Act of 1987,[179] which codified the decision in *Arline*, specifically provides that discrimination against an otherwise qualified handicapped individual solely on the basis that the handicap is a contagious disease is impermissible.[180] In 1988 the Department of Justice, reversing an earlier position, likewise concluded AIDS is a handicap under the Rehabilitation Act.[181]

According to current medical knowledge, AIDS does not present a threat of infection to co-workers or customers through casual workplace contact. Accordingly, most AIDS victims would be considered "qualified" to hold jobs until the disease renders them physically

---

[177]*Id.*

[178]45 C.F.R. §84.3(j) (2) (i) (1988).

[179]Pub. L. No. 100-259, 102 Stat. 28 (enacted Mar. 22, 1988) (amending 29 U.S.C. §706(7) (B) (1982 & Supp. V 1987)).

[180]The relevant provision specifically provides:

For the purpose of sections 503 and 504, as such sections relate to employment, ["individual with handicaps"] does not include an individual who has a currently contagious disease or infection and who, by reason of such disease or infection, would constitute a direct threat to the health and safety of other individuals or who, by reason of the currently contagious disease or infection, is unable to perform the duties of the job.

29 U.S.C. §706(7) (B) (1988).

[181]JUSTICE DEPARTMENT MEMORANDUM ON APPLICATION OF REHABILITATION ACT'S SECT. 504 TO HIV INFECTED PERSONS, Sept. 27, 1988, *reprinted in* AMERICANS WITH DISABILITIES ACT, 1989: HEARINGS ON S. 933 BEFORE COMM. ON LABOR AND HUMAN RESOURCES AND THE SUBCOMM. ON THE HANDICAPPED, 101st Cong., 1st Sess. 338, 343 (1989).

incapable of working.[182] This was the position taken by the Ninth Circuit in *Chalk v. United States District Court Central District of California*,[183] where the court of appeals ruled that a teacher of the hearing impaired, diagnosed as having AIDS, could not be denied his former teaching position in favor of an administrative assignment. If, however, AIDS is later determined to present a significant threat of infection to co-workers or customers, management could arguably discriminate against AIDS victims based on fear of possible contagion. At any rate, numerous states have enacted laws on the subject of HIV and AIDS-related diseases,[184] most of which deal with testing and the confidentiality of test results.[185] Some states have included AIDS within the definition of physical handicap for purposes of their

---

[182]The consensus of opinion holds AIDS qualifies as a handicap or disability under federal antidiscrimination laws. *See* Martinez v. School Bd. of Hillsborough County, 861 F.2d 1502, 1506 (11th Cir. 1988) (holding AIDS a handicap under Rehabilitation Act); Chalk v. United States Dist. Court, 840 F.2d 701, 46 FEP Cases 279 (9th Cir. 1988) (reversing denial of preliminary injunction reinstating teacher with AIDS to classroom duties under Rehabilitation Act); Baxter v. City of Belleville, 720 F. Supp. 720, 730 (S.D. Ill. 1989) (concluding HIV carriers handicapped under Fair Housing Act, 42 U.S.C. §§3601–31); Robertson v. Granite City Community Unit Sch. Dist., 684 F. Supp. 1002, 1006–07 (S.D. Ill. 1988) (holding student with AIDS-related complex (ARC) handicapped under Rehabilitation Act); Doe v. Dolton Elementary Sch. Dist. No. 148, 694 F. Supp. 440 (N.D. Ill. 1988) (finding AIDS handicap under §504 of Rehabilitation Act); Thomas v. Atascadero Unified Sch. Dist., 662 F. Supp. 376, 381 (C.D. Cal. 1986) (holding child with AIDS handicapped under Rehabilitation Act).

[183]840 F.2d 701, 705, 46 FEP Cases 279 (9th Cir. 1988). *See also* Doe v. Centinela Hosp., 57 USLW 2034 (C.D. Cal. 1988) (holding that seropositive persons are "handicapped" under Rehabilitation Act because they are "regarded as having an impairment").

[184]Two-thirds of the states have announced either administratively or judicially that AIDS-related discrimination is illegal under their statutes. *See, e.g.,* Raytheon Co. v. Fair Employment & Housing Comm'n, 46 FEP Cases 1089 (Cal. Super. Ct. 1988), *aff'd,* 261 Cal. Rptr. 197, 50 FEP Cases 921 (1989); District 27 Community Sch. Bd. v. Board of Educ., 130 Misc. 2d 398 (N.Y. Sup. Ct. 1986); M.A.E. v. Doe & Roe, 566 A.2d 285, 287, 51 FEP Cases 529 (Pa. Super. 1989) (Cavanaugh, J., concurring) (stating AIDS a disability or handicap under PHRA); *see also* Arthur S. Leonard, *AIDS, Employment and Unemployment,* 49 OHIO ST. L.J. 929, 939–40 n.74-89 (1989) (collecting decisions).

[185]*See, e.g.,* FLA. STAT. ANN. §760.50(3) (a)-(c) (West 1989) (prohibiting employers from requiring HIV-related tests as a condition of hiring, promotion, or continued employment, unless absence of HIV infection is a BFOQ for the job in question); HAW. REV. STAT. §325-101(c) (1989) (stating "no person shall be compelled . . . to disclose whether that person has been tested for the presence of HIV infection, in order to obtain or maintain . . . employment"); IOWA CODE §601A.6(1) (d) (1989) (prohibiting testing as a condition of employment); N.M. STAT. ANN. §28-10 A-1 (Michie 1989) (prohibiting use of AIDS test as condition of employment unless

fair employment or civil rights statutes.[186] As a result, an employer subject to such a statute cannot take adverse action because an individual is afflicted with full-blown AIDS or is sero-positive (HIV-infected).[187]

Whether a public sector employer can compel an employee to submit to an AIDS test is a more difficult question. Although distinguishable on their facts, the two cases to reach the courts of appeals are arguably split on the issue.[188] Employers who disclose the results of an employee's test risk tort liability for invasion of privacy.[189]

BFOQ present); N.C. GEN. STAT §§130-148 (1989) (prohibiting HIV tests of current employees as basis of determining "suitability" for continued employment; employers permitted to test applicants and may refuse to hire solely on the basis of positive HIV test; statute also permits HIV tests as part of annual medical exams routinely required for all employees); R.I. GEN. LAWS §23-6-22 (1989) (prohibiting HIV testing as condition of employment except in instances where employers can demonstrate, through medical authorities, "clear and present danger" of AIDS transmission if testing were not done); VT. STAT. ANN. §495(a) (7) (1989) (prohibiting HIV-related blood tests as condition of employment); WASH. REV. CODE §49.60.172 (1988) (prohibiting HIV testing as condition of employment absent BFOQ).

[186]*See, e.g.,* MD. REG. CODE ANN. §14.03.02.01-14.03.02.05 (1986) (declaring that HIV infection physical handicap under Maryland law); MO. REV. STAT. §191.655.1 (1986) (including AIDS and AIDS-related complex (ARC) within definition of handicap); PA. HUMAN RTS. COMM'N DIRECTIVE, REAFFIRMATION OF PHRC AIDS POLICY, POLICY NO. 88-01 (June 2, 1988) (declaring AIDS a handicap for person regarded or treated as having AIDS).

[187]Query whether a symptomless HIV-infected person is handicapped under the Rehabilitation Act? *See* Local 1812, AFGE v. United States Dep't of State, 662 F. Supp. 50, 54, 2 IER Cases 47 (D.D.C. 1987) (where the court stated that an HIV-infected person is not an "otherwise qualified individual" for worldwide Foreign Service duty).

Are *all* HIV carriers physically impaired because of measurable deficiencies in their immune systems even where disease symptoms have not yet developed? *Arline* appears to require that management make an individual determination and, thus, an employer covered under the Act cannot make a generalization with respect to all HIV-infected persons.

[188]*Compare* Glover v. East Neb. Community Office of Retardation, 867 F.2d 461, 464, 4 IER Cases 65 (8th Cir.), *cert. denied,* 493 U.S. 932, 4 IER Cases 1504 (1989) (state administrative agency's policy of requiring certain employees to submit to AIDS and hepatitis B test in order to provide safe environment for mentally retarded clients unreasonable search and seizure) with Leckelt v. Board of Comm'rs, 909 F.2d 820, 827, 5 IER Cases 1089 (5th Cir. 1990) (allowing dismissal of male homosexual nurse, who had long-term relationship with man who ultimately died from AIDS-related condition, for failing to disclose results of AIDS test).

See also Doe v. Attorney General, 723 F. Supp. 452, 4 IER Cases 1400 (N.D. Cal. 1989) (upholding testing for physician by health care facility); Local 1812, AFGE v. United States Dep't of State, 662 F. Supp. 50, 53, 2 IER Cases 47 (D.D.C. 1987) (allowing testing by State Department of Foreign Service employees).

[189]Cronan v. New England Tel., 1 IER Cases 651 (Mass. Super. Ct. 1986).

It is of note that arbitrators, when deciding AIDS cases, apply traditional notions of just cause, and require management to demonstrate the afflicted employee cannot perform the assigned work before dismissal is allowed.[190] In this respect, arbitrators track the intent of the Rehabilitation Act.

2. Obesity as a Disability Under Section 504 of the Rehabilitation Act°

While merely being overweight is not typically considered a handicap under the Rehabilitation Act,[191] no court has held that obesity could never be a handicap under section 504 of the Act. Most courts, never bothering to discuss the difference between severe or morbid obesity, and simply being overweight,[192] have concluded "obesity" is not a handicap, and thus failing to hire or discharging an individual based on weight is not unlawful discrimination. Courts have based this conclusion on the fact that the obesity adversely affects job performance,[193] and that employers are entitled to control productivity

---

[190]For an excellent discussion on the rulings of arbitrators in AIDS cases, *see* Roger Abrams & Dennis Nolan, *AIDS in Labor Arbitration*, DAILY JOURNAL REPORT, Mar. 29, 1991, at 24–35.

°We are thankful to Lynette Labinger, of Roney & Labinger, the Rhode Island Affiliate of the American Civil Liberties Union, Providence, Rhode Island, for sharing her pleadings and motions with us from Cook v. State of Rhode Island, C.A. 90-0560-T, a case involving obesity under the Rehabilitation Act.

[191]Underwood v. Trans World Airlines, Inc., 710 F. Supp. 78, 84, 49 FEP Cases 1725 (S.D.N.Y. 1989) (154-pound female flight attendant not handicapped).

[192]As stated by the *Underwood* court, "the difference between 'obesity' and 'overweight' is not merely one of semantics." *Id.* 710 F. Supp. at 83. Obesity is not simply a physical characteristic but a clinically ascertainable and observable medical condition. *See, e.g.*, State Division of Human Rights v. Xerox Corp., 480 N.E.2d 695, 698, 37 FEP Cases 1389 (N.Y. 1985) ("the Commissioner could find that the complainant's obese condition itself, which was clinically diagnosed and found to render her medically unsuitable by the respondent's own physician, constituted an impairment and therefore a disability within the contemplation of the statute").

Being overweight, on the other hand, is a lay term that could refer to being above suggested weight and height tables.

[193]*See* Greene v. Union Pac. R.R., 548 F. Supp. 3, 5 (W.D. Wash. 1981); Missouri Comm'n on Human Rights v. Southwestern Bell Tel., 699 S.W.2d 75 (Mo. Ct. App. 1985); Thomas J. Lipton, Inc. v. New York State Human Rights Appeal Bd., 67 A.D.2d 1029, 30 FEP Cases 400 (N.Y. 1979); Krein v. Marian Manor Nursing Home, 415 N.W.2d 793, 796, 45 FEP Cases 979 (N.D. 1987) (stating in dictum that state law may comprehend condition which significantly impairs person's abilities, but

by refusing to hire or by discharging those employees who are likely to be absent often and who are less productive.[194] Additionally, even though the statute does not differentiate between voluntary and involuntary conditions, courts have found that obesity should not be considered a handicap because the condition is able to be altered, unlike other handicaps such as lameness or blindness.[195]

Suppose a person is clinically obese, or regarded by the employer as clinically obese, or has a record of being clinically obese, through no fault of the individual, and the obesity substantially limits a major life activity (walking, breathing, or even working, for example)? Is that person handicapped under the Act? There is some reason to conclude, under these circumstances, severe or morbid obesity is a handicap under the statute. In *Civil Service Commission of Pittsburgh v. Pennsylvania Human Relations Commission*,[196] the court relied on a "perceived handicap" analysis to affirm an agency finding that obesity is a handicap under Pennsylvania law. A comparison of the Pennsylvania statute with the Rehabilitation Act indicates the state statute tracked the Rehabilitation Act's definition of handicap. Similarly, in *State Division of Human Rights v. Xerox*,[197] the Court of Appeals for New York held that a woman, 5 feet, 6 inches, and weighing 249 pounds, seeking a job as a computer programmer, suffered from a "disability" under New York's Human Rights Law (which included medical impairments in its definition of disability). What is particularly interesting is the court's rejection of management's argument that it could deny employment because of the statistical likelihood her obese condition would produce impairments in the future.[198] The court also rejected the company's argument that the statute applied only to immutable disabilities and not to those that are correctable.[199]

---

holding that plaintiff failed to show that there was genuine issue as to whether her obesity fell within protections of Act); Philadelphia Elec. Co. v. Commonwealth of Pennsylvania Human Relations Comm'n, 448 A.2d 701, 707, 36 FEP Cases 593 (Pa. Commw. Ct. 1982).

[194]Thomas J. Lipton, Inc. v. New York State Human Rights, 413, 67 A.D.2d 1029, 30 FEP Cases 400 (N.Y. 1979).

[195]Philadelphia Elec. Co., 448 A.2d at 707 (accepting principle that morbid obesity could fall within definition of handicap or disability under state law, but holding that it was not a handicap per se).

[196]591 A.2d 281 (Pa. 1991).

[197]480 N.E.2d 695, 698, 37 FEP Cases 1389 (N.Y. 1985).

[198]*Id.* at 697.

[199]*Id.* at 698.

Case law suggests a complaint that clinical obesity is a handicap should not be dismissed by a trial court for failure to state a claim unless it is clear to the court that relief could not be granted under the Act under any set of facts found to be consistent with the allegations.[200] Consistent with the decisions of the Pennsylvania and New York courts, before rejecting a claim of handicap discrimination regarding obesity, an individualized, fact-intensive examination should be conducted. The fact that obesity is not included in the federal definition promulgated by HHS is not dispositive of the issue.

3. Drug and Alcohol Addiction

As noted, under the federal statute the term "handicap" does not include any individual whose current use of alcohol or drugs prevents such individual from performing the duties of the job in question.[201] Thus, drug addicts and alcoholics are not categorically excluded from coverage of the Rehabilitation Act. They are excluded only if their *current use* prevents them from performing the duties of the job or if their employment "would constitute a direct threat to the property or safety of others."[202]

Similarly, several states expressly exclude alcohol or drug abusers from protection under their handicap acts.[203] In those states with

---

[200]Conley v. Gibson, 355 U.S. 41, 45–46, 9 FEP Cases 439 (1957) ("a complaint should not be dismissed for failure to state a claim unless it appears beyond doubt that the plaintiff can prove no set of facts in support of his claim which would entitle him to relief").

[201]29 U.S.C. §706(8) (C) (1982 & Supp. 1986).

[202]*Id.* Query under what conditions addiction to nicotine would prevent someone from currently performing a job or constitute a direct threat to property or to the safety of others? Under the law we see no reason why management cannot exclude smokers as a class because of their economic impact on the organization. *See* Leila B. Boulton, Comment, *Tobacco Under Fire: Developments in Judicial Responses to Cigarette Smoking Injuries*, 36 CATH. U.L. REV. 643, 645 n.11 (1987) (asserting that medical care and lost productivity costs due to cigarette smoking total about $65 billion annually).

[203]ARIZ. REV. STAT. ANN. §41-1461(4) (a) (1956); CAL. FAIR EMPLOYMENT & HOUSING COMM. RULES & REGS. §7293.6(a) (4) Tit. 56 (1988); GA. CODE ANN. §66-502(2) (1988); 56 ILL. ADMIN. CODE §2500.20 (1984); KY. REV. STAT. ANN. §207.140(2) (b) (Baldwin 1985); LA. REV. STAT. ANN. §46:2253(2) (West 1989); N.C. GEN. STAT. §168A-3(4) (a) (1987); S.C. CODE ANN. §43-33-560 (Law. Co-op. 1976); TEX. REV. CIV. STAT. ANN. Art. 5221(k) (2.01) (7) (A) (Vernon 1987); VA. CODE ANN. §51.5.3 (Michie 1991).

Some states expressly *include* drug addiction and alcoholism as protected conditions. *See, e.g.,* ME. REV. STAT. §3.02c.2(a) (West 1991); W. VA. CODE §5-11-3(t) (1991).

statutes addressing the issue, the courts are split.[204] We know of no case under any statute prohibiting the dismissal of an employee who reports for work under the influence of drugs or alcohol.[205]

4. Smoking

It is unclear whether smoking caused by nicotine addiction is a handicap under the Rehabilitation Act. Under the Court's test in *Arline,* an argument can be advanced that a longtime smoker or, alternatively, one addicted to nicotine, is a handicapped individual because he or she has a "physical impairment" of a "body system" which limits "life activities" of breathing and working. Under this logic, management would have to accommodate smokers. One commentator points out that even if smoking is a handicap, smoke-cessation classes, restricted smoking areas, and distribution of nicotine gum might be considered reasonable accommodation for employees who smoke.[206]

An alternative remedy, for smokers excluded from employment consideration or otherwise discriminated against because of their addiction, is a Title VII suit under a disparate impact theory.[207] If it could be demonstrated that blacks as a class have a higher percentage of smokers than whites,[208] management would be compelled to dem-

---

[204]*See, e.g.,* Clowes v. Terminix Int'l Inc., 538 A.2d 794, 52 FEP Cases 1608 (N.J. 1988) (finding alcoholism a handicap); Hazlett v. Martin Chevrolet, Inc., 496 N.E.2d 478, 51 FEP Cases 1588 (Ohio 1986); Connecticut Gen. Life Ins. Co. v. Wisconsin Dep't of Indus., Labor & Human Relations, 273 N.W.2d 206, 212–23, 18 FEP Cases 1447 (Wis. 1979) (alcoholism a handicap); Doe v. Roe, Inc., 539 N.Y.S.2d 876 (1989), *aff'd,* 553 N.Y.S.2d 364, 52 FEP Cases 1012 (N.Y. App. Div. 1990) (drug addiction handicap under New York Human Rights Law).
    Contra Welsh v. Municipality of Anchorage, 676 P.2d 602 (Alaska 1984) (alcoholism a handicap); Phillips v. City of Seattle, 766 P.2d 1099, 1103, 57 FEP Cases 404 (Wash. 1989) (refusing to define alcoholism as handicap).
    [205]*See, e.g.,* Harper v. Louisiana State Bd. of Nursing, 484 So. 2d 857, 858–61 (La. Ct. App. 1986) (permitting discharge if drugs or alcohol makes employee unable safely and substantially to perform job duties); Blitz v. Northwest Airlines, Inc., 363 N.W.2d 94, 96–97, 37 FEP Cases 171 (Minn. Ct. App. 1985) (pilot); Squires v. Labor & Indus. Rev. Comm'n, 294 N.W.2d 48, 49–57, 30 FEP Cases 398 (Wis. 1980).
    [206]Joan Vogel, Comment, *Containing Medical and Disability Costs by Cutting Unhealthy Employees: Does Section 510 of ERISA Provide a Remedy?,* 62 NOTRE DAME L. REV. 1024, 1037 (1987).
    [207]See the discussion of disparate impact theory, *supra* notes 19–26 and accompanying text.
    [208]In 1986, the Centers for Disease Control found that black men smoked at a

onstrate a business necessity for an off-duty, no-smoking rule which, in many cases, may be a difficult burden for management to meet.

D. Americans With Disabilities Act

On July 13, 1990, Congress enacted the Americans with Disabilities Act (ADA),[209] which broadened the scope of protection available under the Rehabilitation Act (the Rehabilitation Act covers only employers who contract with the federal government). While the ADA regulates a variety of areas including real estate transactions and public accommodations, the provisions dealing with employment are particularly important for employers attempting to regulate their employees' lifestyle or, alternatively, divest themselves of employees whose disabilities may result in higher medical or insurance costs.

The ADA defines an employer as any person or his agent having 15 or more employees. Employers with less than 15 employees are not covered by the ADA.[210] The ADA excludes the federal government or any corporation owned by the federal government.[211] All other public employers are covered.

The ADA protects "qualified individuals with disabilities."[212] The statute provides that a qualified individual with a disability may not be discriminated against if with "reasonable accommodation" the individual can perform the essential functions of the position sought or held.[213] The Act defines a qualified individual with a disability as one: "who with reasonable modification of rules, policies, or practices, the removal of architectural, communication or transportation barri-

---

rate of 32.5% while white men smoked at 29.3%. Black women smoked at 25.1% compared to 23.7% for white women. *See* John C. Fox & Bernadette M. Davison, *Smoking in the Workplace: Accommodating Diversity*, LAB. L. J. 387, 388 n.5 (1989) (citing *Cigarette Smoking in the United States*, 1986, MORBIDITY AND MORTALITY WEEKLY REPORT 582 (Sept. 11, 1987)).

[209]42 U.S.C. §§12101–12112 (Supp. 1990). *See generally* Robert E. Stein, *The Americans with Disabilities Act of 1990*, ARB. J. 6, 6–15 (1991).

[210]42 U.S.C. §12111(A) (Supp. 1990); 29 C.F.R. §1630.2(e) (1) (1990). The provisions of the ADA became effective July 26, 1992, for those employers with 25 or more employees. The effective date for those employers with less than 25 but more than 14 employees is July 26, 1994.

[211]42 U.S.C. §12111(5) (B) (Supp. 1990); 29 C.F.R. §1630.2(e) (2) (1990).

[212]42 U.S.C. §12111(8) (Supp. 1990).

[213]*Id.*

ers, or the provisions of auxiliary aids and services, meets the essential eligibility for participation in programs or activities or receipt of service provided by a public entity."[214] This definition also protects the qualified individual from hiring and employment practices that are discriminatory.

Under the ADA a "covered disability" is defined as a "physical or mental impairment that substantially limits one or more major life activities."[215] A record of prior impairment, or being regarded as having such an impairment, is also considered a covered disability.[216] Physical or mental impairments include: (1) physiological disorders or conditions; (2) cosmetic disfigurement; (3) anatomical loss affecting a number of designated systems;[217] (4) mental or psychological disorders, including (a) mental retardation, (b) organic brain syndrome, (c) emotional illness, (d) mental illness, (e) special learning disabilities;[218] (5) disease or infections, including HIV infection (AIDS), cancer, heart disease, drug addiction, and alcoholism.

A physical or mental impairment is not a disability if it does not substantially limit one or more "major life activities."[219] According to the ADA, a major life activity includes "caring for oneself, performing manual tasks, walking, seeing, hearing, speaking, reaching, learning, and working."[220] To have a disability, one must have an actual physical or mental *impairment* and not simply a physical *condition.* Thus, an individual with a visual impairment would be covered, but a person with two broken legs would not be covered even though that condition would impair working. Further, the disability must be serious enough to affect some form of major life activity.

The second and third definition of disability, which tracks the definition in the Rehabilitation Act, includes persons with a record or history of impairment and persons regarded as disabled. Those with a history of past disability are protected by the ADA, even if they have recovered from the impairment.[221] The ADA also covers

---

[214]*Id.* at §12131(2).
[215]*Id.* at §12102(2)A.
[216]*Id.* at §12102(2)B, C.
[217]29 C.F.R. §1630.2(h) (1) (1990).
[218]*Id.* at §1630.2(b)2.
[219]*Id.* at §1630.2(g) (i).
[220]*Id.* at §1630.2(i).
[221]*Id.* at §1630.2(g) (2).

individuals who associate with people with disabilities. Thus, for example, a person may not be excluded from employment because he or she lives with an HIV-infected person.

A number of disabilities are excluded from the statute. Section 114(a) of the ADA states that employees or applicants engaged in illegal drug use are excluded from the Act's protection. The "drug user" exclusion applies to any individual whose drug use is current.[222] Thus, a person who has successfully completed a drug rehabilitation program and is no longer using drugs is protected under the ADA. Similarly, a person who is erroneously regarded as an illegal drug user is protected. The ADA allows testing for illegal drugs.

Also specifically excluded are homosexuals, bisexuals, transvestites, transsexuals, pedophiles, exhibitionists, voyeurs, kleptomaniacs, compulsive gamblers, pyromaniacs, and persons with other sexual disorders.[223] Employees whose lifestyles include any of the above are not protected by the ADA.

The ADA prohibits a covered employer from discrimination with respect to hiring an employee against "qualified individuals with disabilities" because of the person's disability. The ADA lists a number of different forms of discrimination, including (1) limiting, segregating, or classifying disabled persons;[224] (2) participating in contractual relationships that effectuate discrimination;[225] (3) enacting standards, criteria, and methods of administration that effectuate discrimination;[226] (4) excluding or denying jobs or benefits because of a relationship to individuals with disabilities;[227] (5) using qualification standards, employment tests, and all other selection criteria that effectuate discrimination.[228] Employers' medical examinations cannot ask applicants if they have a disability or require applicants to take a medical exam before a job is offered. However, after offering a job the employer can require the employee to take a medical exam but only if required of all employees and the results are kept confidential. Of course, management can always ask an applicant if he can perform the job.

---

[222]42 U.S.C. §12114(a) (Supp. 1990).
[223]29 C.F.R. §1630.3(d) (1) (1990).
[224]42 U.S.C. §12112(b) (1) (Supp. 1990).
[225]*Id.* at §12112(b) (2).
[226]*Id.* at §12112(b) (3)A.
[227]*Id.* at §12112(b)4.
[228]*Id.* at §12112(b)6.

Finally, the ADA provides that failure to make reasonable accommodation may not be actionable if there would be undue hardship on the employer. The Act defines undue hardship as an act requiring significant difficulty or expense.[229] If a qualified individual is discriminated against in violation of the ADA, numerous remedies are available. Temporary or preliminary relief, such as temporary restraining orders, permanent injunctions, additional back pay, and equitable relief are available. The employer may also be forced to pay the employee's attorney's fees if a violation is found.[230]

E. Section 510 of the Employee Retirement Income Security Act

An employee who can establish a causal connection between a medical risk and the loss of benefits and an adverse employment action may have relief under the Employee Retirement Income Security Act (ERISA). Section 510 of ERISA,[231] makes it unlawful

> for any person to discharge, fine, suspend, expel, discipline, or discriminate against a participant or beneficiary for exercising any right to which he is entitled under the provisions of an employee benefit plan, [or this title]. . . . It shall be unlawful for any person to discharge, fine, suspend, expel or discriminate against any person because he has given information or has testified or is about to testify in any inquiry or proceeding relating to this [Act]. . . .[232]

---

[229]*Id.* at §12111(10) (B) (i), (iii), (iv). Various factors taken into account include: (1) the nature of the cost accommodation required; (2) the overall financial resources of the facility invoked in the provision of the reasonable accommodation; (3) the number of persons employed at the facility; (4) the effect of the reasonable accommodation on expenses and resources; (5) the impact of the accommodation on the operation of the facility; (6) the overall financial resources of the covered entity; (7) the overall size of the covered entity's business with respect to the number of employees; (8) the number, type, and location of its facilities; (9) the type of operations of the covered entity, including the composition, structure, and function of its work force; (10) the geographic separateness of the facility; and (11) the administration or fiscal relationships of the facility to the covered entity. *Id.* All factors should be taken into account when determining whether a particular accommodation is reasonable under the ADA.

[230]*Id.* at §12117(a).
[231]29 U.S.C. §§1001–1461 (1988).
[232]*Id.*

Section 510 is relevant because it may provide redress for employees who are dismissed or otherwise discriminated against because they are considered insurance or medical risks.[233] Section 510 also applies to beneficiaries—a person designated by a participant or one entitled to receive benefits under the terms of an employee's benefit plan. It does not cover job applicants or employees who do not receive benefits. Accordingly, an applicant who is refused employment because of his anticipated medical costs has no cause of action under section 510.

In a decision with far-reaching implications for employees with AIDS or drug or alcohol problems, the Fifth Circuit, in *McGann v. H & H Music Co.*,[234] ruled that a self-insured employer can change its policy to reduce coverage for workers who develop costly illnesses.[235] An employee of H & H Music discovered he was afflicted with AIDS in December 1987. McGann submitted his first claims for reimbursement under the employer's group medical plan and informed management he had AIDS.[236] In July 1988, H & H Music informed its employees that changes would be made in their medical coverage. These changes included limiting benefits for AIDS-related claims to a lifetime maximum of $5,000. Before the change, the lifetime coverage was $1 million. Other changes included increased individual and family deductibles, elimination of coverage for chemical dependency treatment, adoption of a preferred provider plan, and increased contribution requests. No limitation was placed on any other catastrophic illness. H & H Music also became a self-insurer under the new plan. By January 1990, McGann had exhausted the $5,000 limit on coverage for his illness.

In August 1989, McGann sued H & H Music under section 510 alleging the company discriminated against him in violation of both prohibitions of section 510. He claimed the coverage limitation for AIDS-related expenses was directed specifically at him in retaliation for exercising his rights under the plan and for the purpose of interfering with the attainment of a right to which he was entitled as a beneficiary under the plan. The employer, conceding the factual allegations of McGann's complaint, moved for summary judgment.

---

[233]*See generally* Vogel, *supra* note 206, at 1024.

[234]946 F.2d 401, 14 EB Cases 1729 (5th Cir. 1991), *cert. denied,* Greenberg v. H & H Music Co., 1992 U.S. LEXIS 7177, 113 S.Ct. 482, 16 EB Cases 1432 (1992).

[235]*Id.* at 402–05.

[236]*Id.* at 402.

The district court granted summary judgment, reasoning management had an absolute right to alter the terms of the plan, regardless of intent. The district court also held that even if the issue of discriminatory motive were relevant, summary judgment would still be proper because the employer's motive was to ensure the future existence of the plan and not specifically to retaliate against McGann.[237]

In sustaining the lower court, the appellate court pointed out that, at trial, McGann would bear the burden of proving the existence of the employer's discriminatory intent as an element of either of his claims.[238] McGann conceded the reduction in AIDS benefits will apply equally to all employees filing AIDS-related claims and the effect of this reduction will not be felt only by him. Also, he did not allege the company's reduction had any other purpose other than to reduce costs. As such, McGann could not make the necessary showing sufficient to show management had a specific intent to retaliate against him to survive summary judgment.

Similarly, McGann failed to adduce evidence of the existence of "any right to which [he] may become entitled under the plan."[239] The court made it clear the right referred to in section 510 "is not simply any right to which an employee may conceivably become entitled, but rather any right to which an employee may become entitled pursuant to an existing, enforceable obligation assumed by the employer."[240] There was nothing to indicate H & H Music ever promised the $1 million coverage limit was permanent and there was no evidence of any oral or written representations made to McGann that the coverage limit would not be lowered. The court refused to rule that section 510 prohibits any discrimination in the alteration of an employee benefit plan which results in an identifiable employee or group of employees being treated differently than other employees. Reflecting the better weight of authority, the court concluded:

> [Section 510] does not prohibit welfare plan discrimination between or among categories of diseases. Section 510 does not mandate that if some, or most, or virtually all catastrophic illnesses are covered, AIDS (or any other particular catastrophic illness) must be among them. It does not prohibit an employer from electing not to cover or continue

---

[237]*Id.*
[238]*Id.* at 403–04.
[239]*Id.* at 404.
[240]*Id.* at 404–05.

to cover AIDS, while covering or continuing to cover other catastrophic illnesses, even though the employer's decision in this respect may stem from some "prejudice" against AIDS or its victims generally. The same, of course, is true of any other disease and its victims. That sort of "discrimination" is simply not addressed by section 510.[241]

The implications of *McGann,* and similar cases,[242] are staggering for employees who develop a catastrophic illness and work for a self-insured employer.[243] Under federal law, employers are free to discriminate in the creation, alteration, or termination of employee benefits plans. Employers are not free to retaliate against an employee, such as effecting a dismissal, or to deprive an employee of an *existing* right. A fair reading of the law is that companies that adopt self-insurance programs, and thus are able to avoid state regulation, are, in effect, free to classify risks and eliminate coverage at whim. It is difficult to imagine any employer who cannot articulate a legitimate business purpose, such as saving money, for eliminating coverage.

As this text was going to press the EEOC issued its first formal guidance on the relationship between employer-provided insurance and the Americans with Disabilities Act (ADA). The complex policy (described as "interim enforcement guidance"), effective June 8, 1993, declares that the 1990 ADA "prohibits employers from discriminating on the basis of disability in the provision of health insurance to their employees." The policy suggests that an employer may not set a lower level of benefits for a specific disability, like AIDS, or a discrete group of disabilities, like cancer. However, under the guidelines an employer could make very broad distinctions. For example, an employer could elect reduced coverage for eye care or mental/nervous conditions. In the words of the Commission, "such broad distinctions, which apply to the treatment of a multitude of dissimilar conditions and which constrain individuals both with and without disabilities, are not distinctions based on disability." The Commission said that an employer does not violate the law if it refuses, as a general proposition, to cover

---

[241]*Id.* at 405.

[242]*See, e.g.,* Owens v. Storehouse, Inc., 773 F. Supp. 416, 14 EB Cases 1550 (N.D. Ga. 1991) (unilateral modification of existing plan to provide a $25,000 cap on AIDS coverage not supportive of §510 claim).

[243]Over half of all employees work for companies that are partially or fully self-insured. R. Pear, *Court Approves Cuts in Benefits in Costly Illness,* N.Y. TIMES, Nov. 27, 1991, at 1.

experimental drugs and treatments since such distinctions are not based on disability and may affect people with different illnesses.

While the Commission made it clear that "health-related insurance conditions that are based on disability may violate the ADA," the Commission would permit employers to make disability-based distinctions on the basis of cost or actuarial data in some circumstances. In such cases employers would have to establish that the plan is bona fide and that the distinction is not a subterfuge to evade the ADA. The EEOC said that an employer could rely on costs and on "legitimate actuarial data" for making a disability-based distinction, but would have to provide evidence to support its decision to show that other alternatives are not available. An employer may not use data based on myths, fears, or stereotypes. Thus, an employer cannot justify exclusion of epilepsy from its insurance plan based on an unsupported assumption that people with epilepsy will have more accidents and file more claims. Similarly, an employer who asserts that it restricted coverage of certain disabilities to avoid a huge increase in insurance premiums or to prevent insolvency of its plan will have to show that management considered ways to save money without discriminating against the disabled. A "detailed explanation of the rationale" for its decision will be required.

In response to the *McGann* case discussed above, the Commission said that the 1990 ADA would probably prohibit an employer from setting grossly unequal limits of $5,000 a year for treatment of AIDS and $100,000 a year for other physical conditions.[244]

II. STATE STATUTES

Virtually all states have enacted statutes or ordinances prohibiting discrimination on the basis of race, color, religion, sex, national origin, or age. Because Title VII requires the EEOC to initially defer processing charges of employment discrimination to those states that have enacted a comprehensive fair employment statute (defined as

---

[244]*See generally,* "EEOC Issues Guidance on ADA and Insurance," 143 LRR 208 (BNA News and Background Information)(June 14, 1993).

a "706 agency"),[245] the operation of a state or local statute should have particular relevance for the labor or management practitioner. As noted, state statutes are important to employees with unconventional lifestyles because many states will cover forms of discrimination (marital status and sexual orientation, for example) that are excluded under Title VII.[246] Because of the importance of these state statutory provisions, they deserve some review.

A. Laws Aimed at Preserving an Employee's Privacy-Type Rights

Some states have enacted statutes or have constitutions that apply constitutional-type rights, such as privacy, to all employees, regardless of whether they work for a public or private sector employer.[247] When applicable, employees may find a safe harbor for lifestyle protection.

B. Laws Protecting Sexual Orientation

If an employee, discriminated against because of sexual preference, has any statutory recourse it is at the state or local level. Many states now have some form of statutory protection or executive order prohibiting discrimination against a person's sexual orientation.

In California, for example, discrimination based upon an employee's sexual preference is prohibited by executive order.[248] In *Hinman v. Department of Personnel Administration*,[249] an employee of a Cali-

---

[245]42 U.S.C. §2000e-5(d) (1988).

[246]See *supra* note 1 and accompanying text.

[247]*See, e.g.*, Paradis v. United Technologies Pratt & Whitney Div., 672 F. Supp. 67, 2 IER Cases 1221 (D. Conn. 1987); Luedtke v. Nabors Alaska Drilling Inc., 768 P.2d 1123, 4 IER Cases 129 (Alaska 1989); Garrett v. Los Angeles City Unified Sch. Dist., 172 Cal. Rptr. 170, 174 (Cal. Ct. App. 1981) (holding that chest x-ray for tuberculosis as condition of employment not violative of state constitutional right of privacy); Cort v. Bristol-Myers Co., 431 N.E.2d 908, 115 LRRM 5127 (Mass. 1982).

[248]CAL. EX. OR. B-54-79. *See also* AB 2601 L. 1992, effective Jan. 1, 1993 (LAB. CODE §11-2.1, prohibiting discrimination or different treatment in any aspect of employment or opportunity for employment based on actual or perceived sexual orientation).

[249]213 Cal. Rptr. 410, 37 FEP Cases 1246 (Cal. Ct. App. 1985).

fornia state agency had sought to enroll his homosexual partner as his "mate," "spouse," or "family partner" under the state dental plan.[250] The Executive Order provides that the state shall not "discriminate in state employment against any individual solely upon that individual's sexual preference."[251] The court found, however, that the Executive Order in question only prohibited discrimination that was based "solely" on an individual's sexual preference. Therefore, according to the court, there is no discrimination by refusing to enroll a homosexual's "family partner" in an employee benefit plan when the plan was limited to spouses or dependents.[252] The court found that the state had treated unmarried homosexual and heterosexual employees equally.

In another California Court of Appeal case, *Soroka v. Dayton Hudson*,[253] the employee was required as a condition of employment to take a psychological test. The test included questions that attempted to reveal the applicant's sexual orientation. The questions included: "I wish I were not bothered by thoughts about sex, . . . I have never been in trouble because of my sex behavior, . . . I have been in trouble one or more times because of my sexual behaviour, . . . My sex life is satisfactory, . . . I am very strongly attracted by members of my own sex, . . . I have often wished I were a girl. (Or if you are a girl) I have never been sorry that I am a girl, . . . I have never indulged in any unusual sex practices, . . . I am worried about sex matters, . . . I like to talk about sex, . . . Many of my dreams are about sex matters."[254]

The court noted that the California law prohibits private employers from discriminating against an employee on the basis of his or her sexual orientation. The court went on to find that questions such as "I am very strongly attracted by members of my own sex" were intended to reveal an applicant's sexual orientation. Thus, "as a matter of law, this practice tends to discriminate against those who express a homosexual orientation. It also constitutes an attempt to coerce an applicant to refrain from expressing a homosexual orientation by threat of loss of employment."[255] Therefore, the court found that the

---

[250]*Id.* 37 FEP Cases at 1247.
[251]Ex. Or. B-54-79.
[252]*Hinman,* 37 FEP Cases at 1253.
[253]235 Cal. App. 3d 654, 6 IER 1491 (1991).
[254]*Id.* 6 IER Cases at 1493.
[255]Id. at 1499.

employee did state a cause of action for the employer's violation of the sexual orientation prohibition.

Similarly, a Washington state executive order prohibits state agencies and higher education institutions from discrimination based upon sexual orientation.[256] In a somewhat related case, *Doe v. Boeing Co.*,[257] a Washington State Court of Appeals recognized gender dysphoria or transsexualism as a handicap under the Washington law prohibiting discrimination of the handicapped.

Other states having statutes or executive orders prohibiting public or private employers from discriminating against employees due to sexual orientation include: Connecticut,[258] District of Columbia,[259] Hawaii,[260] Massachusetts,[261] Minnesota,[262] New Jersey,[263] New Mex-

---

[256]WASH. EX. OR. 85-09.

[257]64 Wash. App. 234, 58 FEP Cases 107 (1992).

[258]Connecticut's Fair Employment Practice law prohibits discrimination on the basis of sexual orientation. CONN. GEN. STAT. ANN. §46a-60(a) (West Supp. 1991).

[259]District of Columbia's Human Rights Act and an Order of the Mayor both prohibit discrimination based upon sexual orientation. D.C. CODE, Tit. 1, Chap. 25, §1-2512(a) (1992); D.C. Ex. Ord. 85-85. The District of Columbia's Human Rights Act defines sexual orientation as including male or female homosexuality, heterosexuality, and bisexuality, by preference or practice. D.C. CODE, Tit. 1, Chap. 25, §1-2502(29) (1992). The statute applies to both private and public employers. D.C. CODE, Tit. 1, Chap. 25, §1-2512(a) (1) (1992); *see also* D.C. CODE, Tit. 1, Chap. 25, §1-2543 (1992).

[260]Hawaii's Fair Employment Practice law prohibits discrimination based upon sexual orientation. HAW. REV. STAT., Tit. 21, §378-2(1) (1989). Under the Hawaii law, which applies to private employers, sexual orientation is defined as having a preference for heterosexuality, homosexuality, or bisexuality, or having a history of any one or more of these preferences, or being identified with any one or more of these preferences. HAW. REV. STAT., Tit. 21, §378-1 (1989).

[261]Massachusetts' Fair Employment Practice Act prohibits discrimination based upon sexual orientation. MASS. GEN. LAWS, Chap. 151B, §4.1, 4.2, 4.3 (West Supp. 1991). Sexual orientation under the Massachusetts law is defined as having orientation for or being identified as having an orientation for heterosexuality, bisexuality, or homosexuality. MASS. GEN. LAWS, Chap. 151B, §3.6 (West Supp. 1991). The law, which also applies to public and private employers, specifically excludes sexual orientation that involves minor children as sex objects. MASS. GEN. LAWS, Chap. 151B §3.6, 3.9, 4.1, 4.2, 4.3, 4.15 (West Supp. 1991).

[262]A Minnesota state government executive order protects state employees from discrimination or harassment based upon sexual orientation. MINN. EX. OR. 86-14, §1.

[263]New Jersey prohibits employment discrimination based upon affectional or sexual orientation. N.J. STAT. ANN., Tit. 10, Chap. 5, §10:5-12 (1992). Affectional or sexual orientation is defined as "male or female heterosexuality, homosexuality or bisexuality by inclination, practice, identity or expression." N.J. STAT. ANN., Tit. 10, Chap. 5, §10:5-5(hh) (1992).

ico,[264] New York,[265] Oregon,[266] Pennsylvania,[267] Rhode Island,[268] Vermont,[269] and Wisconsin.[270]

C. Laws Prohibiting Discrimination Based Upon Marital Status

A number of states also prohibit discrimination based upon marital status. In many states, this prohibition extends to unmarried couples as well as married couples. For example, in *State v. Porter Farms*,[271] an employee was discharged because he refused to marry a woman with whom he was living. The court found that Minnesota's Human Rights Act protected the employee from discrimination because the employee refused to marry.[272]

---

[264]New Mexico's executive order prohibits sexual preference discrimination by certain public employers. N.M. Ex. Or. 85-15.

[265]New York's executive order prohibits sexual orientation discrimination by certain public employers. N.Y. Ex. Or. No. 28, 11/18/83, policy 2.

[266]Oregon prohibits sexual orientation discrimination under the State Personnel Relations Law when the employment decisions are based upon non–job-related factors. Or. Rev. Stat. §243.320 (Supp. 1990).

[267]Pennsylvania prohibits sexual orientation discrimination in public employment by executive order. Pa. Ex. Or. 1975-5.

[268]Rhode Island prohibited discrimination based on sexual orientation under a public employment and government executive order. R.I. Ex. Or. 85-11, §4. In Rhode Island, however, that executive order was superseded by a public employment and government contractor law that does not prohibit sexual orientation discrimination. R.I. Gen. Stat. §28-5.1-4, -8, and -16 (1989). Some argument may be made that the executive order is still enforceable based upon a provision in the new law that purports to keep all consistent implementing directives of the prior executive order in full force. R.I. Gen. Stat. §28-5-7(5) (1989).

[269]Vermont's Fair Employment Practice Act prohibits employment discrimination on the basis of sexual orientation. Vt. Stat. Ann., Tit. 21, Chap. 5, Subchapter 6, §495 (1991). Vermont provides for an exception to the sexual orientation bias prohibition for religious organizations who give preference to members of the same religion. Vt. Stat. Ann., Tit. 21, Chap. 5, Subchapter 6, §495(e) (1991).

[270]Wisconsin's Fair Employment Act, public employment law, and government contracts statute prohibit sexual orientation discrimination. Wis. Stat. Ann. §111.31(1), .31(2), and .31(3) (West 1988); Wis. Stat. Ann. §230.01(2) (1988); Wis. Stat. Ann. §16.765(1) (1989–90). All three Wisconsin statutes adopt a definition of sexual orientation as having a preference for heterosexuality, homosexuality, or bisexuality, or having a history of, or being identified with, such preference. Wis. Stat. Ann. §111.32(13m) (West 1988).

[271]55 FEP Cases 48 (Minn. Ct. App. 1986).

[272]*Id.* at 51. Minnesota's Human Rights Act prohibits an employer from refusing

Most state statutes that prohibit marital discrimination extend the protection to so-called antinepotism policies. In *River Bend Community Unit School District No. 2 v. Illinois Human Rights Commission*,[273] an Illinois Court of Appeals found that the employer violated the Illinois Human Rights Act when it transferred an employee whose husband had been assigned as her supervisor. The transfer was based upon an employment policy prohibiting one spouse from directly supervising another spouse. The court found the Human Rights Act to be applicable and that the transfer imposed a direct burden on the marriage.

States having some statutory prohibition against discrimination based upon marital status include: Alaska,[274] California,[275] Connecticut,[276] District of Columbia,[277] Florida,[278] Hawaii,[279] Illinois,[280] Iowa,[281] Kansas,[282] Maine,[283] Maryland,[284] Massachusetts,[285] Minnesota,[286] Montana,[287] Nebraska,[288] New Hampshire,[289] New Jersey,[290] New York,[291] North Dakota,[292] Oregon,[293] Puerto Rico,[294] Washington,[295] and Wisconsin.[296]

---

to hire or from discharging an employee based upon marital status. MINN. STAT. §363.03(2) (1992).

[273] 597 N.E.2d 842 (Ill. App. Ct. 1992).

[274] ALASKA STAT. §18.80.220 (1987).

[275] CAL. LAB CODE §12940 (West Supp. 1991).

[276] CONN. GEN. STAT. ANN. §46a-60 (West Supp. 1991).

[277] D.C. CODE ANN. §1-2505 (1992).

[278] FLA. STAT. §760.10 (West 1989).

[279] HAW. REV. STAT. §378-2 (SUPP. 1990).

[280] ILL. REV. STAT., Ch. 68, §1-102 (1991).

[281] IOWA CODE ANN. §601A.6 (West 1989)

[282] KAN. STAT. ANN. §44-1001 (1991).

[283] ME. REV. STAT. ANN., Tit. 5, §7051 (West 1989) (limited to discrimination in public employment).

[284] MD. ANN. CODE Art. 49B, §16 (1986).

[285] MASS. GEN. LAWS ANN., Ch. 151B, §1 *et seq.* (West Supp. 1991).

[286] MINN. STAT. ANN. §363.03, Subd. 1 (2) (West 1991).

[287] MONT. CODE ANN. §49-2-303(1) (a) (1990).

[288] NEB. REV. STAT. §48-1104 (1988).

[289] N.H. REV. STAT. ANN. §354-A:7 (1991).

[290] N.J. REV. STAT. 10:5-12 (1992).

[291] N.Y. EXEC. LAW §296 (McKinney 1991).

[292] N.D. CENT. CODE §14-02.4-03 (1991).

[293] OR. REV. STAT. §659.020, .030 (Supp. 1990).

[294] P.R. LAWS ANN., Chap. 7, §146 (1989).

[295] WASH. REV. CODE ANN. §49.60.180 (West 1990).

[296] WIS. STAT. ANN. §111.31 (West 1988).

D. Laws Prohibiting Discrimination Based Upon Handicap

The Vocational Rehabilitation Act of 1973, as amended,[297] provides protection for individuals with a physical or mental handicap employed by an employer receiving federal financial assistance. The protection of individual employees with a disability has been extended by the Americans with Disabilities Act (ADA).[298] The ADA expands the scope of protection available under the Rehabilitation Act to private employers having 15 or more employees.[299] In addition to the Rehabilitation Act and the ADA, individual employees with a handicap or physical disability may find discrimination protection under various state laws.

The application of specific state statutes, however, is usually narrowly applied based upon the statute's definition of handicap or disability. Such a narrow approach can be seen in *City of Columbus v. OCRC*,[300] where applicants for the position of police officer with the City of Columbus, Ohio, were denied consideration for employment due to their failure to meet visual acuity requirements. The Ohio Fair Employment Practice Law defined a handicap as any

> abnormal condition which is expected to continue for a considerable length of time, whether correctable or uncorrectable by good medical practice, which can reasonably be expected to limit the person's functional ability, including, but not limited to seeing, hearing, thinking, ambulating, climbing, descending, lifting, grasping, sitting, rising, any related function, or any limitation due to weakness and significantly decreased endurance, so that he can not perform his everyday routine living and working without significantly increased hardship and vulnerability to what are considered the everyday obstacles and hazards encountered by the nonhandicapped.[301]

---

[297]29 U.S.C. §§701–96 (1982). See discussion *supra* notes 149–208 and accompanying text.

[298]42 U.S.C §§12101–12112 (Supp. 1990). See discussion *supra* notes 209–230 and accompanying text.

[299]42 U.S.C. §12111(A) (Supp. 1990).

[300]55 FEP Cases 147 (Ohio Ct. App. 1985).

[301]OHIO REV. STAT., Tit. 41, §4112.01(A) (13) (1992). This definition has been subsequently amended to read:

> a physical or mental impairment that substantially limits one or more major life activities, including the functions of caring for one's self, performing manual tasks, walking, seeing, hearing, speaking, breathing, learning, and working; a record of a physical or mental impairment; or being regarded as having a physical or mental impairment. *Id.* amended by H.B. 321 L. 1992.

The Act made it unlawful for an employer to refuse to hire a person because of a handicap.[302]

The court determined that the individual applicants failed to meet the definition as defined in the statute. Thus, the court upheld the trial court's finding that the applicants failed to demonstrate that they could not perform "everyday routine living and working without significantly increased hardship and vulnerability to what are considered the everyday obstacles and hazards encountered by the nonhandicapped."[303]

Most of the state statutes that provide protection for disabled employees also require the employer to make reasonable accommodations for the particular disability or handicap of the employee. Thus, in *Kennedy v. Dixon*,[304] the court held that the District of Columbia's Human Rights Act and the Mayor's Order applying the Act's protection to D.C. employees prohibited the D.C. Fire Department from enforcing a no-beard policy against firefighters who suffered from pseudofolliculitis barbae. The court held that reasonable accommodations could be made by allowing the disabled firefighter to wear a one-quarter inch beard.[305]

Similarly, in *Clarke v. Shoreline School District No. 412*,[306] the Supreme Court of the State of Washington held that the Washington State Law Against Discrimination required a school district to take an affirmative step in placing a legally blind and hearing-impaired teacher in a position within the district if a position existed and the teacher was qualified to fill it. However, the state law did not require the district to hire or employ a handicapped employee who was unable to perform essential job functions. Thus, even without attempting to accommodate the employee, if the employee is otherwise not qualified to teach because of a handicap, the district would not violate the state law by discharging or failing to hire the individual.[307]

In *LaMott v. Apple Valley Health Center*,[308] interpreting the Minnesota Human Rights Act,[309] the court noted that the goal of the

---

[302]OHIO REV. STAT. TIT. 41, §4112.02(a) (1992).
[303]OCRC, 55 FEP Cases at 149.
[304]57 FEP Cases 494 (D.C. Sup. Ct. 1991).
[305]*Id.* at 499.
[306]57 FEP 442 (Wash. 1986).
[307]*Id.* at 448.
[308]55 FEP Cases 55 (Minn. Ct. App. 1991).
[309]MINN. STAT. ANN. §363.01-.14 *et seq.* (West 1991).

Act was to "facilitate the return of disabled persons into the work force."[310] In *LaMott*, the employee was not allowed to return to work after suffering a severe cerebral hemorrhage resulting from an aneurysm.[311] The employee's supervisor testified that the employee could complete her tasks 50 percent of the time while using a "memory log," or 100 percent of the tasks when using a combination of memory log and personal supervision. Based upon this testimony, the court concluded that the "evidence showed that with reasonable accommodation, [the employee] had the ability to perform the essential functions required of all applicants for the job.[312]

All 50 states have some statutory restriction on discrimination based upon a mental or physical disability or handicap.[313] The three states of Alabama, Arkansas, and Mississippi, however, extend handicapped discrimination protection only to governmental employees.[314]

[310]*LaMott* 55 FEP Cases at 60.

[311]*Id.* at 57.

[312]*Id.* at 59.

[313]ALASKA STAT. §18.80.220 *et seq.* (1987); ARIZ. REV. STAT. ANN. §41-1461(4) (1992); CAL. GOV'T CODE §12940(1) (West Supp. 1991); COLO. REV. STAT. §24-34-801 (1992); CONN. GEN. STAT. §46a-60 (West Supp. 1991); DEL. CODE ANN., Tit. 19, §724 (1985); D.C. CODE ANN. §6-1701 (1992); FLA. STAT. §413.08 (West 1991); GA. CODE ANN. §34-6A-4 (1992); HAW. REV. STAT. §378-1 (Supp. 1990); IDAHO CODE §67-5909 (1992); ILL. REV. STAT. Ch. 68, §1-102 (1991); IND. CODE §22-9-1-3(q) (1992); IOWA CODE §601A.6 (West 1989); KAN. STAT. ANN. §44-101 (1992); KY. REV. STAT. ANN. §207.150 (Michie/Bobbs-Merrill 1991); LA. REV. STAT. ANN., Tit. 23, Ch. 9, §2251 *et seq.* (West 1992); ME. REV. STAT. ANN., Tit. 5, §4572 (West 1989); MD. ANN. CODE Art. 49B, §15(g) (1986); MASS. GEN. L. Ch. 151B, §4 (West Supp. 1991); MICH. COMP. LAWS §37.1101 *et seq.* (1991); MINN. STAT. ANN. §363.03, Subd. 1(2) (West 1991); MO. REV. STAT. §213.055 (1986); MONT. CODE ANN. §49-2-303(1) (a) (1990); NEB. REV. STAT. §48-1104 (1988); NEV. REV. STAT. 613.330 (1991); N.H. REV. STAT. ANN. §354-A:7 (1991); N.J. REV. STAT. §10:5-4.1 (1992); N.M. STAT. ANN. §28-1-7 (Michie 1989); N.Y. STAT. EXEC. LAW, Art. 15, §292(21) (McKinney 1991); N.C. GEN. STAT. §143-422.2 (1992); N.D. CENT. CODE §14-02.4-03 (1991); OHIO REV. CODE ANN. §4112.02 (Anderson 1992); OKLA. STAT., Tit. 25, Ch. 21, §1301(4) (1992); OR. REV. STAT. §659.400 (Supp. 1990); PA. CONS. STAT., Tit. 43, §955 (1991); R.I. GEN. LAWS, Tit. 28, §28-5-7 (1989); S.C. CODE ANN. 43-33-530 (Law. Co-op. 1991); S.D. CODIFIED LAWS ANN. §20-13-1(4) (Supp. 1991); TENN. CODE ANN. §4-21-102(9) (1992); TEX. HUM. RES. CODE ANN., Tit. 83, Ch. 16, Art. 5221k, §2.01(4) (Vernon 1993); UTAH CODE ANN. §34-35-2(9) (1986); VT. STAT. ANN., Tit. 21, Ch. 5, Subchapter 6, §495 (1992); VA. CODE ANN. §2.1-715 (Michie 1991); WASH. REV. CODE §49.60.180 (West 1990); W. VA. CODE §5-11-9(a) (1) (1992); WIS. STAT. §111.34 (1988); WYO. STAT. §27-9-105 (1992).

[314]ALA CODE §21-7-1 *et seq.* (1988); ARK. STAT. ANN. §20-14-301 *et seq.* (Michie 1988); MISS CODE ANN §43-6-15 (1989).

E. Laws Prohibiting Discrimination Based Upon Political Affiliation

Many states have statutes protecting employees from discrimination based upon political affiliation. State court application, however, depends exclusively upon the wording of the individual statute. Thus, in *Dudycz v. City of Chicago*,[315] where a City of Chicago police officer was forced to seek a leave of absence from his police duties after being elected to the Illinois State Senate, the state court narrowly interpreted the state statute to exclude the City from the statutory prohibition. The court noted that Illinois has a statute that prohibits certain municipal governments from restricting the political activities of their employees.[316] The court, however, went on to hold that the City of Chicago was a home rule unit and did not operate under the applicable statutes which prohibited the restriction of an employee's political activities.[317] Thus, in a narrow interpretation of the statute, the court held that the City of Chicago was not subject to the prohibitions against political activity restrictions and could require its employees to take leave-of-absences without violating state law.[318]

In *Eldridge v. Sierra View Local Hospital District*,[319] the court enforced a state statute which provided that "no restriction shall be placed on the political activities of any officer or employee of a state or local agency."[320] In *Eldridge*, after a nurse employed by Sierra View Hospital announced her candidacy for a vacant position as a director of the Hospital's Local Board of Directors, the Hospital Board passed a conflict of interest bylaw which required an employee elected or appointed to the Board to resign from hospital employment.[321] The court held that the Hospital Board could not "burden the exercise of the statutory rights contained in §3203 with the penalty of loss of employment."[322]

---

[315]563 N.E.2d 1112 (Ill. Ct. App. 1990), *cert. denied*, 567 N.E.2d 340 (Ill. 1991).
[316]*Id.* at 1124, citing ILL. REV. STAT., Ch. 24, paras. 10-1-27.1; 10-2.1-5.1 (1985).
[317]*Id.* at 19.
[318]*Id.* at 20.
[319]273 Cal. Rptr. 654 (Cal. Ct. App., 5th Dist. 1990).
[320]*Id.* at 658, citing CAL. GOV'T CODE §3202 (West Supp. 1991).
[321]*Id.* at 655.
[322]*Id.* at 658.

Forty-two states have enacted some degree of protection for employee political affiliation.[323]

---

[323]ARIZ. REV. STAT. ANN. §41-772(A)-(L) (1992); ARK. STAT. ANN. §1, as enacted by Act 580, L. 1991, 8, as enacted by Act 564, L. 1991; CAL. LAB. CODE §1101 *et seq.* (West Supp. 1991); CAL. GOV'T CODE §3203 (West Supp. 1991); COLO. REV. STAT. §80-2-108 (1992); CONN. GEN. STAT. §2-3a, §31-511, and §7-421 (West Supp. 1991); DEL. CODE. ANN., Tit. 29, §5110, Tit. 15, §5161 *et seq.* (1992); FLA. STAT. §104.081 (West 1989); IDAHO CODE §67-5311(1) and (2) (1992); ILL. REV. STAT., Ch. 24, paras. 10-1-27.1; 10-2.1-5.1 (1985); IND. CODE §3-14-3-21(1) and (2) (1992); KY. REV. STAT. ANN. §121.310 (Baldwin 1992); LA. REV. STAT. ANN. §23:961 (1992); MD. ANN. CODE Art. 33, §28-1 (1986); MASS. GEN. L., Ch. 56, §33 (West Supp. 1991); MICH. COMP. LAWS §168.931(a) and (d) (1991); MINN. STAT. §§202A.135 and 204B.195 (West 1991); MISS. CODE ANN. §23-15-871 (1991); MO. REV. STAT. §115.637 (1986); MONT. CODE ANN. §2-18-620(1) to (3) (1990); NEB. REV. STAT. §§32-1223, 32-1050, 23-3001 (1988); NEV. REV. STAT. §613.040 (1991); N.H. REV. STAT. ANN. §98-E:1 (1991); N.J. REV. STAT. §19:34-27 (1992); N.M. STAT. ANN. §1-20-13 (1992); N.Y. LAB. LAW §201-d(5) to (7) (McKinney 1992); N.C. GEN. STAT. §126-14(a) (1992); N.D. CENT. CODE §39-01-04 (1991); OHIO REV. CODE ANN. §3599-05 (Anderson 1992); OKLA. STAT., Tit. 26, §7-101, Tit. 40, §187 (West 1991); OR. REV. STAT. §171.120, and 171.122 (Supp. 1990); PA. CONS. STAT., Tit. 25, §3547 (1991); P.R. LAWS ANN. §§131 and 133 (1989); R.I. GEN. LAWS §17-23-6 (1989); S.C. CODE ANN. §16-17-560 (1991); S.D. CODIFIED LAWS 12-26-13 (1992); TENN. CODE ANN. §2-19-134(a) to (c); §38-8-351 (1992); TEX. GOV'T CODE §150.001 to .003 (1993); UTAH CODE ANN. §20-13-6 (1986); V.I. CODE ANN., Tit. 24, Ch. 7, 160 (1992); W. VA. CODE §3-9-15 (West 1992); WIS. STAT. §12.07(3) and (4), and §103.18 (West 1988); and WYO. STAT. §22-26-112(a) (v) to (vii), §22-26-116, -117, and -118 (1992).

Chapter 4

Constitutional Standards

To what extent is the Constitution a "safe harbor" for employees with bizarre or unconventional lifestyles? Suppose management disapproves of the sexual partners, associations, or speech of its employees? Can a public employer dismiss or fail to hire such employees? Under what circumstances can management "test" an employee for the results of his or her off-duty misconduct, such as the use of illegal drugs? This chapter addresses the Constitution as a limitation on management's power to regulate the lifestyles of its employees.

A public sector employee dismissed because of off-duty lifestyle conduct may be protected under the Constitution. Specifically, at the state level the Fourteenth Amendment prohibits deprivations of life, liberty, or property without due process of law. Application of this prohibition requires a two-stage analysis: a court will first determine whether the asserted individual interests are encompassed within the Fourteenth Amendment's protection of "life, liberty, or property"; if protected interests are implicated, the court then decides what procedures constitute "due process of law" or, stated differently, the type of notice and hearing to which the individual is entitled under the Amendment.[1] As the Supreme Court has noted, "The question

---

[1] Robb v. City of Philadelphia, 733 F.2d 286, 292, 1 IER Cases 1787 (3d Cir. 1984).
The Fourteenth Amendment provides in part that "[no state] shall . . . deprive any person of life, liberty, or property, without due process of law; nor deny to any person within its jurisdiction equal protection of the laws." U.S. CONST. amend. XIV. The Fifth Amendment is a limitation only upon the actions of the federal government,

117

is not merely the 'weight' of the individual's interest, but whether the nature of the interest is one within the contemplation of the 'liberty or property' language of the Fourteenth Amendment."[2]

The significance of concluding that an individual has a protected property or liberty interest in some aspect of his employment is that he cannot be denied or deprived of that interest without due process of law. From a procedural standpoint, an employee facing discipline or discharge for questionable conduct who has some property or liberty interest in continued employment is entitled to procedural due process. Equally important, substantive guarantees are also inherent in the Due Process Clause. Justice John Harlan, rejecting the view that the Due Process Clause is a guarantee only of procedural fairness, declared that the Due Process Clause contains both a substantive and a procedural component. As stated by Justice Harlan, if due process was simply "a procedural safeguard it would fail to reach those situations where the deprivation of life, liberty or property was accomplished by legislation which by operating in the future could,

---

Public Utility Comm'n v. Pollak, 343 U.S. 451 (1952), and in part provides that "no person shall . . . be deprived of life, liberty, or property, without due process of law." U.S. CONST. amend. V. It is settled that although not explicitly drafted in the language of the Fifth Amendment, the Due Process Clause of the Fifth Amendment contains an equal protection component prohibiting the United States from invidiously discriminating among individuals or groups. Bolling v. Sharpe, 347 U.S. 497, 499 (1954).

While most case law regarding off-duty conduct involves a state as employer, the discussion in this chapter has applicability to the federal government as employer although, in many instances, the forum for resolving federal employee constitutional claims will not be the courts but arbitration under a collective bargaining agreement. *See* 5 U.S.C. §7121 (1988) (providing that all collective bargaining agreements in the federal sector contain a procedure for settlement of grievances, including questions of arbitrability). Moreover, arbitration decisions involving employee removals, suspensions for more than 14 days, reductions in grade or pay, or furloughs of 30 days or less ("Category II" claims) are subject to review by the U.S. Court of Appeals for the Federal Circuit. 28 U.S.C. §1295(a) (9) (1988); 5 U.S.C. §7121(f) (1988). Alternatively, a federal employee may elect to process a grievance through the Merit Systems Protection Board (MSPB), with appeal to the Federal Circuit. For Category II issues, the arbitrator is governed by the same criteria and standards that would govern the MSPB. *See* FRANK ELKOURI & EDNA ASPER ELKOURI, HOW ARBITRATION WORKS, 54–55 (4th ed. BNA Books, 1985). In both the arbitral and the MSPB forum, as well as on appeal to the Federal Circuit, employees may argue that the federal government is precluded by the Fifth Amendment's Due Process Clause from adversely affecting an individual's employment status.

[2]Morrissey v. Brewer, 408 U.S. 471, 481 (1972).

given even the fairest possible procedure in application to individuals, nevertheless destroy the enjoyment of all three. Thus the guarantees of due process, . . . have in this country 'become bulwarks also against arbitrary legislation.' "[3]

In a nutshell, substantive due process means fundamental fairness. The test applied for finding a violation of substantive due process involves a "balancing of the nature of the individual interest allegedly infringed, the importance of the government interests furthered, the degree of infringement, and the sensitivity of the government entity responsible for the regulation to more carefully tailored alternative means of achieving its goals."[4] Thus, an employee with an unconventional lifestyle asserting a violation of due process must convince a court that his conduct encompasses a property or liberty interest worthy of constitutional protection.

I. PROPERTY INTERESTS

In a 1985 case, the Supreme Court declared that property interests "are not created by the Constitution, 'they are created and their dimensions are defined by existing rules or understandings that stem from an independent source such as state law. . . .' "[5] The leading case in this area continues to be *Board of Regents v. Roth*,[6] where the Court discussed the basis for a public employee's claim of a property right in continued employment. In that case a university professor argued that his employer's failure to provide any reason or hearing for his nonrenewal violated procedural due process.[7] The Court reasoned that, prior to determining what form of hearing is required under the Due Process Clause, it must first be ascertained whether a liberty or property interest has been denied.[8] Although

---

[3]Poe v. Ullman, 367 U.S. 497, 541 (1961) (Harlan, J., dissenting) [citations omitted] (quoting Hurtado v. California, 110 U.S. 516, 532 (1884)).

[4]Beller v. Middendorf, 632 F.2d 788, 807, 24 FEP Cases 289 (9th Cir. 1980), *cert. denied*, 452 U.S. 905, 26 FEP Cases 1687 (1981).

[5]Cleveland Bd. of Educ. v. Loudermill, 470 U.S. 532, 538–39, 1 IER Cases 424 (1985) (quoting Board of Regents v. Roth, 408 U.S. 564, 577, 1 IER Cases 23 (1972)).

[6]408 U.S. 564, 1 IER Cases 23 (1972).

[7]*Id.* at 565.

[8]*Id.*

the Court recognized that the reemployment of Roth by the university was of major concern to him, the Court nevertheless held that the nonrenewal decision violated neither a liberty nor a property interest where the state did not make any charge that might seriously damage Roth's standing in the community or impose on him a stigma or other disability that foreclosed his freedom to take advantage of other employment.[9] The Court further stated that in order to have a property interest in a benefit one must have more than an abstract demand for it; a "legitimate claim of entitlement" is mandated.[10] Roth's property interest in employment, the Court reasoned, was created and defined in the terms of his employment, and since the university made no provisions whatsoever for renewal, no procedural infirmity existed in the denial of a hearing.

In *Perry v. Sindermann*,[11] a companion case to *Roth*, the Court made it clear that implied promises may give rise to a property interest under the Due Process Clause. *Sindermann* involved another professor serving on a year-to-year basis whose employment was not renewed and who had not been granted a hearing. The Court ruled that a potential property interest in continued employment existed where the university had a *de facto* tenure system for professors after seven or more years of service.[12] In remanding the case to the district court, the Court found that Sindermann, who had taught at a state college for 10 years, must be accorded the opportunity to establish that his property interest was secured by explicit rules and understandings of the institution.[13]

The Court, in *Bishop v. Wood*,[14] stated that where a property interest is created by state law, the issue of what satisfies due process is determined by reference to the appropriate state statute creating that right. Of particular note in the employment area, the Court declared that the Due Process Clause "is not a guarantee against incorrect or ill-advised personnel decisions."[15] More recently, however, the Court said in 1985 that " '[w]hile the legislature may

---

[9]*Id.*
[10]*Id.* at 577.
[11]408 U.S. 593, 1 IER Cases 33 (1972).
[12]*Id.* at 600.
[13]*Id.* at 602-03.
[14]426 U.S. 341 (1976).
[15]*Id.* at 350.

elect not to confer a property interest in [public] employment, it may not constitutionally authorize the deprivation of such an interest, once conferred, without appropriate procedural safeguards.' "[16] Therefore, it now seems clear that state law is only used to determine whether a property right exists; once such a right is found, it cannot be terminated without constitutional due process.[17]

II. LIBERTY INTERESTS

In *Meyer v. Nebraska*,[18] the Supreme Court, discussing the nature of a liberty interest, stated:

> [Liberty] denotes not merely freedom from bodily restraint but also the right of the individual to contract, to engage in any of the common occupations of life, to acquire useful knowledge, to marry, establish a home and bring up children, to worship God according to the dictates of his own conscience, and generally to enjoy those privileges long recognized . . . as essential to the orderly pursuit of happiness by free men.[19]

The Supreme Court, in a series of cases, has placed several limitations upon a public employee's ability to prove a deprivation of liberty under the Constitution.[20] The Court has held that in order to make a successful claim of liberty deprivation, an employee must demonstrate that the dismissal resulted in the publication of information[21] that either put the employee's reputation or integrity

---

[16]Cleveland Bd. of Educ., 470 U.S. at 541 (quoting Arnett v. Kennedy, 416 U.S. 134, 167 (1974) (Powell, J., concurring in part and concurring in result in part)).

[17]Loehr v. Ventura County Community College Dist., 743 F.2d 1310 (9th Cir. 1984).

[18]262 U.S. 390 (1923).

[19]*Id.* at 399.

[20]In Robb v. City of Philadelphia, 733 F.2d 286, 294, 1 IER Cases 1787 (1984), the Third Circuit stated that

> [a]n employment action implicates a fourteenth amendment liberty interest only if it (1) is based on a "charge against [the individual] that might seriously damage his standing and associations in the community . . . for example, that he had been guilty of dishonesty, or immorality" or (2) "impose[s] on him a stigma or other disability that forecloses his freedom to take advantage of other employment opportunities."

Id. at 294 (citing Board of Regents v. Roth, 408 U.S. 564, 573, 1 IER Cases 23 (1972)).

[21]Bishop v. Wood, 426 U.S. 341, 348 (1976).

at stake, or was stigmatizing.[22] The information must have the general effect of curtailing the employee's future freedom of choice or action.[23] A liberty interest is not implicated merely because nonretention on one job, taken alone, might make an individual somewhat less attractive to other employers.[24] As pointed out by one commentator, "To rise to the level of a deprivation of liberty, the foreclosure of other employment opportunities [has] to be more severe, like the foreclosure achieved through regulations barring an employee from future employment in a particular jurisdiction."[25] Simply stated, "[t]he mere fact of discharge from a government position does not deprive a person of a liberty interest,"[26] although it may deprive an individual of a property interest, as in the case of a tenured public employee.

In *Paul v. Davis*,[27] and *Siegert v. Gilley*,[28] the Court held that reputation alone is not a protected liberty interest when the action is not accompanied by an alteration of the individual's legal status. As such, a defamation unaccompanied by an adverse personnel action or, alternatively, minor "personnel actions—such as reprimands, internal transfers, and investigatory-reports—now escapes procedural scrutiny under" the *Davis* and *Gilley* decisions.[29]

III. WHAT PROCESS IS DUE?

Once an individual proves that a property or liberty interest has been or is about to be impermissibly infringed upon by the state, a

---

[22]*Roth*, 408 U.S. at 573.

[23]Sipes v. United States, 744 F.2d 1418, 1422 (10th Cir. 1984) ("a liberty interest may be impinged if the Government 'imposed on him a stigma or disability that foreclosed his freedom to take advantage of other employment opportunities' ") (quoting *Roth*, 408 U.S. at 573, citing Asbill v. Choctaw Housing Auth., 726 F.2d 1499, 1 IER Cases 843 (10th Cir. 1984) (no denial of liberty interest because intragovernment dissemination of reasons for employee's dismissal does not constitute "published")).

[24]*Roth*, 408 U.S. at 574 n.13.

[25]*Developments in the Law—Public Employment*, 97 HARV. L. REV. 1780, 1788 (1984).

[26]Beller v. Middendorf, 632 F.2d 788, 806, 24 FEP Cases 289, 300 (9th Cir. 1980), *cert. denied*, 452 U.S. 905, 25 FEP Cases 254, *cert. denied*, 454 U.S. 1069, 17 FEP Cases 289 (1981).

[27]424 U.S. 693, 1 IER Cases 1827 (1976).

[28]111 S. Ct. 1789, 6 IER Cases 705 (1991) (stating that "[d]efamation, by itself, is a tort actionable under the laws of most States, but not a constitutional deprivation").

[29]*See Developments in the Law, supra* note 25, at 1790.

determination must be made as to what procedural process is due. It is often the case that a state statute, an ordinance, or even a collective bargaining agreement[30] sets out the specific procedures to be followed where an individual has been adversely affected. In this situation the procedures must be substantially followed and must not be less restrictive than the minimal constitutional constraints of due process.[31] With respect to the minimal constitutional guarantees, the Court, as early as 1884, made it clear that a government entity is not free to make any process "due process," and that the courts, in effecting the due process guarantee, must examine "not [the] particular forms of procedure, but the very substance of individual rights to life, liberty, and property."[32] In this respect, due process does not necessarily mandate a court proceeding in every case where property or liberty interests are affected.[33]

More recently, the Court stated that " 'the root requirement' of the Due Process Clause [is] 'that an individual be given an opportunity for a hearing *before* he is deprived of any significant property interest' ";[34] however, the Court, in a footnote, did recognize that there are "some situations in which a post deprivation hearing will satisfy due process requirements,"[35] commenting, "[i]n general,

---

[30]*See, e.g.,* Parrett v. City of Connersville, 737 F.2d 690, 696 (7th Cir. 1984) (indicating in dictum that grievance procedure providing for arbitration might be procedurally adequate); Hamilton v. Adult Educ. Dist., 118 LRRM 3197 (E.D. Wis. 1985) (holding that plaintiff-janitors' collective bargaining agreement "provided all the process that was due them").

[31]*See* the discussion by Justice White, writing for the majority, in Cleveland Bd. of Educ. v. Loudermill, 470 U.S. 532, 540, 1 IER Cases 424 (1985) (rejecting the argument that where the legislature which confers the substantive right also sets out the procedural mechanism for enforcing that right the individual "must take the bitter with the sweet").

[32]Hurtado v. California, 110 U.S. 516, 532 (1884).

[33]The late Justice Felix Frankfurter, in suggesting a balancing test, stated that every case must be considered by itself:

The precise nature of the interest that has been adversely affected, the manner in which this was done, the reasons for doing it, the available alternatives to the procedure that was followed, the protection implicit in the office of the functionary whose conduct is challenged, the balance of hurt complained of and good accomplished—these are some of the considerations that must enter into the judicial judgment.

Joint Anti-Fascist Refugee Comm. v. McGrath, 341 U.S. 123, 163 (1951) (Frankfurter, J., concurring).

[34]Cleveland Bd. of Educ., 470 U.S. at 534–35 (emphasis in original quoting Boddie v. Connecticut, 401 U.S. 371, 379 (1971)).

[35]*Id.* at 542.

something less' than a full evidentiary hearing is sufficient prior to adverse administrative action."[36] What is particularly interesting is that, in balancing the competing interests, the Court appeared to accord more than passing note to "the significance of the [employee's] private interest in retaining employment."[37] With respect to the government's interests in immediate termination, the Court said:

> [A]ffording the employee an opportunity to respond prior to termination would impose neither a significant administrative burden nor intolerable delays. Furthermore, the employer shares the employee's interest in avoiding disruption and erroneous decisions; and until the matter is settled, the employer would continue to receive the benefit of the employee's labors. It is preferable to keep a qualified employee on than to train a new one. A governmental employer also has an interest in keeping citizens usefully employed rather than taking the possibly erroneous and counter-productive step of forcing its employees onto the welfare rolls. Finally, in those situations where the employer perceives a significant hazard in keeping the employee on the job, it can avoid the problem by suspending with pay.[38]

Case law suggests that a public employer, in dismissing a nonprobationary employee, should provide either oral or written notice of the charges and an opportunity for a pretermination hearing *of some kind.* The hearing need not be a full adversarial evidentiary hearing prior to governmental action,[39] but may simply be a request that the employee provide his or her side of the story in person or in writing to management. While the pretermination hearing "need not definitively resolve the propriety of the discharge," it should serve as an initial check against clearly incorrect decisions.[40] As stated by the Court, it should be "essentially, a determination of whether there are reasonable grounds to believe that the charges against the employee are true and support the proposed action."[41]

---

[36]*Id.* at 545 (quoting Mathews v. Eldridge, 424 U.S. 319, 343 (1976)).

[37]*Id.* at 543.

[38]*Id.* at 544 [footnotes omitted].

[39]The Court, in *Cleveland Bd. of Educ.*, 470 U.S. at 546–47, noted that in only one case, Goldberg v. Kelly, 397 U.S. 254 (1970), has the Court required a hearing of this type.

[40]Cleveland Bd. of Educ., 470 U.S. at 532–33.

[41]*Id.* at 533.

IV. DEPRIVATION OF PROTECTED INTERESTS

There is no question that otherwise "terminable-at-will" government employees, while they may generally be discharged for any number of reasons or for no reason at all, may not be discharged for exercising their constitutional rights."[42] At the same time, the courts have indicated that the state may have a greater interest in regulating the conduct of its employees than the activities of the population at large.[43] Although there is overlap between them, four areas are of particular interest in the off-duty lifestyle areas: (1) political affiliation or patronage, (2) privacy, (3) association and speech, and (4) morality standards.

A. Political Association

The Seventh Circuit has stated the black letter law regarding limitations on a public employee's political affiliations as follows: "A public agency that fires an employee because of his political beliefs or political affiliations infringes his freedom of speech."[44] The court went on to note that "there are exceptions to this principle, carved out to minimize its adverse impact on the effective functioning of government."[45] Employees at the policy-making level of government can therefore be fired on political grounds.[46] The Seventh Circuit, for example, has recognized that a public employer cannot run a government with officials who are forced to keep political enemies as their confidential secretaries.[47]

In *Elrod v. Burns*,[48] the plaintiffs, all Republican employees of the Cook County, Illinois, Sheriff's Department, alleged that they

---

[42]McMullen v. Carson, 568 F. Supp. 937, 943, 115 LRRM 2051 (M.D. Fla. 1983) (upholding dismissal of clerk typist for active membership in Ku Klux Klan).

[43]Kelley v. Johnson, 425 U.S. 238 (1976).

[44]Soderbeck v. Burnett County, 752 F.2d 285, 288 (7th Cir. 1985).

[45]*Id.*

[46]Shakman v. Democratic Org. of Cook County, 722 F.2d 1307 (7th Cir. 1983).

[47]*Soderbeck,* 752 F.2d at 288; *see also* De La Cruz v. Pruitt, 590 F. Supp. 1296, 116 LRRM 3334 (N.D. Ind. 1984) (reversing dismissal of government non-policy-making and nonconfidential employee for political beliefs).

[48]427 U.S. 347, 1 IER Cases 60 (1976).

were discharged solely because they were not affiliated with or sponsored by the Democratic party. It had long been a practice of a new Sheriff of a different political party to replace non-civil-service employees with members of his own party. The Supreme Court first concluded that the practice of patronage dismissals clearly infringed upon the First Amendment rights of the employees.[49] In justifying this infringement, however, the defendants argued that there is a compelling need to ensure effective government and the efficiency of public employees. Further, there is a "need for political loyalty of employees, not to the end that effectiveness and efficiency be ensured, but to the end that representative government not be undercut by tactics obstructing the implementation of policies of the new administration, policies presumably sanctioned by the electorate."[50] And finally, according to the defendants, political patronage was justified to preserve the democratic process.

The Court, however, found these arguments ineffective for the "wholesale" validation of patronage dismissals. The Court reasoned that patronage dismissals limited to policy-making positions are sufficient to achieve the government's end. Non-policy-making individuals usually have only limited responsibility and, therefore, are not in a position to thwart the goals of the incumbent party.[51]

The Court concluded that patronage dismissals severely restrict political belief and association. In the Court's words,

> [t]hough there is a vital need for government efficiency and effectiveness, such dismissals are on balance not the least restrictive means for fostering the end. There is also a need to insure that policies which the electorate has sanctioned are effectively implemented. That interest can be fully satisfied by limiting patronage dismissals to policymaking positions. Finally, patronage dismissals cannot be justified by their contributions to proper functioning of our democratic process through their assistance to partisan politics since political parties are nurtured by other, less intrusive and equally effective methods. More fundamentally, however, any contribution of patronage dismissals to the democratic process does not suffice to override their severe encroachment on First Amendment Freedoms. We hold, therefore, that the practice of patronage dismissals is unconstitutional under the First and Fourteenth Amendment. . . .[52]

---

[49]*Id.* 1 IER Cases at 65.
[50]*Id.* at 67.
[51]*Id.*
[52]*Id.* at 69.

The arguable broad "policymaking" exception recognized by the Supreme Court in *Elrod,* however, was subsequently redefined and narrowed in *Branti v. Finkel.*[53] In *Branti,* the Supreme Court stated that "the ultimate inquiry is not whether the label 'policymaker' or 'confidential' fits a particular position; rather, the question is whether the hiring authority can demonstrate that party affiliation is an appropriate requirement for the effective performance of the public office involved."[54] Applying this test, the Court concluded the continued employment of an assistant public defender could not properly be conditioned upon his allegiance to the political party in control of the county government. If an employer cannot demonstrate that the employee's party affiliation is an appropriate requirement for the effective performance of the job, dismissal cannot be effected. The focus is on the powers of the office and not on the tasks of the officeholder.

In *Rutan v. Republican Party of Illinois,*[55] the Supreme Court again addressed the issue of employee political affiliation. In *Rutan,* according to a number of lower level employees of the State of Illinois, Illinois Governor James Thompson had been "using the Governor's office to limit state employment and beneficial employment-related decisions to those who are supported by the Republican Party."[56] The Court framed the issue as "whether promotion, transfer, recall, and hiring decisions involving low-level public employees may be constitutionally based on party affiliation and support."[57] Arguing that this case was different from *Elrod* and *Branti,* the State of Illinois asked the Court to find its failure to transfer, failure to promote, and failure to recall did not arise to the same deprivation as patronage dismissals. The State of Illinois also sought a finding that because the employment decisions in question were not punitive and in no way adversely affected employment, they did "not chill the exercise of protected belief and association by public employees."[58]

The Court, however, found that the conclusions in *Elrod* and *Branti* were equally applicable to the state's patronage practices. The Court found that "[e]mployees who do not compromise their beliefs

---

[53]445 U.S. 507, 1 IER Cases 91 (1980).
[54]*Id.* at 518.
[55]497 U.S. 62, 5 IER Cases 673 (1990).
[56]*Id.* 5 IER Cases at 674.
[57]*Id.*
[58]*Id.* at 677.

stand to lose the considerable increases in pay and job satisfaction attendant to promotions, the hours and maintenance expenses that are consumed by long daily commutes, and even their jobs if they are not rehired after a temporary layoff."[59] Thus, because these are significant penalties imposed for exercising their rights as guaranteed by the First Amendment, "[u]nless these patronage practices are narrowly tailored to further vital government interests,"[60] they must be found to encroach on First Amendment freedoms.

In *Rutan*, the Court went on to find that

> [a] government's interest in securing effective employees can be met by discharging, demoting or transferring staffmembers whose work is deficient. A government's interest in securing employees who will loyally implement its policies can be adequately served by choosing or dismissing certain high-level employees on the basis of their political views. . . . We therefore determine that promotions, transfers, and recalls after layoffs based on political affiliation or support are an impermissible infringement on the First Amendment rights of public employees.[61]

Subsequent lower court cases have attempted to interpret the Supreme Court's test in *Elrod, Branti,* and *Rutan*. It is unclear from these cases, however, whether the broad *Elrod* "policymaker" label is still applicable, or whether the court's narrower *Branti* test has replaced it. In *Savage v. Corski,*[62] the Court of Appeals for the Second Circuit read *Branti* to mean that "political affiliation is an appropriate requirement when there is a rational connection between shared ideology and job performance."[63] Deciding to the contrary, according to the Second Circuit, would limit a new administration's ability to effectuate its policies and thus undercut the electorate's vote.[64]

In *Regan v. Boogertman,*[65] the District Court for the Eastern District of New York, held that it was not necessary for the defendants to demonstrate the employee in question "actually functioned in a policymaking capacity in order to justify [their] use of political affiliation as a qualification for the position. . . . It is sufficient to show [that the defendant] was legally empowered to delegate his authority to

---

[59]*Id.*
[60]*Id.*
[61]*Id.* at 677–78
[62]850 F.2d 64 (2d Cir. 1988).
[63]*Id.* at 68.
[64]*Id.*
[65]791 F. Supp. 625, 7 IER Cases 911 (E.D. N.Y. 1992).

[the employee] and intended to do so."[66] Adopting language from another Eastern District of New York case, the court stated:

> Among the indicia that locate a job along the spectrum between policymaker and clerk are: relative pay, technical competence, power to control others, authority to speak in the name of policymakers, public perception, influence on programs, contact with elected officials, authority to hire and fire employees, authority to prepare budget, and responsiveness to partisan politics and political leaders.[67]

Similarly, in *Myers v. City of Fort Wayne*,[68] an Assistant Chief-Fire Marshal for the City of Fort Wayne, Indiana, was demoted to Platoon Captain allegedly because of her political affiliation and her refusal to support the new mayor's election bid. The City argued that the Assistant Chief-Fire Marshal is a policy-making position which is exempt from the political firing prohibitions. To determine whether the policy-maker exception applies, the court quoted the Seventh Circuit in noting

> whether the position held by the individual authorizes, either directly or indirectly, meaningful input into government decisionmaking on issues where there is room for principled disagreement on goals or their implementations.[69]

The court then stated:

> The purpose behind the policymaking exception is to ensure that the first amendment's protection not interfere with the workings of democratic governments and the ability of duly elected officials to implement their policies.[70]

After reviewing the job descriptions of the Assistant Chief-Fire Marshal, the court concluded that based upon the position's lack of control or political responsibility, and the fact that the Assistant Chief-Fire Marshal had no authority to enter into contracts for the city, no authority to prepare budgets, no authority to make fire codes or orders controlling the government of the fire department, and no direct access to the mayor or city counsel, "[a]n inference can be

---

[66]*Id.* 7 IER Cases at 914.

[67]*Id.* at 914, quoting Ecker v. Cohalan, 542 F. Supp. 896, 901 (E.D.N.Y. 1982).

[68]729 F. Supp. 625, 6 IER Cases 1829 (N.D. Ind. 1990).

[69]*Id.* 6 IER Cases at 1835, quoting Shakman v. Democratic Org. of Cook County, 722 F.2d 1307, 1310 (7th Cir.), *cert. denied,* 464 U.S. 916 (1983).

[70]*Id.,* also quoting *Shakman,* 722 F.2d at 1310.

drawn that [the Assistant Chief-Fire Marshal] position was not a policymaking one. . . ."[71]

What is clear from these decisions is that the government may not infringe upon an individual employee's political association First Amendment rights without compelling justification. It appears that the most predominate factors in finding such a compelling justification are the government's efficiency and effectiveness and the protection of policies sanctioned by the electorate. Public jobs not having significant nexus between these compelling governmental interests and party affiliation will likely be protected by the individual's First Amendment rights.

B. Privacy

Although the Constitution does not explicitly mention any right of privacy, in a line of decisions going back to 1891, the Supreme Court has recognized a right of personal privacy, or a guarantee of certain areas or "zones of privacy," that exist under the First, Fourth, Fifth, and Ninth Amendments, or in the concept of liberty granted by the Fourteenth Amendment.[72] "[O]nly rights that are 'fundamental' or 'implicit in the concept of ordered liberty' " are included in the right to privacy.[73] Privacy rights extend to two types of interests: "[o]ne is the individual interest in avoiding disclosure of personal matters, and another is the interest in independence in making certain kinds of important decisions."[74]

The Supreme Court has developed a three-tier test to review a state's ability to regulate personal liberties. The top-tier or strict scrutiny test applies to fundamental rights or suspect classifications. Under this test a regulation limiting the exercise of a fundamental right must be justified by a "compelling state interest and that legislative enactments must be narrowly drawn to express only the legitimate state interest."[75] When a fundamental right is not present, the lower

---

[71]*Id.* at 1836.

[72]Roe v. Wade, 410 U.S. 113, 152–53 (1973).

[73]Dronenburg v. Zech, 741 F.2d 1388, 1396, 35 FEP Cases 898 (D.C. Cir. 1984) (Navy's policy of discharge for homosexual conduct not violative of any constitutional right to privacy or equal protection).

[74]Whalen v. Roe, 429 U.S. 589, 599–600 (1977).

[75]*Roe,* 410 U.S. at 115–20.

tier test is applied and requires only that the regulation have a rational relationship to some legitimate state objective.[76] The Court has developed a middle-tier analysis to apply to conduct which is not considered a fundamental right, but is significantly sensitive or intimate. This analysis requires that a regulation must "serve important governmental objectives and must be substantially related to achievement of those objectives."[77]

Many public employees have successfully argued that regulation of off-duty behavior by the state, unaccompanied by any nexus to the job, is an unconstitutional invasion of privacy. Case law indicates that public management can discipline employees for off-duty conduct without constitutional infirmity if that conduct does not involve a "fundamental" right. If it is determined that an employee's conduct involves a "fundamental right," it can only be abridged to the extent necessary to achieve a strong, clearly articulated state interest. The Supreme Court has not exhaustively articulated those rights that are "fundamental" or the kinds of interests that are within the "zone of privacy" protected against unwarranted government intrusion. Instead, the Court has taken a case-by-case approach. In certain contexts the Court has extended a guarantee of privacy to marriage,[78] procreation, contraception, family relationships, child rearing and education, abortion,[79] and the private possession of obscene matter.[80]

Most of the decisions that define the parameters or boundaries of legitimate employer concern with an employee's off-duty conduct are those dealing with an employee's sexual practices. For example, several courts have refused to recognize homosexual conduct as a privacy interest, although the better view is that a public employee cannot be dismissed from employment merely because he is a homosexual.[81] One federal court pointed out that the rationale for these

---

[76]*See* McGowan v. Maryland, 366 U.S. 420, 425 (1961).

[77]Craig v. Boren, 429 U.S. 190 (1976); Reed v. Reed, 404 U.S. 71 (1971).

[78]*See* Griswold v. Connecticut, 381 U.S. 479, 484 (1965), where the Supreme Court, holding that sexual relations betwen a married couple are within the constitutionally protected right to privacy, stated that the Constitution created individual rights and that "penumbras, formed by emanations from those guarantees . . . help give them life and substance."

[79]*See Roe*, 410 U.S. at 152–53.

[80]Stanley v. Georgia, 394 U.S. 557 (1969).

[81]Norton v. Macy, 417 F.2d 1161, 1164-65, 42 FEP Cases 787 (D.C. Cir. 1969) (prohibiting discharge on basis of sexual preference absent proven nexus between

decisions is that dismissal solely because of one's status as a homosexual is "so arbitrary and capricious as to violate due process."[82] Where dismissals or other disciplinary actions have been upheld, there has generally been a showing that the homosexual conduct was open and notorious, or a finding that the state's interest in discipline, morale, or efficiency outweighed the employee's privacy interests.[83] In *Padula v. Webster*,[84] for example, the D.C. Circuit, applying an equal protection analysis, found permissible the FBI's refusal to hire Margaret Padula because she was a homosexual. Ruling that a challenged classi-

---

homosexual conduct and disruption of agency efficiency); Swift v. United States, 649 F. Supp. 596, 602 (D.D.C. 1986) (denying government's motion to dismiss homosexual White House stenographer's privacy claim, reasoning that "the government has not offered any explanation as to how plaintiff's dismissal is related to a legitimate governmental purpose"); Baker v. Wade, 553 F. Supp. 1121, 1148 (N.D. Tex. 1982) ("right of privacy extends to private sexual conduct between consenting adults—whether husband and wife, unmarried males and females, or homosexuals"); benShalom v. Secretary of the Army, 489 F. Supp. 964, 977, 22 FEP Cases 1396 (E.D. Wis. 1980) (no "nexus" between homosexuality and military capability); Saal v. Middendorf, 427 F. Supp. 192, 17 FEP Cases 1243 (N.D. Cal. 1977) (military service); Society for Indiv. Rights, Inc. v. Hampton, 63 F.R.D. 399, 12 FEP Cases 534 (N.D. Cal. 1973) (Civil Service Commission can discharge for immoral behavior only if behavior "impairs the efficiency" of the service), *aff'd on other grounds,* 528 F.2d 905 (9th Cir. 1975).

[82]Shuman v. City of Philadelphia, 470 F. Supp. 449, 459 n.8 (E.D. Pa. 1979) (quoting Society for Indiv. Rights, 63 F.R.D. at 400); *see also* Morrison v. State Bd. of Educ., 461 P.2d 375, 391 (Cal. 1969) (holding that male teacher who engaged fellow male teacher in noncriminal physical homosexual relationship not subject to disciplinary action under statute authorizing revocation of teacher's life diploma for immoral or unprofessional conduct or moral turpitude absent nexus to ability to teach, stating "[management] offered no evidence that a man of petitioner's background was any more likely than the average adult male to engage in any untoward conduct with a student").

[83]*See* Rich v. Secretary of the Army, 735 F.2d 1220, 1228, 37 FEP Cases 598 (10th Cir. 1984) ("even if privacy interests were implicated in this case, they are outweighed by the Government's interest in preventing armed service members from engaging in homosexual conduct"); McConnell v. Anderson, 451 F.2d 193, 3 FEP Cases 1106 (8th Cir. 1971) (denial of university employment because of "activist" role concerning the social status to be accorded homosexuals), *cert. denied,* 405 U.S. 1046, 4 FEP Cases 631 (1972); Endsley v. Naes, 673 F. Supp. 1032, 1038, 45 FEP Cases 1352 (D. Kan. 1987) (upholding dismissal of female police officer because of rumors of her relationship with other deputy); Naragon v. Wharton, 572 F. Supp. 1117, 1124, 33 FEP Cases 61 (M.D. La. 1983) (sustaining reassignment of graduate assistant for having homosexual relationship with university student not her student, rejecting argument that employee's freedom of association was restricted).

[84]822 F.2d 97, 2 IER Cases 454 (D.C. Cir. 1987).

fication of homosexuality need only satisfy a minimum standard of rationality,[85] the court refused to recognize homosexuality as comparable to race, alienage, and national origin, the three classifications recognized by the Supreme Court as deserving of heightened scrutiny.[86] Citing the Supreme Court's decision in *Bowers v. Hardwick*,[87] a decision holding that the right to engage in consensual homosexual sodomy[88] is not constitutionally protected, the appellate court reasoned that "[i]f the Court was unwilling to object to state laws that criminalize the behavior that defines the class [homosexual], it is hardly open to a lower court to conclude that the state-sponsored discrimination against the class is invidious."

In a particularly bizarre case reported by the federal District Court of South Carolina involving a privacy claim and alleged homosexual conduct, *Dawson v. State Law Enforcement Division*,[89] a 16-year police officer and a co-worker's husband were accused of masturbating in each other's presence. The federal court rejected the officer's claim that the dismissal was violative of his constitutional rights to privacy and association. Although the court conceded "that some portions of a public official's private sexual life may be within the zone of protected privacy,"[90] the court refused to extend a privacy right to conduct committed between two males, reasoning that "such activity clearly bears no relationship to marriage, procreation, or family life."[91] The court also declined to find a violation of equal protection, concluding that courts have refused to recognize homosexuality as a suspect classification. In this case there was a rational basis for the administration's dismissal for consensual homosexual conduct with or in the presence of the husband of a fellow employee.

---

[85]*Id.* at 104.

[86]*Id.* at 102.

[87]478 U.S. 186 (1986).

[88]The crime of "sodomy," punishable by imprisonment for up to 20 years, was defined by Georgia law as "any sexual act involving the sex organs of one person and the mouth or anus of another." GA. CODE ANN. §16-6-2 (Michie 1984). The statute applies to all persons, whether married or single, heterosexual or homosexual. Georgia is one of 19 states that outlaw all forms of sodomy, in contrast to those states that criminalize only homosexual acts. *See, e.g.,* ARK. CODE ANN. §41-1813 (Michie 1988); KAN. STAT. ANN. §21-3505 (1989).

[89]7 IER Cases 629 (S.C. 1992).

[90]7 IER Cases at 633.

[91]*Id.* at 634.

Similarly, extramarital heterosexual cohabitation has sometimes been accorded constitutional protection[92] but, more often, courts have denied this activity protected status.[93] Some public sector employers,

[92]*See, e.g.,* Eastwood v. Department of Corrections, 846 F.2d 627, 631, 46 FEP Cases 1869 (10th Cir. 1988) (upholding 42 U.S.C. §1983 claim against individual who investigated sexual harassment claim of employee and forced her to reveal facts about her sexual history); Schowengerdt v. General Dynamics Corp., 823 F.2d 1328, 1330–31, 2 IER Cases 545 (9th Cir. 1987) (stating that Navy engineer "had a constitutional right to be free from unnecessary, overbroad, or unregulated employer investigations into his sexual practices"); Thorne v. City of El Segundo, 726 F.2d 459, 470, 33 FEP Cases 441 (9th Cir. 1983) (holding that reliance on private, non–job-related questions on police officer application form regarding possible pregnancy, abortion, and identity of sexual partners violates constitutionally protected association and privacy interests), *cert. denied,* 469 U.S. 979, 1 IER Cases 1136 (1984); Kukla v. Village of Antioch, 647 F. Supp. 799, 808 (N.D. Ill. 1986) (police sergeant and female police dispatcher unmarried but living together fall within "personal intimacies of the home"); Briggs v. North Muskegon Police Dep't, 563 F. Supp. 585, 591, 1 IER Cases 195 (W.D. Mich. 1983) (upholding constitutional right of police officer to sexual privacy absent showing that cohabitation affected job performance); Shuman v. City of Philadelphia, 470 F. Supp. 449, 459 (E.D. Pa. 1979) (holding that regulations permitting inquiry into off-duty relationship of police officers violated officer's constitutional rights, stating: "a party's private sexual activities are within the 'zone of privacy' protected from unwarranted government intrusion"); Mindel v. Civil Serv. Comm'n, 312 F. Supp. 485 (N.D. Cal. 1970) (postal clerk's extramarital cohabitation protected).

[93]*See* Shawgo v. Spradlin, 701 F.2d 470, 482-83, 1 IER Cases 164, (5th Cir.) (stating that "right to privacy has not been infringed by the scope of the regulation proscribing, as conduct prejudicial to good order, cohabitation of two police officers", or proscribing a superior officer from sharing an apartment with one of lower rank"), *cert. denied,* 464 U.S. 965 (1983), discussed *infra* notes 111–17 and accompanying text; Suddarth v. Slane, 539 F. Supp. 612 (W.D. Va. 1982) (dismissal of police officer for adultery permissible); Johnson v. San Jacinto Junior College, 498 F. Supp. 555, 576 (S.D. Tex. 1980) (extramarital affair not protected within scope of privacy); Hollenbaugh v. Carnegie Free Library, 436 F. Supp. 1328, 1332–33 (W.D. Pa. 1977) (sustaining dismissal of public employees who were living together in a state of "open adultery," applying minimum rationality test), *aff'd,* 578 F.2d 1374 (3d Cir.), *cert. denied,* 439 U.S. 1052 (1978); Fabio v. Civil Serv. Comm'n of Philadelphia, 414 A.2d 82 (Pa. 1980) (upholding discharge). *But see In re* Dalessandro, 397 A.2d 743, 758 (Pa. 1979) (judge's open and notorious adulterous relationship not subject to discipline).
   Aside from consensual homosexual sodomy, the Supreme Court has yet to answer the question whether and to what extent the Constitution prohibits state statutes from regulating private consensual sexual behavior among adults. In addition, "[n]o Supreme Court case has held that married persons have a constitutional right to engage in adultery." Andrade v. City of Phoenix, 692 F.2d 557, 563 (9th Cir. 1982). *See generally* K. Karst, *The Freedom of Intimate Association,* 89 YALE L.J. 624 (1980); Michael A. Woronoff, Note, *Public Employees or Private Citizens: The Off-Duty Sexual Activities of Police Officers and the Constitutional Right of Privacy,* 18 U. MICH. J.L. REF. 195, 211 (1984).

with concurrence from selected courts, have asserted that extramarital off-duty relationships are permissible so long as the affair is "clandestine" rather than "open." When the affair is exposed or, for whatever reason, becomes "unconventional" (practicing polygamy, for example),[94] the employee's privacy interest is often outweighed (in the eyes of the courts) by the public employer's interest in "conventional" employees. In *Shuman v. City of Philadelphia*,[95] for example, a federal district court recognized that even though activities may be within the protected "zone of privacy," this protection is by no means absolute. It stated that "if the sexual activities of a public employee were open and notorious, or if such activities took place in a small town, the public employer might very well have an interest in investigating such activities and possibly terminating an employee."[96] According to the court, "[i]n such a case, the actions of the public employee with respect to his or her private life could be deemed to have a substantial impact upon his or her ability to perform on the job."[97]

Likewise, an individual may give up any reasonable expectation of privacy when he or she makes public the conduct that is arguably protected.[98] Joining swingers clubs,[99] appearing on televised talk shows,[100] and having your picture in *Beaver* or *Screw Magazine*[101] is

---

[94]*See, e.g.*, Potter v. Murray City, 760 F.2d 1065, 37 FEP Cases 1652 (10th Cir.), *cert. denied*, 474 U.S. 849 (1985), where the court of appeals rejected the argument that a constitutional right of privacy prevented the State of Utah from discharging a police officer for entering into a polygamous marriage.

[95]470 F. Supp. 449, 459 (E.D. Pa. 1979).

[96]*Id.*

[97]*Id.*

[98]*See, e.g.*, Lovisi v. Slayton, 539 F.2d 349, 351 (4th Cir.) (presence of onlooker in bedroom of married couple defeated couple's reasonable expectation of privacy), *cert. denied*, 429 U.S. 977 (1976); Johnson v. San Jacinto Junior College, 498 F. Supp. 555, 576 n.5 (S.D. Tex. 1980) (admitting extramarital affair to several persons).

[99]*See* Pettit v. State Bd. of Educ., 513 P.2d 889, 890–91 (Cal. 1973) (holding that teacher who joined "swingers" club, and who was observed by undercover police officer committing 3 separate acts of oral copulation with 3 different men at a party, was properly terminated for immoral and unprofessional conduct evidencing unfitness to teach).

[100] *Id.* at 890 ("appearing on Joe Pyne show discussing 'nonconventional sexual life styles' "). *But see* Caron v. Silvia, 588 N.E.2d 711, 7 IER Cases 522 (Mass. App. Ct. 1992) (holding government social worker, dismissed from the Department of Public Welfare after she appeared on 3 talk shows to protest statewide policy restricting workplace smoking, stated cause of action under First Amendment).

[101]Borges v. McGuire, 107 A.D.2d 492 (N.Y. 1985) (reversing dismissal for

not consistent with the assertion that one's privacy rights have been violated. An employee who commences a tort action may also relinquish what would otherwise be a privacy right as part of the discovery process.[102]

Applying the better rule, in *Swope v. Bratton*,[103] a federal court stated that a police department has an interest in and may investigate some areas of the personal sexual activities of its employees "*if* the activities have an impact upon job performance."[104] The court noted, however, that "in the absence of a nexus between the personal, off-duty activities and poor job performance, inquiry into these activities violates the constitutionally protected right of privacy; a party's private sexual activities are within the 'zone of privacy' and protected from unwarranted governmental intrusion."[105] In this case the court concluded that a police chief did not have the right to order a policeman to refrain from developing a "more than casual relationship" with a police dispatcher, at least where the relationship was not "open and notorious" and there was no "public outcry" or complaints by any citizen. *Swope* suggests that public outcry and citizen complaints can be critera in determining constitutional rights, a position long accepted by labor arbitrators[106] in deciding off-duty misconduct cases.

C. Association and Speech

There is no question that the constitutional guarantee of freedom of association is, like speech and assembly, a fundamental right. As noted by one judge, "[s]ince speech, assembly and association all

---

posing nude in BEAVER, SCREW, and other "men's magazines" prior to becoming police officer).

   [102]Ferrel v. Glen-Gery Brick, 678 F. Supp. 111, 46 FEP Cases 502 (E.D. Pa. 1987) (employee bringing claim for intentional infliction of emotional distress not entitled to protective order forbidding disclosure of notes of psychiatrist, reasoning that when an employee places her physical or mental condition at issue the privacy right is waived). *But see* Vinson v. Superior Court, 740 P.2d 404, 410, 2 IER Cases 727 (Cal. 1987) (recognizing some privacy interest for employee commencing sexual harassment action).

   [103]541 F. Supp. 99 (W.D. Ark. 1982).

   [104]*Id.* at 108.

   [105]*Id.*

   [106]*Id.* at 109.

serve a common purpose—to promote the free exchange of ideas—defeating any one of these rights might defeat them all. Freedom of association therefore stands as a fundamental right in a free society."[107] The Supreme Court has made it clear that mere membership in an organization without specific advocacy of any illegal conduct by the organization is protected by the Constitution.[108] At the same time, however, not all public employees can rely on this standard. For example, the courts have been consistent in holding that law enforcement agencies are qualitatively different from other branches of government. In *McMullen v. Carson*,[109] the Eleventh Circuit stated:

> The First Amendment does not protect personal behavior in the law enforcement context to the same extent that it does in other areas of Governmental concern. The need for high morale and internal discipline in a police force led this Court to hold that "a reasonable likelihood of harm generally is . . . enough to support full consideration of the police department's asserted interests in restricting its employees' speech."[110]

Illustrating the extent to which a public employer *can* discipline a protective service employee for off-duty association is *Shawgo v. Spradlin*,[111] a decision by the Fifth Circuit. In that case a patrolwoman

---

[107]Curle v. Ward, 389 N.E.2d 1070, 1072 (N.Y. 1979) (Wachtler, J., dissenting).

[108]Hess v. Indiana, 414 U.S. 105, 109 (1973) (advocating illegal conduct at some indefinite future time protected by First Amendment); Brandenburg v. Ohio, 395 U.S. 444, 447 (1969) (First Amendment protects advocacy of illegal conduct except where conduct is "directed to inciting or producing imminent lawless action"); United States v. Robel, 389 U.S. 258 (1967); Elfbrandt v. Russell, 384 U.S. 11 (1966).

The legal standards by which First Amendment claims are judged have been outlined by the Supreme Court in Mt. Healthy City Bd. of Educ. v. Doyle, 429 U.S. 274, 1 IER Cases 76 (1977). First, the court must determine whether the employee's activity was protected by the First Amendment. *Id.* at 287. If so, the employee still has the burden of showing that the activity was a substantial or motivating factor in the public employer's decision to take adverse employment action against the employee. *Id.* Having done so, the burden then shifts to the employer to demonstrate that the same action would have taken place absent the protected conduct. *Id.*

[109]754 F.2d 936 (11th Cir. 1985).

[110]*Id.* at 939–40 (quoting in part Waters v. Chaffin, 684 F.2d 833, 839 n.12 (11th Cir. 1982)). *See also* Baron v. Meloni, 556 F. Supp. 796, 800 (W.D.N.Y. 1983), *cert. denied*, 474 U.S. 1058 (1986) ("An individual joining a police agency must recognize that acceptance of such an important and sensitive position requires the individual to forgo certain privileges and even some rights that an ordinary citizen often exercises without restrictions or thoughts of sanctions, because a police force is a para-military organization with all the attendant requirements and circumstances.").

[111]701 F.2d 470, 1 IER Cases 164 (5th Cir. 1983).

and a police sergeant were suspended from their jobs, and the sergeant demoted to patrolman, because they dated and spent several nights together. These punishments were imposed even though the department failed to provide any notice that their conduct was prohibited.[112] The district court ruled that the officers did not have a protected property or privacy interest.[113] The Fifth Circuit, although recognizing a property interest, affirmed the decision, and the Supreme Court, declining to review,[114] let the ruling stand. The court of appeals rejected the officers' argument that the state could not regulate their off-duty association, reasoning that "th[e] argument fails to take into account the fact that the right to privacy is not unqualified, . . . and that the state has more interest in regulating the activities of its employees than the activities of the population at large."[115] The court went on to point out that the burden on the police officer is onerous in attacking management's regulations: the officer, to sustain an attack, must demonstrate "that there is no rational connection between the regulation, based as it is on the county's method of organizing its police force, and the promotion of safety of persons and property."[116] In this case the court found a rational connection between "forbidding members of a quasi-military unit, especially those different in rank, to share an apartment or to cohabit."[117]

---

[112]*Id.* at 478.

[113]*Id.* at 473.

[114]464 U.S. 965, 1 IER Cases 174 (1983). Justice Brennan, joined by Justices Marshall and Blackmun, dissented to the denial of a writ of certiorari, because he believed that petitioners' conduct involved a fundamental right. Justice Brennan commented, "[t]he intimate, consensual, and private relationship between petitioners involved both the 'interest in avoiding disclosure of personal matters [and] the interest in independence in making certain kinds of important decisions' . . . that our cases have recognized as fundamental." *Id.* at 971 (Brennan, J., dissenting) (quoting Whalen v. Roe, 429 U.S. 589, 599–600 (1977)).

[115]Shawgo, 701 F.2d at 482–83 (quoting Kelley v. Johnson, 425 U.S. 238, 245 (1976)).

[116]*Id.* at 483 (quoting *Kelley*, 425 U.S. at 245).

[117]*Id.; see also Swank v. Smart*, 898 F.2d 1247, 1250, 5 IER Cases 323 (7th Cir.) (upholding discharge of police officer for giving female student off-duty motorcycle ride, rejecting claim that ride constituted First Amendment right to speech or association), *cert. denied*, 111 S. Ct. 147 (1990); Baron v. Meloni, 556 F. Supp. 796 (W.D.N.Y. 1983) (sheriff's order that deputy sheriff cease associating with wife of reputed mobster not violative of deputy's constitutional right of privacy), *cert. denied*, 474 U.S. 1058 (1986); Wilson v. Swing, 463 F. Supp. 555, 563–64 (M.D.N.C. 1978) (no First Amendment right of association protecting police officer who had extramarital affair with another officer, reasoning that state has substantial

There are limits, however, even in the protective services. The Fifth Circuit, in *Wilson v. Taylor*,[118] overturned a decision of a lower court that had ruled in favor of a police department that had fired an officer because of his association with the daughter of a convicted felon and reputed crime figure. The court of appeals pointed out that the fact that the individual is a policeman does not obviate the need to balance the interests of the employee against the interests of the governmental employer: "[P]olicemen, like teachers and lawyers, are not relegated to a watered-down version of constitutional rights."[119] Still, the court noted that "several courts have read into the balance more deference to the state interest in preserving the morale and integrity of police departments than might be appropriate in other contexts."[120] Similarly, the Fifth Circuit, in *Battle v. Mulholland*,[121] ruled that a black police officer could not be dismissed because he and his wife permitted two single white women to board with them. Absent a showing that his associations "would materially and substantially impair his usefulness as a police officer," the court rejected the argument that his living situation may have an adverse impact upon the racial tension in a southern town.[122] Another federal court, in *Burns v. Pomerleau*,[123] held that a police department could not refuse the application for position of probationary patrolman solely because the applicant was a member of a nudist club. Applying strict scrutiny, the court reasoned that, "[i]t is too late in the day to doubt that this freedom of association extends only to political or conventional associations and not to the social or the unorthodox."[124]

In *Curle v. Ward*,[125] the New York Court of Appeals upheld the decision of the trial court directing reinstatement of a correctional officer for membership in the Ku Klux Klan. Since the employer

---

interest in discouraging adulterous conduct); Morrisette v. Dilworth, 89 A.D.2d 99 (N.Y. 1982) (discipline sustained for police officer's association with "Jukebox Tony," a known felon, applying "exacting scrutiny" test).

[118]658 F.2d 1021 (5th Cir. 1981).

[119]*Id.* at 1027 (quoting Garrity v. New Jersey, 385 U.S. 493, 500 (1967)).

[120]*Id.* at 1027 (citing Byrd v. Gain, 558 F.2d 553 (9th Cir. 1977), *cert. denied*, 434 U.S. 1087 (1978); Gasparinetti v. Kerr, 568 F.2d 311 (3d Cir. 1977).

[121]439 F.2d 321, 9 FEP Cases 1150 (5th Cir. 1971).

[122]*Id.* at 324.

[123]319 F. Supp. 58 (D. Md. 1970).

[124]*Id.* at 65.

[125]389 N.E.2d 1070 (N.Y. 1979).

failed to tender sufficient evidence of the claimed detrimental impact of employee membership in the Klan upon the operation of the facility or the inmates, the court of appeals refused to address the broader constitutional issue of association.[126]

In an education case, a school board dismissed a middle-aged female teacher for engaging in "social misbehavior that is not conducive to the maintenance of the integrity of the public school system" because she allowed a 26-year-old male visitor to stay at her apartment overnight.[127] The Eighth Circuit, declining to consider the dismissal on the basis of association or privacy, instead reversed the termination on substantive due process grounds.[128] Applying a *de facto* nexus requirement, the court of appeals found the teacher could successfully argue that her dismissal was arbitrary and capricious if she could prove "that each of the stated reasons [underlying her dismissal] is trivial, or is unrelated to the educational process or to working relationships within the educational institution, or is wholly unsupported by a basis in fact."[129]

Another federal court, in *High Tech Gays v. Defense Industrial Security Office,*[130] held that the Department of Defense could not require an expanded security investigation because an applicant belonged to a gay organization. The court found that there was no rational basis for the government subjecting all gay applicants to expanded investigations while not doing the same for "straight" applicants.[131] Further, the court ruled that subjecting gays to additional scrutiny interferes with their First Amendment right to associate.[132] "Governmental actions that significantly impair an individual's First Amendment rights must survive exacting scrutiny,"[133] and this, said the court, "is clearly not the least restrictive means to achieving the governmental interests in protecting national security."[134]

---

[126]*Id.* at 1071.
[127]Fisher v. Snyder, 476 F.2d 375, 377 (8th Cir. 1973).
[128]*Id.* at 376.
[129]*Id.* at 377 (citing McEnteggart v. Cataldo, 451 F.2d 1109, 1111 (1st Cir. 1971), *cert. denied,* 408 U.S. 943 (1972)).
[130]668 F. Supp. 1361, 44 FEP Cases 1023 (N.D. Cal. 1987).
[131]*Id.* at 1373.
[132]*Id.* at 1378.
[133]*Id.*
[134]*Id.*

In a case with far-reaching implications for government employers, *Federal Employees v. Greenberg*,[135] Judge Harold Green, writing for the federal court for the District of Columbia, held invalid the Department of Defense's request that all employees, regardless of position in the organization, subject to a security clearance fill out a questionnaire naming all organizational affiliations since the age of 16, with the exception of labor unions and religious and political organizations.[136] Employees were also required to list each individual with whom they had associated if those individuals were members of the described organizations "and the organizations with which they were or are affiliated."[137] Rejecting a blanket security argument advanced by the administration, Judge Green reasoned that "security concerns do not, under the American system of ordered liberty, ipso facto override all constitutional and privacy considerations. The purpose of national security is to protect American citizens, not to overwhelm their rights."[138]

With respect to questions requiring information about any past or present mental, emotional, or psychological problems or treatments, Judge Green stated that "the requirement that thousands upon thousands of individuals must reveal the most intimate details of their lives under this rubric is so intrusive that on any balancing privacy considerations will prevail."[139] According to Judge Green, "[i]t is plain that, at a minimum, individuals—even those working for the Department of Defense—may not be routinely required, consistently with the Constitution and the Privacy Act, to reveal in detail past emotional or psychological problems, much less treatment for such problems."[140]

Judge Green also found that questions relating to an employee's drug use suffered from the same problems and, in addition, raised self-incrimination concerns under the Fifth Amendment where the questionnaire itself stated that the disclosed information may be made available to federal, state, or local law enforcement agencies, including the Department of Justice. Noting that as a general matter, a govern-

---

[135]789 F. Supp. 430, 7 IER Cases 621 (D.D.C. 1992).
[136]The questionnaire was also used for employees who were not required to have a security clearance. 7 IER Cases at 623 n.1.
[137]7 IER Cases at 626 n.11.
[138]*Id.* at 627.
[139]*Id.* at 625.
[140]*Id.* at 625.

ment agency may maintain in its records "such information about an individual as is relevant and necessary to accomplish a purpose of the agency required to be accomplished by statute or by executive order of the President,"[141] the court found impermissible the employer's request for arrest and financial information from all applicants. Judge Green did acknowledge that the Department·may be entitled to some information from selected applicants (a confidential assistant to the Joint Chiefs of Staff or in the nuclear weapons program). The infirmity here was that the Department's inclusion of all employees, such as plaintiff David Wiefing, a publicity specialist at the Rock Island facility, was too sweeping to pass constitutional muster. Applying a nexus rule, Judge Green stated that "such hypothetical and minimal security considerations are not permitted to trump the vested rights of citizens."[142]

Courts have held that while a state's interest in regulating the speech of its employees differs from the state's interest in regulating the speech of the general citizenry, an employee's First Amendment rights may be restricted only if "the employer shows that some restriction is necessary to prevent the disruption of official functions or to insure effective performance by the employee."[143] Thus, in *National Gay Task Force v. Board of Education*,[144] the Tenth Circuit declared unconstitutional a portion of a statute that allowed punishment of teachers for "public homosexual conduct," defined as "advocating, soliciting, imposing, encouraging or promoting public or private homosexual activity in a manner that creates a substantial risk that such conduct will come to the attention of school children or school employees."[145] According to the court, although a teacher could properly be dismissed for public homosexual conduct, discipline for mere "advocacy" would be barred since it does not necessarily imply incitement to immediate action.[146] First Amendment rights have also been found for a police officer who had part ownership in a video store

---

[141]*Id.* at 624, citing 5 U.S.C. §552a(e) (1).

[142]*Id.*

[143]National Gay Task Force v. Board of Educ., 729 F.2d 1270, 1274, 34 FEP Cases 459 (10th Cir. 1984) (citing Childers v. Independent Sch. Dist. No. 1, 676 F.2d 1338, 1341 (10th Cir. 1982)).

[144]729 F.2d 1270, 34 FEP Cases 459 (1984), *aff'd*, 470 U.S. 903, 37 FEP Cases 459 (1985).

[145]*Id.* at 1272.

[146]*Id.* at 1274.

that stocked sexually explicit videos. The Tenth Circuit, in *Flanagan v. Munger*,[147] ruled that a police department could not require removal of objectionable films from the store's stock by the owner, who was also an officer in the department.[148]

In *Rowland v. Mad River Local School District*,[149] the Supreme Court in 1985 let stand the Sixth Circuit's holding that it was permissible for a school district not to renew the contract of Marjorie Rowland, a high school guidance counselor, because she was bisexual and revealed her sexual preference.[150] Although a jury found that the employee's mention of her bisexuality did not in any way "interfere with the proper performance of [her or other school staff members'] duties or with the operation of the school generally,"[151] the Sixth Circuit nevertheless reasoned that nonrenewal based on her workplace statements was permissible under the First Amendment because, under the Supreme Court's test in *Connick v. Myers*,[152] her speech was not "a matter of public concern."[153]

---

[147]890 F.2d 1557 (10th Cir. 1989).
[148]*Id.*
[149]470 U.S. 1009, 37 FEP Cases 188 (1985).
[150]730 F.2d 444, 34 FEP Cases 175 (6th Cir. 1984).
[151]*Id.* at 447.
[152]461 U.S. 138, 1 IER Cases 178 (1983).
[153]*Rowland*, 730 F.2d at 447. In Connick v. Myers, 461 U.S. 138, 1 FEP Cases 178 (1983), the Supreme Court considered the discharge of a state employee for circulating a questionnaire concerning internal office matters. The plaintiff, Sheila Myers, as assistant district attorney, circulated a questionnaire soliciting the views of her fellow staff members concerning office transfer policy, office morale, the need for a grievance committee, the level of confidence in supervisors, and whether employees felt pressured to work in political campaigns. After distributing the questionnaire to 15 assistant district attorneys, Myers was terminated. The Supreme Court, reversing the district and appellate courts, pointed out that the repeated emphasis in Pickering v. Board of Educ., 391 U.S. 563, 1 IER Cases 8 (1964), "on the right of a public employee 'as a citizen, in commenting on matters of public concern,' was not accidental." Justice Byron White, writing for the majority, noted that, unlike the issues that Myers addressed, the subject matter in *Pickering* "was 'a matter of legitimate public concern' upon which 'free and open debate is vital to informed decision-making by the electorate.' " *Connick*, 461 U.S. at 145 (quoting *Pickering*, 391 U.S. at 571–72.) Justice White wrote:

> We hold only that when a public employee speaks not as a citizen upon matters of public concern, but instead as an employee upon matters only of personal interest, absent the most unusual circumstances, a federal court is not the appropriate forum in which to review the wisdom of a personnel decision taken by a public agency allegedly in reaction to the employee's behavior. . . . Our responsibility is to ensure that citizens are not deprived

The Seventh Circuit has stated that "public employers do not lose their ability to control behavior and speech in the workplace merely because they are governmental bodies subject to the restraints of the First Amendment."[154] The key is whether the employee's speech touches a matter of "public concern," and according to the *Connick* Court, this is determined by the content, form, and context of a given statement.[155]

Hawkins v. Department of Public Safety,[156] is especially illustrative of the approach taken by courts in First Amendment cases. A probationary prison guard, while off-duty and out-of-uniform, stated to a bank teller who had declined to cash his payroll check: "Hitler should have gotten rid of all you Jews . . . and all the Poles too."[157] Applying *Pickering* and *Connick*, the Maryland Court of Appeals found no First Amendment violation in the dismissal of Hawkins. The court reasoned that the speech did not touch a matter of public concern. Even if protected, the court found a nexus to the employer's interest. The dissent, believing that no nexus existed, noted that "it should only be the rare case in which non-employee speech—speech of a public employee that is not about work and does not occur at work, or under circumstances identifying the speaker to bystanders with work—is outweighed by the State's interest in an efficient workplace."[158]

In a particularly fascinating case, *Sims v. Metropolitan Dade County*,[159] the U.S. Court of Appeals for the Eleventh Circuit upheld the three-day suspension of a black employee for Dade County Department of Community Affairs, who, while in his off-duty capacity as a pastor of the Greater New Faith Missionary Baptist Church,

---

of fundamental rights by virtue of working for the government; this does not require a grant of immunity for employee grievances not afforded by the First Amendment to those who do not work for the state.
Connick, 461 U.S. at 147 [citation omitted].
    According to the majority, "Myers' questionnaire touched upon matters of public concern in only a limited sense." *Id.* at 153. The Court concluded that the survey "is most accurately characterized as an employee grievance concerning internal office policy." *Id.*
    [154]Yoggerst v. Hedges, 739 F.2d 293, 295 (7th Cir. 1984).
    [155]*Connick*, 461 U.S. at 147-48.
    [156]602 A.2d 712, 7 IER Cases 382 (Md. App. 1992).
    [157]*Id.* 7 IER Cases at 383.
    [158]*Id.* at 393.
    [159]972 F.2d 1230, 7 IER Cases 1289 (11th Cir. 1992).

declared from his pulpit that Miami blacks should not spend their money at businesses that did not hire blacks, nor should their money be spent on businesses that have not shown sensitivity toward blacks in the past, and that "[s]ometimes we are made to feel like foreigners in our own homeland because of the way Spanish is spoken in many of our public facilities and businesses. . . ."[160] The court noted that "it is clear that the First Amendment does not provide a right to continued government employment in a capacity that is inconsistent with, and undermined by, one's off-duty expressive conduct. Stated more simply, one who cheers for the robbers has no right to ride with the police."[161] The court went further to state the standard of review in such cases as:

> [a] determination whether a public employer has improperly sanctioned an employee on the basis of the employee's speech requires "a balance between the interest of the [employee], as a citizen, in commenting upon matters of public concern and the interest of the State, as an employer, in promoting the efficiency of the public services it performs through its employees."[162]

In applying this standard, the court concluded that even though Sims' statements were a matter of public concern, the Department had a compelling interest in the accomplishment of its mission to avoid urban violence by fostering understanding and tolerance.[163] Thus, the court concluded: "The First Amendment does not require that Sims be allowed to continue his weekday employment drenching the fires of racial animosity for the Department while he fans those flames during his weekend sermons."[164]

Case law indicates that when the employee's speech deals with personnel disputes or individual grievances with management, it will not be protected under the Constitution. Such information, however meritorious, adds little to the public's evaluation of the performance

---

[160]*Id.* at 1290.

[161]*Id.* at 1294, citing L. TRIBE, AMERICAN CONSTITUTIONAL LAW, §12–26 at 1018 (2d ed. 1978) ("those associational rights that are demonstrably incompatible with the mission of a given public agency or calling may be forbidden—not on a theory that public servants lose their constitutional rights when they assume government duty, but on a theory that such rights cannot be defined independent of the contexts in which they are asserted").

[162]*Id.*, quoting Kurtz v. Vickrey, 855 F.2d 723, 726 (11th Cir. 1988).

[163]*Id.* at 1295.

[164]*Id.*

of government, and, accordingly, is not a matter of concern to the public. Even when the speech does touch a matter of public concern, if the speech or activity adversely affects the efficiency, discipline, or administration of the public employer,[165] the employee's conduct may still be subject to regulation if management can establish some nexus. Arbitrators have taken a similar approach when issues of speech have triggered discharges.[166] In a majority of cases the key for public management is establishing a nexus between the conduct and job performance.

D. Morality Standards

When considering the issue of public employers' promulgation of rules and regulations relating to an employee's lifestyle or off-duty

---

[165]*See, e.g.,* Rankin v. McPherson, 483 U.S. 378, 383, 2 IER Cases 257, 260 (1987) (statement by clerical employee in county constable's office concerning assassination attempt on President that "if they go for him again, I hope they get him," protected speech under First Amendment, holding statement of public concern).

[166]*See, e.g.,* City of Detroit, 83-2 Lab. Arb. Awards (CCH) ¶ 8562 (1983) (McCormick, Arb.), where an arbitrator, citing *Pickering,* sustained the suspension of a city auditor who, during an interview on a network television station, implicated city officials in a coverup of improprieties in a contract with an oil company; Town of Plainville, 77 LA 161, 162–63 (1981) (Sacks, Arb.) (finding *Pickering* "and the host of decisions which have followed it" relevant); Douglas County, 79-2 Lab. Arb. Awards (CCH) ¶ 8522 (1979) (Doyle, Arb.) (upholding suspension of employee for making public statements that care provided by hospital-employer was inadequate; *Pickering* distinguished); *see also* Los Angeles Harbor Dep't, 84 LA 860, 862 (1985) (Weiss, Arb.) (quoting *Pickering,* 391 U.S. at 568) (holding city employer properly suspended employee for writing letter to newspaper referring to department head as "head inquisitor," and applying both *Pickering* and *Connick,* stating "[h]ere, it is the interest 'of the State, as an employer, in promoting efficiency of the public services it performs through its employees' which must take precedence"); Department of the Navy, 75 LA 889 (1980) (Aronin, Arb.) (holding employees' use of media to resolve grievance disputes was permitted, reasoning, in part, that the activity was protected under the First Amendment).

In a particularly interesting case, Circleville Bd. of Educ., 98 LA 271 (1991) (Stanton, Arb.), Arbitrator David Stanton ruled that just cause existed for a principal's written reprimand to a teacher who showed a Madonna music video, "Justify My Love" (with nudity and sexually explicit scenes), offered by a student who had taped it from a late-night television program (Nightline), to two American Government classes (high school seniors) studying censorship in the media. The arbitrator, while declaring that it would be inappropriate for him to impose his moral standards upon the educational system, *id.* at 279, nevertheless found that the teacher did not exercise sound prudent judgment. *Id.* The constitutional issue was never argued nor addressed.

conduct, two additional considerations should be addressed. The first is whether a public employer possesses the power to enact a morality standard for its employees. The second issue, applicable only if the employer is found to have this power, is whether the power has been exercised consistently with the mandates of due process. The courts considering the validity of enacting standards of morality have consistently held that the state may indeed enact rules prescribing the moral standards of its employees, especially in teaching and the protective services.[167] The Supreme Court, however, has stated that if a state designates some form of moral character as a criterion for bestowing a benefit or imposing a burden, it must be based on *present* moral character.[168]

V. OFF-DUTY MISCONDUCT AND UNREASONABLE SEARCHES AND SEIZURES

There are times when management will actually "test" an employee to determine whether the employee engaged in off-duty

---

[167]*See, e.g.,* Beilan v. Board of Public Educ., 357 U.S. 399, 405, 408–09 (1958); Hoska v. United States Dep't of the Army, 677 F.2d 131, 135 (D.C. Cir. 1982) (stating that "a pronouncement of 'immorality' tends to discourage careful analysis because it unavoidably connotes a violation of divine, Olympian, or otherwise universal standards of rectitude," and holding that Army failed to provide any "careful analysis" of connection between incidents of alleged immoral or improper behavior and employee's ability to execute responsibilities); Velasquez v. City of Colorado Springs, 23 FEP Cases 621 (D. Colo. 1980) (noting that "lack of sufficient moral character" defense is suspect on its face because it is highly subjective); Dolter v. Wahlert High Sch., 483 F. Supp. 266, 21 FEP Cases 1413 (N.D. Iowa 1980) (rejecting argument that Catholic Church cannot be held liable for sex discrimination where standards of morality for teachers were not in accord with moral and religious precepts of church concerning unwed pregnancy); Andrews v. Drew Mun. Separate Sch. Dist., 371 F. Supp. 27, 6 FEP Cases 872 (N.D. Miss. 1973), *aff'd,* 507 F.2d 611, 9 FEP Cases 235 (5th Cir. 1975); *see also* Thorne v. City of El Segundo, 726 F.2d 459, 470 (9th Cir. 1983) ("[we] do not hold that the City is prohibited by the Constitution from questioning or considering the sexual morality of its employees"), *cert. denied,* 469 U.S. 979, 36 FEP Cases 234 (1984); Smith v. Price, 616 F.2d 1371 (5th Cir. 1980) (providing for dismissal of employee for failure to meet prescribed standards of work, morality, and ethics, to an extent that makes employee unsuitable for any kind of employment in city's service); Bruns v. Pomerleau, 319 F. Supp. 58, 67 (D. Md. 1970) ("[behavioral pattern] can only be limited to such associations or off duty activities that affect his morals and integrity or are inimical to the Department").

[168]Schware v. Board of Bar Examiners, 353 U.S. 232 (1957).

misconduct. Drug testing, for example, frequently results in reports to management of the employee's off-duty activities.[169] This section concerns situations where public management elects to "search" an employee's system for evidence of off-duty drug use through urinalysis or some other test.[170]

Most of the reported decisions involving legal challenges to drug testing have arisen in the public sector, although common law challenges are becoming more frequent in the private sector.[171] As noted throughout this text, governmental employers are bound by the requirements of the Fourth Amendment, which preserves the individual's right to be free from unreasonable governmental searches and seizures.[172] In the public employment setting, the Fourth Amendment interplays sharply with the individual's privacy rights. For instance, drug and alcohol testing procedures, such as urinalysis and blood, respectively, can obtain information concerning the employee's off-duty activities and lifestyle choices. As noted by one court:

> We would be appalled at the specter of the police spying on employees during their free time and then reporting their activities to employers.

---

[169]Certain drugs (marijuana, for example) may be present "in the system" and detected by a test (generally urinalysis) several weeks after use. Other drugs, like cocaine, are present for only 2 to 3 days. (Should a marijuana user be subject to more punishment than a cocaine abuser because the latter is more likely to escape detection?) While arbitrators have generally regarded off-duty conduct beyond the reach of management absent a nexus to the job or employer's business, exceptions may exist where management's rule permits discipline of employees who have drugs "in their system" even when what is in the employee's system has no discernible effect on the employee's job performance. See Chapter 5, notes 257–76 and accompanying text.

See generally TIA SCHNEIDER DENENBERG & R.V. DENENBERG, ALCOHOL AND OTHER DRUGS: ISSUES IN ARBITRATION 220–24 (BNA Books, 1991).

[170]Besides the cases in this section, see also the discussion, *supra* Chapter 2, part II, at B.5., and *infra* Chapter 5, at part VIII.

[171]Absent a state statute or state constitutional prohibition, or a prohibition in a collective bargaining agreement, private sector employers are generally unrestricted with respect to testing employees for drugs. Common law issues are discussed in Chapter 2.

[172]The Fourth Amendment, states:

The right of the people to be secure in their persons, houses, papers, and effects, against unreasonable searches and seizures, shall not be violated, and no Warrants shall issue, but upon probable cause, supported by Oath or affirmation, and particularly describing the place to be searched, and the persons or things to be seized.

U.S. CONST. amend. IV.

Drug testing is a form of surveillance, albeit it is a technological one. Nonetheless, it reports on a person's off-duty activities just as surely as someone had been present and watching. It is George Orwell's "Big Brother" society come to life.[173]

Private sector employers, on the other hand, are not restrained by the Fourth Amendment unless the testing procedures are attributable to governmental action. However, due to the heavy involvement of federal governmental regulations in the drug testing area,[174] the courts may find governmental or state action on behalf of the private employer. This was the case in *Skinner v. Railway Labor Executives Ass'n*,[175] where the Supreme Court held that a drug testing program performed by a private employer amounted to government action due to the federal regulations which mandated and authorized such testing. Thus, in industries where the federal government demands random, routine, mass, suspicion-based, or post-accident drug testing, the regulations and the actions by the private employer must comply with the individual's Fourth Amendment rights.

Application of the Fourth Amendment to individual drug testing, however, raises many search and seizure issues. Is blood, breath, or urine collection and analysis a "search" that is protected by the Fourth Amendment? If such procedures are searches, must some level of suspicion or probable cause be met before a public employer demands that an employee submit to a blood, breath, or urine test?

---

[173]Capua v. City of Plainfield, 643 F.Supp. 1507, 1510, 1 IER Cases 625, 626 (D.N.J. 1986).

[174]Under the Drug-Free Workplace Act of 1988, 102 Stat. 4181 (1988), private employers with federal contracts or grants must certify that they will provide a drug-free workplace. Covered employers (those employers with federal contracts of $25,000 or more) must publish rules against drug use and establish an awareness program informing employees about the dangers of drug use. Employees must notify management of any criminal conviction of a drug violation occuring in the workplace within 5 days of the conviction. Employers who receive such notice must take action against the employee, up to and including dismissal, or require participation in a rehabilitation program. Drug testing is not required. Failure to comply with the requirements can lead to termination of the contract or suspension of payments. Absent a mandate to test, or absent a close nexus between the government and the employer's drug testing, the Fourth Amendment does not apply. *See, e.g.,* Stevenson v. Panhandle Eastern Pipe Line Co., 680 F. Supp. 859 (S.D. Tex. 1987) (no state action notwithstanding federal government's encouragement of drug-free workplace).

[175]489 U.S. 602, 4 IER Cases 224 (1989).

Alternatively, can the employer simply order its employees to undergo suspicionless, random, mass, or even routine drug testing at any time without violating the Constitution? Further, as most cases in the area demonstrate, is there a difference in the Fourth Amendment's protection as applied to over-the-road truck drivers versus law enforcement officials? Custodians versus agricultural employees? In 1989, the Supreme Court, in two major companion cases, answered many of these questions.[176]

For the most part, prior to 1989, it was settled law that government drug testing of employees, either urine or blood, may constitute a search or seizure for purposes of the Fourth Amendment.[177] Thus, any time the government sought to obtain evidence of a physical nature from an individual's person, the application of the Fourth Amendment was frequently at issue. However, even though drug testing was generally considered a search prior to 1989, some concurring opinions asserted that drug testing by urinalysis was not a Fourth Amendment search.[178] Without a Fourth Amendment search, the government would be without constitutional Fourth Amendment restraints in performing such urinalysis testing—even without probable cause or suspicion of drug use.

In *Skinner*, the Supreme Court was faced with the issue whether regulations promulgated by the Federal Railroad Safety Act of 1970, which authorized the Secretary of Transportation to "prescribe, as necessary, appropriate rules, regulations, orders, and standards for all areas of railroad safety,"[179] were constitutional. The government

---

[176]Skinner v. Railway Labor Executives Ass'n, 489 U.S. 602, 4 IER Cases 224 (1989), and National Treasury Employees Union v. Von Raab, 489 U.S. 656, 4 IER Cases 246 (1989).

[177]Skinner v. Railway Labor Executives Ass'n, 489 U.S. 602, 4 IER Cases 224 (1989).

[178]Turner v. Fraternal Order of Police, 500 A.2d 1005, 120 LRRM 3294 (D.C. App. 1985) (concurring opinion of Judge Nebeker), stating:

> [W]e must first consider whether a police officer holds a subjective expectation of privacy in his body waste. It is obvious that body waste is forever discarded upon release from the body. An individual cannot retain a privacy interest in a waste product that, once released, is flushed down the drain.... Once the officer urinates he cannot logically retain any possessory or privacy interest in it. In fact, in the interest of public health and safety, it is difficult to conceive of any possessory interest the officer should be allowed to retain in his urine.

Id. at 1011; *See also* National Treasury Employees Union v. Von Raab, 808 F.2d 1057, 1 IER Cases 1433 (5th Cir. 1987) (concurring opinion of Judge Higginbotham).

[179]45 U.S.C. §431(a).

mandated blood and urine tests for employees who were involved in certain train accidents, and authorized railroads to administer breath and urine tests to employees who violated certain safety rules. The Ninth Circuit had found that such testing was an unreasonable search and seizure. Reversing, the Court found that it has long been recognized that "compelled intrusio[n] into the body for blood to be analyzed for alcohol content" was deemed a Fourth Amendment search.[180] It has also been consistently held that "physical intrusion, penetrating beneath the skin, infringes an expectation of privacy that society is prepared to recognize as reasonable."[181] Further, similar implications are at issue for breath testing, which, according to the Court, implies similar concerns about bodily integrity, and thus should be considered a search.

However, unlike blood testing, testing urine samples does not entail "surgical intrusions into the body."[182] Prior to *Skinner*, the courts were split on the issue of whether urine collection and testing was a search for Fourth Amendment purposes.[183] In *Skinner*, the Supreme Court laid to rest the issue once and for all. Adopting the language of a Fifth Circuit case, the Court, holding that a drug test is indeed a search and not just a mere medical examination, reasoned that there are few activities in society more personal or private than the passing of urine. In the words of the Court, "[m]ost people describe it by euphemisms if they talk about it at all. It is a function traditionally performed without public observation; indeed, its performance in public is generally prohibited by law as well as social custom."[184] As

---

[180]*Skinner*, 4 IER Cases at 231, citing Schmerber v. California, 384 U.S. 757, (1966).

[181]*Id.*

[182]*Id.*

[183]*See* McDonall v. Hunter, 809 F.2d 170 (5th Cir. 1987) (noted a "proper administered [urinalysis] is not as intrusive as a strip search or a blood test"); Mack v. United States, 653 F.Supp. 70 (S.D.N.Y. 1986), *aff'd*, 814 F.2d 120 (2d Cir. 1987) (finding that a urinalysis had little in common with stomach pumping and body cavity searches); Turner v. Fraternal Order of Police, 500 A.2d 1005, 120 LRRM 3294 (D.C. App. 1985) (concluding that a urinalysis was not an "extreme bodily invasion"). *But see* Patchogue-Medford Congress of Teachers v. Board of Educ., 510 N.E.2d 325, 2 IER Cases 198 (1987) ("[r]equiring a person to urinate in the presence of a government official or agent. . . is at least as intrusive as a strip search"); and Ensor v. Rust Eng'g Co., 704 F. Supp. 808 (E.D. Tenn. 1989) (random "observed" testing may be intrusive and thus unconstitutional).

[184]National Treasury Employees Union v. Von Raab, 816 F.2d 170, 2 IER Cases 15 (5th Cir. 1987), *affirmed in part, vacated in part*, 489 U.S. 656, 4 IER Cases 246 (1989).

such, because the collection and testing of urine intrudes upon the individual's reasonable expectations of privacy, such intrusions, according to the Court, "must be deemed searches under the Fourth Amendment."[185]

However, the Fourth Amendment does not proscribe all searches and seizures, but only those that are unreasonable, and "[w]hat is reasonable . . . depends on all the circumstances surrounding the search or seizure and the nature of the search or seizure itself."[186] Thus, the constitutionality of a drug test depends on whether it was reasonably based upon the individual's expectation of privacy, and, to some extent, the degree of the governmental interest in the invasion.

Once the Court determined that breath and urine collection and analysis were searches as defined by the Fourth Amendment, the Court went on to determine whether the particular intrusions were reasonable. In addressing this issue, the Court pointed out that in criminal cases, a search and seizure is not reasonable unless it is performed pursuant to a judicial warrant. The Court stated:

> An essential purpose of a warrant requirement is to protect privacy interests by assuring citizens subject to a search or seizure that such intrusions are not the random or arbitrary acts of government agents. A warrant assures the citizen that the intrusion is authorized by law, and that it is narrowly limited in its objectives and scope. . . . A warrant also provides the detached scrutiny of a neutral magistrate, and thus ensures an objective determination whether an intrusion is justified in any given case.[187]

However, in special cases, the Court has recognized exceptions to the rule requiring individualized suspicion.[188] In these "special needs" cases, the courts have "balance[d] the governmental and privacy interests to assess the practicality of the warrant and probable cause requirements in the particular context."[189] Even though breath

---

[185]*Skinner,* 4 IER Cases at 231.

[186]*Id.* at 232, quoting United States v. Montoya de Hevendez, 473 U.S. 531, 537 (1985).

[187]*Id.* at 233 [citation omitted].

[188]New York v. Burger, 482 U.S. 691 (1987) (search of premises of certain highly regulated businesses); O'Connor v. Ortega, 480 U.S. 709, 1 IER Cases 1617 (1987) (work-related searches of employees' desks and offices); New Jersey v. T.L.O., 469 U.S. 325 (1985) (search of student's property by school officials); Bell v. Wolfish, 441 U.S. 520 (1979) (body cavity searches of prison inmates).

[189]*Skinner,* 4 IER Cases at 232.

and urine collection and analysis are considered searches under the Fourth Amendment, the *Skinner* Court found the objectives of the warrant requirements would not be furthered in employee drug testing cases.[190] Moreover, the *Skinner* Court found the government's interest in bypassing the warrant requirement is strongest when "the burden of obtaining a warrant is likely to frustrate the governmental purpose behind the search."[191] Thus, because time delays would make it impossible to determine whether drugs were in an employee's system when an accident or safety violation occurred, blood and urine samples need to be obtained as soon as possible. Requiring a warrant would stymie the government's investigation.

Even without a warrant requirement, in non-drug-testing Fourth Amendment cases, searches cannot be performed without probable cause,[192] or "some quantum of individualized suspicion."[193] For the purpose of employee drug testing cases, however, the Court abandoned this approach for a simple balancing test. The Court declared that "where privacy interests implicated by the search are minimal, and where an important governmental interest furthered by the intrusion would be placed in jeopardy by a requirement of individualized suspicion, a search may be reasonable despite the absence of such suspicion."[194]

Thus, the Court found that breath and blood collection and analysis were minimal in their impact upon the individual's privacy interests. Therefore, due to important governmental safety interests, no individualized suspicion was needed prior to drug testing. For urine testing, however, the Court limited the lack of individualized suspicion exception to testing procedures that do not require the direct observation of a monitor.[195] The Court reasoned that such procedures do not impact on privacy concerns as severely as direct observation type testing.

---

[190]*Id.*
[191]*Id.*
[192]*Id.* at 234.
[193]*Id.*, citing United States v. Martinez-Fuerte, 428 U.S. 543 (1976).
[194]*Id.* at 234.
[195]*Id.* The presence of observation does not determine whether a testing procedure is a search. Observation is considered only to determine the reasonableness of the search. *See* National Fed'n of Fed. Employees v. Weinberger, 651 F. Supp. 726, 1 IER Cases 1137 (S.D. Ga. 1986).

In further justifying nonsuspicion testing, the Court found that the employees' expectations of privacy were diminished by reason of their participation in an industry that was regulated pervasively to ensure safety. According to the Court, the governmental interest in drug testing in such situations was compelling because the employees subject to the tests discharge duties fraught with such risk of injury to others and even a momentary lapse of attention can have disastrous consequences to the public. Similar to persons who have routine access to dangerous nuclear power facilities, employees who are subject to testing under the regulations can cause great human loss before any signs of impairment become noticeable to supervisors or others.[196] Even though the testing in question implicated the Fourth Amendment, "in light of the limited discretion exercised by the railroad employers under the regulations, the surpassing safety interests served by toxicological tests in this context, and the diminished expectation of privacy that attaches to information pertaining to the fitness of covered employees,"[197] the Court held that it was reasonable to conduct such tests in the absence of a warrant or reasonable suspicion.

In the companion case to *Skinner, National Treasury Employees Union v. Von Raab*,[198] the Court was faced with a related issue of general drug testing as a condition of employment. The U.S. Customs Service implemented a drug testing program for employees seeking employment in positions where the employee was (1) involved with drug interdiction or enforcement of related laws, (2) carried a firearm, or (3) handled "classified" material. The Court again addressed the circumstances in which the government may require warrantless and suspicionless drug testing of employees. In the Court's view, where the constitutional intrusion serves special governmental needs, beyond the normal need for law enforcement, "it is necessary to balance the individual's privacy expectations against the government's interest to determine whether it is impractical to require a warrant or some level of individualized suspicion in the particular context."[199]

---

[196]*Skinner,* 4 IER Cases at 236.
[197]*Id.* at 238.
[198]489 U.S. 656, 4 IER Cases 246 (1989).
[199]*Id.* at 665–66.

In *Von Raab*, the Court held that the Customs Service's drug testing was not designed to "serve the ordinary needs of law enforcement."[200] Thus, because the purpose of the testing was to deter drug use, the substantial interest of the government presented a "special need" that eliminated the ordinary warrant and probable cause requirements. The Court concluded that employees who are directly involved in the interdiction of illegal drugs or who are required to carry firearms in the line of duty have a diminished expectation of privacy with respect to the intrusions occasioned by a urine test. The Court recognized that the test infringed upon the employee's privacy expectations, but found that these expectations did not outweigh the government's compelling interest in safety and in the integrity of the borders.[201] The Court remanded the third category (those employees dealing with classified materials) for a determination of the scope of the "classified materials" requirement.

To what extent can a public employer require drug testing under the Supreme Court's balancing test outlined in *Skinner* and *Von Raab*? Are certain public employment positions more likely to implicate safety concerns and, if so, how does this impact management? How much governmental interest must be recognized before a public employee can be *randomly* tested (i.e., testing without reason or individualized suspicion) for drug use (neither *Skinner* nor *Von Raab* involved a truly random testing program)? Relying upon the Supreme Court's pronouncements in *Skinner* and *Von Raab*, the lower courts have addressed these issues.

In *Bolden v. Southeastern Pennsylvania Transportation Authority*,[202] the employee, a maintenance custodian, was discharged as a result of failing a random drug test. The Authority had implemented a drug testing policy without prior notice or consultation with the employees' unions. The Authority's plan was to administer random urinalysis tests to detect the presence of psychotropic drug metabolites and alcohol in employees' body systems.[203] The Authority

---

[200]4 IER Cases at 251.

[201]*Id.* at 253.

[202]953 F.2d 807, 7 IER Cases 94 (3d Cir. 1991).

[203]*See* Transport Workers Local 234 v. SEPTA, 863 F.2d 1110, 4 IER Cases 1 (3d Cir. 1988), for a discussion of the background and details of the proposed SEPTA policy.

claimed that the random drug testing was justified due to "substantial risk of harm to [the employee] and others."[204]

The court of appeals noted that in both *Skinner* and *Von Raab* the employees subjected to suspicionless testing were found to have diminished privacy expectations due to pervasive governmental regulations of the jobs they performed.[205] Further, the court pointed out that the Supreme Court had not "endorsed the proposition that compulsory, suspicionless drug testing may be conducted to prevent an employee from causing harm to himself, rather than to others."[206] Because the employee's duties did not involve an unusual amount of personal danger and the Authority's maintenance custodians were not "pervasively regulated" by the government, the Authority had "no special need to subject [the employee] to a drug test."[207]

In *Harmon v. Thornburgh*,[208] the court recapped *Skinner* and *Von Raab* stating:

> Urinalysis, if compelled by the government, is a "search" subject to the restrictions of the Fourth Amendment. However, individualized suspicion of a particular employee is not required by the Constitution. Nor is it necessary that a documented drug problem exist within the particular workplace at issue. . . . Rather, where a Fourth Amendment intrusion serves special governmental needs, beyond the normal need for law enforcement, it is necessary to balance the individual's privacy expectation against the Government's interests to determine whether it is impractical to require a warrant or some level of individualized suspicion in the particular context.[209]

The court went on to note that three distinct governmental interests have been recognized which may be sufficient to justify drug testing in the absence of individualized suspicion:

> First, the government's interest in maintaining the integrity of its workforce. . . . Second, the suspicionless testing of . . . employees who carry firearms. . . . Finally, the . . . government's compelling interest in protecting truly sensitive information. . . .[210]

In *Harmon*, the U.S. Department of Justice implemented drug testing procedures whereby five categories of employees in "sensitive"

---

[204]*Bolden*, 7 IER Cases at 102–03.
[205]*Id.* at 104.
[206]*Id.*
[207]*Id.*
[208]878 F.2d 484, 4 IER Cases 1001 (D.C. Cir. 1989).
[209]*Id.* 4 IER Cases at 1003 [citations omitted].
[210]*Id.*

positions would be subjected to random drug testing. These categories included: (1) all employees who were authorized to have access to top secret classified information; (2) all attorneys responsible for conducting grand jury proceedings; (3) all employees serving under presidential appointments; (4) all employees whose assigned position duties included the prosecution of criminal cases; and (5) all employees whose assigned position duties included maintaining, storing, or safeguarding a controlled substance.[211]

The Department of Justice argued that its interest in "ensuring the integrity of its workforce would justify the random drug testing of every federal employee." The court, however, found that "federal employment alone is not a sufficient predicate for mandatory urinalysis."[212] The court interpreted the *Von Raab* decision to require a clear and direct nexus between the nature of the employee's duty and the nature of the feared violation.[213]

The Department also argued that the duties of the covered employees raise public safety concerns comparable to those of *Skinner* and *Von Raab*. The court found this argument to be unpersuasive, noting that a "blunder by a Justice Department lawyer may lead, through a chain of ensuing circumstances, to a threat [to] public safety. That sort of indirect risk, however, is wholly different from the risk posed by a worker who carries a gun or operates a train."[214] The *Skinner* and *Von Raab* public safety rational looked to the "immediacy" of the threat.

Finally, the government contended that the covered employees had access to confidential information, and the government had a compelling interest to protect that information. The court accepted this argument based upon the *Von Raab* decision. The court noted that only the category of employees who had access to truly sensitive information could be tested under the proposed policy.

A further interpretation of *Skinner* and *Von Raab* was addressed in *National Treasury Employees Union v. Yeutter.*[215] In *Yeutter*, the Department of Agriculture developed a "Drug Free Workplace Program" that provided for the urinalysis testing of applicants, random

[211]*Id.* at 1002.
[212]*Id.* at 1005.
[213]*Id.*
[214]*Id.* at 1006.
[215]918 F.2d 968, 5 IER Cases 1605 (D.C. Cir. 1990), *aff'g in part,* 733 F. Supp. 403, 5 IER Cases 9 (D.D.C. 1990).

testing of all employees, reasonable suspicion testing of employees, injury, illness, unsafe or unhealthful practice testing of employees, voluntary testing, and testing as part of or as follow-up to counseling or rehabilitation.[216]

In analyzing the employees' claim that the testing violated their Fourth Amendment rights, the court noted that in applying the Supreme Court's *Skinner* and *Von Raab* decisions, it must "weigh the strength of the government's asserted interests supporting the urinalysis testing program against the individual's privacy interests to determine if the intrusion is reasonable under the Fourth Amendment."[217] According to the court, the employees of the Department of Agriculture to be tested included Plant Protection and Quarantine Officers who were responsible for preventing pests and animal diseases from entering the United States. The officers are administrative employees not law enforcement personnel. They do not carry weapons and are not authorized to make arrests. Thus, the court found that "[s]imply put, these PPQ officers do not remotely resemble this nation's first line of defense against one of the greatest problems affecting the health and welfare of our population."[218] Thus, the court found

> neither a sufficient "clear, direct nexus" between the duties of these employees and the feared violation nor a "compelling reason" to expect that drug use by these PPQ officers will result in misplaced sympathy to their essential mission of eradicating the scourge of plant pests and animal diseases in this country.[219]

Further, the court found that the PPQ officers did not have a diminished expectation of privacy because of their relatively nonsensitive positions, concluding:

> [B]ecause the government's integrity interest in randomly testing these PPQ officers falls far short of the compelling interest that the Supreme Court identified in Von Raab and because these PPQ officers do not have a diminished expectation of privacy, the court finds that this portion of the plan's random testing provision is unreasonable under the Fourth Amendment.[220]

---

[216]*Id.* 5 IER Cases at 11.
[217]*Id.* at 13.
[218]*Id.* at 14, citing *Von Raab*, 4 IER Cases at 252.
[219]*Id.* at 15.
[220]*Id.*

The court went on to find that the proposed drug testing plan was unreasonable with respect to Computer Specialists. The Department of Agriculture had argued that these Specialists were responsible for safeguarding highly sensitive information. However, according to the court, because the "risk presented to the government, and to the public in general, from the damage or loss of some or all of this information is simply not the type of compelling risk that would justify the random urinalysis testing proposed by the Department."[221]

After finding that proposed urinalysis testing of the PPQ officers and the Computer Specialists was unreasonable under the Fourth Amendment, the court addressed the proposed test as relating to the Department's Motor Vehicle Operators. The Department argued that the governmental interest in testing these employees is compelling "because these positions are fraught with such risks of injury to others that even a momentary lapse of attention can have disastrous consequences."[222] The Department further argued that these employees had a diminished expectation of privacy "because successful performance of their duties depends uniquely on their judgment and dexterity."[223]

The court upheld the proposed testing of Motor Vehicle Operators, concluding that strong safety interests support the testing of most operators who are responsible for the transportation of visiting foreign dignitaries and key department officials and the operation of passenger-laden shuttle buses.[224]

The similar application of the Fourth Amendment's restriction upon unreasonable searches was addressed by the Ninth Circuit in *Electrical Workers (IBEW) v. NRC.*[225] In that case, the International Brotherhood of Electrical Workers appealed the Nuclear Regulatory Commission's refusal to exempt clerical, warehouse, and maintenance employees from industry-wide drug testing programs. The Union argued that the testing, performed in a highly regulated private industry, was unconstitutional because the employees who would be tested under the regulations did not have access to vital areas of the

[221]*Id.* at 16.
[222]*Id.* at 17.
[223]*Id.*
[224]*Id.* at 18, citing Government Employees (AFGE) v. Skinner, 885 F.2d. 884, 892, 4 IER Cases 1153 (D.C. Cir. 1989).
[225]966 F.2d 521, 7 IER Cases 890 (9th Cir. 1992).

plant, were closely supervised, and their job duties did not involve work which could compromise plant safety.

The regulations of the Nuclear Regulatory Commission required all commercial nuclear plants to implement random drug testing programs for workers who had "unescorted access to protected areas."[226] After Pacific Gas and Electric Company, the owner and operator of Diablo Canyon Nuclear Power Plant, implemented the Nuclear Regulatory Commission's regulations, the Union (representing warehouse, clerical, and maintenance employees at the Diablo plant) filed a request with the Commission to exempt its members from random drug testing. The Commission denied the exemption, asserting that "all workers with access to protected areas of the plant had the potential both to distribute illegal substances to other plant employees and to threaten the safety of the plant."[227]

The court recognized that drug testing performed in the private sector which is mandated by governmental regulations may involve state action sufficient to implement constitutional restrictions.[228] However, the court refused to find that the Commission's regulations were too broad in scope because the evidence substantiated that clerical workers, warehouse employees, and maintenance employees all were involved in safety-sensitive jobs.

Absent reasonable suspicion of drug use, it is clear that public and private sector employers acting under governmental regulations, must demonstrate *special* needs, beyond the normal need for law enforcement and the normal concern for the employee's own welfare, before requiring random drug testing. The special needs test requires a balancing of the privacy interests of the employee and the interests of the government. The courts have continually recognized three governmental interests that can support drug testing without particular or individual suspicion of drug use and impairment. These include (1) promotion of the public safety, (2) protection of truly sensitive information, and (3) maintenance of employee integrity.[229]

What is the employer's right to test an employee when there *is* reasonable suspicion of drug use? Is the employer's ability to test

---

[226]*Id.*

[227]*Id.* 7 IER Cases at 891.

[228]*Id.* at 892, citing Bluestein v. Skinner, 908 F.2d 451, 455, 5 IER Cases 887 (9th Cir. 1990). *See also* Transportation Inst. v. Coast Guard, 727 F. Supp. 648 (D.D.C. 1989) (drug testing of private citizens on commercial vessels upheld).

[229]*See Skinner,* 489 U.S. at 628; *Von Raab,* 489 U.S. at 670–71, 677.

based upon reasonable suspicion limited to the same compelling governmental interest as suspicionless testing?

In *Government Employees v. Barr*,[230] the federal District Court for Northern District of California had before it a challenge to the Federal Bureau of Prisons' drug testing policy. The drug testing program required random testing of all Bureau employees; regular testing of job applicants, probationary employees, and management employees; testing in connection with on-the-job accidents or unsafe activities; and testing upon reasonable suspicion that an employee was under the influence of drugs.[231] With respect to the proposed random testing, the court found that "only those employees in primary law enforcement positions whom in the regular course of their duties, are issued or given access to firearms for use on a daily or weekly basis may be subject to random testing under [the] public safety rationale."[232] Further, "those licensed physicians and dentists in primary law enforcement positions who, in the regular course of their duties, must diagnose, treat, or directly supervise the diagnosis or treatment of patients on a daily or weekly basis may be subject to random urinalysis."[233] The court also found that "the interest of employee integrity justify the testing of only those employees in primary law enforcement positions who (1) have direct contact with inmates (2) on a daily or weekly basis (3) for periods of one hour or more each day of contact."[234] Finally, the court also found that "the Bureau may test those employees in primary law enforcement positions who apparently cause accidents or engage in unsafe practices (1) involving personal injury that requires immediate medical treatment, or (2) resulting in more than $2,000 damage."[235]

Under its testing plan, the Bureau also proposed to test employees if reasonable suspicion warrants "rational inferences that a person is using drugs."[236] Under the proposed plan, for those employees in positions subject to random testing, the suspicion may apply to "conduct either on or off duty."[237] For all other employees,

---

[230]794 F. Supp. 1466, 7 IER Cases 823 (N.D. Cal. 1992).
[231]*Id.* 7 IER Cases at 825.
[232]*Id.* at 828.
[233]*Id.* at 829.
[234]*Id.* at 831.
[235]*Id.* at 832.
[236]*Id.* at 833.
[237]*Id.*

the plan required suspicion based upon "on-duty illegal use or impairment."[238] The court noted that in *Von Raab* and *Skinner* the Supreme Court recognized a government interest in off-duty drug use only with respect to those employees with extraordinary duties, including drug interdiction, firearm use, access to truly sensitive information, and railroad work.[239] Thus, those employees who carried firearms, or were licensed physicians or dentists in direct contact with inmates on a daily or weekly basis, or involved in law enforcement with direct contact with the inmates, could be tested based upon reasonable suspicion of "off-duty" drug use.[240]

Drug use and testing of employees while "on-duty," however, could be performed on any employee based upon reasonable suspicion. Thus, the court upheld the program's proposed reasonable suspicion "on-duty" testing when supported by specific, personal observations concerning job performance, appearance, behavior, speech, or bodily odors of the employee; or, if the suspicion is based on hearsay evidence, corroborative evidence from a manager or supervisor with training and experience in the evaluation of drug induced impairment.[241]

In a Ninth Circuit case, *Jackson v. Gates*,[242] the appellate court addressed the issue of whether a urinalysis drug test was reasonable under the Fourth Amendment absent a reasonable individualized and articulated suspicion of drug use, impairment, or ingestion. Jackson, a Los Angeles police officer, was suspected of illegal drug use by the Department's Internal Affairs Division (IAD). Jackson had been seen associating on a number of occasions with another officer who frequented a suspected "narcotics location."[243] After the other officer was taken into custody, and pursuant to a warrant, his car searched, revealing "a tinfoil bundle which in size and shape was consistent with the packaging of cocaine,"[244] the IAD officers formally ordered Jackson to provide a urine sample under contemporaneous

---

[238]*Id.*

[239]*Id.* at 833, citing *Von Raab* 489 U.S. at 670–71, 676–77; *Skinner*, 489 U.S. at 632–33; National Treasury Employees Union v. Yeutter, 918 F.2d at 974–75.

[240]*Id.*

[241]*Id.*

[242]975 F.2d 648, 7 IER Cases 1249 (9th Cir. 1992).

[243]*Id.* 7 IER Cases at 1250.

[244]*Id.*

observation by the officers in a public restroom. Officer Jackson refused the order and was subsequently terminated for insubordination for refusing to comply with a lawful order.

Through established grievance procedures, Jackson submitted his discharge to binding arbitration. The arbitrator found that the labor agreement between the union and the Los Angeles Police Department did not authorize compulsory urinalysis. Jackson was reinstated in accordance with the arbitrator's decision.

Subsequent to the reinstatement, Jackson filed suit against the Department alleging a violation of his rights under the Fourth, Fifth, and Fourteenth Amendments. Following a trial, the jury returned a $154,747 verdict for Jackson. The Department appealed the decision to the Ninth Circuit, claiming that the order for Jackson to submit to urinalysis was reasonable under the Fourth Amendment even absent an individualized and articulated suspicion. The Department relied upon *Von Raab* and *Skinner* for the argument that no degree of individualized suspicion is necessary before ordering a police officer to submit to an administrative drug test.

The Ninth Circuit, however, distinguished both *Von Raab* and *Skinner,* noting that the employer could demonstrate no special compelling interests which would justify a search because there was no triggering event or employment pre-promotion requirement involved.[245] The appellate court also found that *National Federation of Federal Employees v. Chaney*[246] did not authorize police officer drug testing without individualized suspicion. In *Chaney,* civilian police officers employed by the Army were subjected to drug testing with no "limiting factor" other than randomness. In *Chaney,* the testing was found to be constitutional without individual suspicion. However, according to the Ninth Circuit, Jackson had not been ordered to submit to urinalysis as part of a "random drug testing program targeted at the entire police force. Rather, Jackson was singled out for testing based only on his association with another officer who was under IAD surveillance."[247] The court concluded that the IAD had no articulable, individualized basis for suspecting that Jackson was using narcotics. Further, the Department could not

---

[245]*Id.* at 1252.
[246]884 F.2d 603, 4 IER Cases 1164 (D.C. Cir 1989).
[247]*Jackson,* 7 IER Cases at 1252.

demonstrate a compelling interest which would justify the order given to Jackson. Accordingly, it was unreasonable under the Fourth Amendment for the IAD to order Jackson to provide a urine sample for drug testing.[248]

Under the current status of the law, the testing of employees for drug use does not constitute an unreasonable search and seizure under the Fourth Amendment if the employer can either demonstrate a reasonable suspicion of drug use, or that the employer's interest in public safety, protection of sensitive information, or employee integrity is considered substantial. It helps management's case if there is some diminished expectation of privacy by the employee and the searches are nonprosecutorial in character (i.e., justified by management's immediate need for information or investigation rather than its desire to "get the goods" on an employee). Without such special governmental needs, or demonstrated suspicion, or diminished employee expectation, the testing becomes unreasonable under the Fourth Amendment. Further, the public employer's interest in employees' off-duty drug use must be limited to employees with "extraordinary duties." When an employee is protected by the Fourth Amendment, the employer's concern with the employee's "off-duty" drug use cannot be justified without the demonstrated nexus between the on-duty responsibilities and the off-duty conduct.

VI. SYNTHESIS: CASES INVOLVING OFF-DUTY CONDUCT, LIFESTYLE, AND EXISTING CONSTITUTIONAL RESTRAINTS

Case law indicates that when a public employer regulates the off-duty conduct or lifestyle of its employees, it must do so consistent with the mandates of procedural and substantive due process. At a minimum, this means that there must be some rational connection between the off-duty behavior and the employee's job. An employer will not be able to effect the dismissal of an employee for off-duty conduct if management can articulate no interest whatsoever for its

---

[248]*Id.*

action. If the employee's conduct involves a fundamental right such as association or speech, or is within an individual's recognized "zone of privacy," a public employer will have to show more than a *de minimis* interest before it can justify a discharge for engaging in protected conduct. At times the employer's interest must be "compelling," depending upon the particular occupation at issue and the specific conduct of the employee. Finally, if a court finds that the employee has a property interest in continued employment, or that the discharge affects a "liberty" interest, certain procedural guarantees must be accorded the individual prior to the dismissal.

When, then, should freedom to associate or engage in an unconventional lifestyle bow to the government's interest? As the cases indicate, the easy answer is when there is a significant nexus between the employee's job and his or her off-duty conduct. The most difficult cases involve military and para-military organizations, such as police, fire, or security-sensitive positions in government. While these organizations have an acknowledged interest in promoting security and effectiveness this, however, does not mean that simple declarations that the state's interests outweigh the employee's privacy interests should be enough for a reviewing court or arbitrator. In the privacy area, for example, courts should not rule that any employee should be disqualified from employment simply because that employee is a homosexual. Moreover, we do not believe that the Supreme Court's decision in *Hardwick,* which held that consensual homosexual sodomy is not constitutionally protected,[249] is dispositive of anything.[250] Just as an individual cannot be punished for mere membership in an organization that has both illegal and legal objectives, under the Constitution an individual should not be presumed to violate sodomy (or similar) statutes because that person professes an "unconventional" sexual preference or orientation.[251]

[249]*Hardwick* is discussed *supra* notes 87–88 and accompanying text.

[250]In Doe v. Casey, 796 F.2d 1508, 1522, 41 FEP Cases 618 (D.C. Cir. 1986), the appellate court pointed out that *Hardwick* "did not reach the difficult issue of whether an agency of the federal government can discriminate against individuals merely because of [their] sexual *orientation.*" *See also* Watkins v. United States Dep't of the Army, 837 F.2d 1428, 2 IER Cases 1836 (9th Cir. 1988) (distinguishing *Hardwick*), *reh'g,* 875 F.2d 699, 49 FEP Cases 1763 (9th Cir. 1989).

[251]Jantz v. Muci, 759 F. Supp. 1543 (D. Kan. 1991) (reversing school district's denial of employment to teacher because of perception that he had "homosexual tendencies," distinguishing *Hardwick*).

Other dimensions of the problem of balancing the rights of employers and employees in lifestyle cases are explored in the next section and in the conclusion. One proposition advanced is that an employee with a lifestyle repugnant to management may fare better in an arbitration proceeding than in a court applying a mere rational basis test.

Chapter 5

Arbitral Standards Under "Just Cause" Provisions in Collective Bargaining Agreements

This chapter[1] concerns arbitral rulings when unions challenge management's right to discipline or discharge an employee under a just cause provision of a collective bargaining agreement[2] because

---

[1]This chapter is taken in part from MARVIN F. HILL, JR., & ANTHONY V. SINICROPI, MANAGEMENT RIGHTS 193–217 (BNA Books, 1986); Marvin F. Hill, Jr., & Mark Kahn, *Discipline and Discharge for Off-Duty Misconduct: What Are the Arbitral Standards, in* ARBITRATION 1986: CURRENT AND EXPANDING ROLES, PROC. OF THE 39TH ANN. MEETING, NAT'L ACADEMY OF ARBITRATORS 121–54 (1986); Marvin F. Hill, Jr., & Emily Delacenserie, *Procrustean Beds and Draconian Choices: Lifestyle Regulations and Officious Intermeddlers—Bosses, Workers, Courts, and Labor Arbitrators,* 57 MISSOURI L. REV. 51 (Winter 1992).

[2]Recent survey reports by The Bureau of National Affairs, Inc. (BNA), reveal that discharge and discipline provisions are found in 98% of collective bargaining agreements analyzed in a sample of 400. These clauses are included in all but 1 manufacturing agreement and excluded in only 8 nonmanufacturing contracts. BNA also reports that grounds-for-discharge provisions, found in 97% of its sample, are generally of 2 types—discharge for "cause" or "just cause" (found in 91% of the agreements), or discharge for a specific offense (found in 84% of the contracts in the database). THE BUREAU OF NATIONAL AFFAIRS, INC., *Basic Patterns in Union Contracts* 7 (13th ed. 1992).

Even if no "just cause" provision is found in the collective bargaining agreement, the better weight of authority holds that absent a clear indication to the contrary, a

management disagrees with certain aspects of an employee's lifestyle the results of that lifestyle, or off-duty conduct that management finds offensive.[3] What jurisdictional basis does management have regarding the employee's off-duty, off-premises conduct? What rules or standards do arbitrators follow? Does it make a difference whether the arbitrator is deciding a case in the public as opposed to the private sector? Do arbitrators track court rulings and apply a balancing or a multitier test[4] depending on the conduct at issue and the interest asserted by the employer? Most (but not all) of the cases dealing with lifestyle issues involve off-duty conduct and whether management can establish a relationship or nexus between the employee's conduct and his or her job or, alternatively, the employer's product or reputation. In general, arbitrators are reluctant to sustain discipline or discharge based on off-duty misconduct or lifestyle absent some relationship or nexus to the job. The reason for this principle was well expressed by Arbitrator Clair Duff in his 1961 *Chicago Pneumatic Tool Co.* decision.[5] Arbitrator Duff sustained the dismissal of a welder with

---

just cause standard is implied in the labor agreement. *See, e.g.,* B.F. Goodrich Tire Co., 36 LA 552, 556 (1961) (Ryder, Arb.); David E. Feller, *The Remedy Power in Grievance Arbitration,* 5 INDUS. REL. L.J. 128, 134–35 (1982).

Despite the high frequency of arbitration cases dealing with discharge and discipline (about 1 out of 3 grievances deals with discharge or discipline), few contracts contain a definition of "just cause." While no set criteria exist, arbitrators have uniformly held that any determination of just cause requires 2 separate considerations: (1) whether the employee is guilty of misconduct or a serious or faulty lapse in job performance, and (2) assuming guilt, whether the discipline imposed is a reasonable penalty under the circumstances of the case.

Professors Abrams and Nolan propose that:

Just cause . . . embodies the idea that the employee is entitled to continued employment, provided he attends work regularly, obeys work rules, performs at some reasonable level of quality and quantity, and refrains from interfering with his employer's business by his activities on or off the job.

Roger I. Abrams & Dennis R. Nolan, *Toward a Theory of "Just Cause" in Employee Discipline Cases,* 1985 DUKE L.J. 594, 601.

The universal rule in grievance arbitration is that the employer must carry the burden of proof on just cause in a discharge case.

[3]In a select few cases unrelated to any character infirmities, management may attempt to prohibit certain kinds of off-duty conduct by its employees. *See, e.g.,* Oregon State Police, 98 LA 944 (1992) (Wilkinson, Arb.) (denying detective's request to work 8 hours per month at pawn shop on ground that work in pawn shop never is suitable for police officer). A number of decisions involve an employee's "loyalty" to management. See *infra* notes 189–256 and accompanying text for a discussion of loyalty as it relates to misconduct by an employee.

[4]See *infra* Chapter 6 notes 1–3 and accompanying text.

[5]38 LA 891 (1961) (Duff, Arb.).

16 years' seniority who pleaded guilty to a narcotics offense:
attempting twice to obtain cocaine by misrepresentation of a physician's prescription obtained by another person. Arbitrator Duff found
that the grievant had become addicted to cocaine, although he had
never been shown to have reported for work under the influence.
Duff warned that arbitrators should be reluctant to sustain discharges
for off-duty conduct "lest Employers become censors of community
morals," but he nevertheless agreed that "where socially reprehensible
conduct and employment duties and risks are closely related, conviction for certain types of crimes may justify discharge."[6]

It is of note that Arbitrator Duff, quoting with approval the
company's answer in the lower steps of the grievance procedure,
recognized "reputation" and the morale of fellow workers as legitimate
company considerations.[7] Duff also relied on the fact that the grievant
was not available for work, agreeing with management that it was
"under no obligation to hold his job open for an indefinite period of
one to twenty-four months, as is the length of his sentence."[8]

Likewise, in *Fairmont General Hospital*,[9] Arbitrator Alfred
Dybeck outlined the controlling principle as follows:

> While generally an employee's conduct away from the place of business
> is normally viewed as none of the employer's business, there is a signifi-
> cant exception where it is established that the employee's misconduct
> off the premises can have a detrimental effect on the employer's reputa-
> tion or product, or where the off-duty conduct leads to a refusal,
> reluctance or inability of other employees to work with the employee
> involved.[10]

Arbitrator Harvey Nathan, in an unpublished decision (April 12,
1984), expressed the principle adopted by most arbitrators this way:

> [T]he generally accepted standard among arbitrators is that proof of
> off-duty misconduct, even when serious and/or criminal, does not justify
> automatic discharge. An employer must show that the conduct has a

---

[6]*Id.* at 893.
[7]The Employer had answered as follows:
The Company is not obligated to continue in its employ employees who commit
offenses involving moral turpitude especially where a conviction is involved. To do
so would be injurious to the reputation of the Company, in the community and
among its customers[,] and would have an adverse effect on employee morale.
Id.
[8]*Id.*
[9]58 LA 1293 (1972) (Dybeck, Arb.).
[10]*Id.* at 1295.

demonstrable effect on the employer's business. In this regard, saying it does not make it so. An employer must do more than simply make the pronouncement that it has or will be injured by retaining an employee who has engaged in off-duty misconduct. It is always possible that any employer could theoretically lose a customer, lose face with the public or suffer some general loss of business reputation by employing "convicts." An employer must demonstrate some meaningful nexus between the off-duty conduct and the employee's employment. [Emphasis in original.]

Arbitrator Nathan concluded that the employer, a large city, had been justified in its decision to discharge a firefighter who had pleaded guilty to felony-theft, given the characteristics of the firefighter's job. After recognizing the special nature of the work involved, requiring "highly skilled personnel engaged in a variety of public health and safety functions," Nathan had this to say:

Their work is an integral and critical part of the functioning of the public body for which they serve. They are recipients of public trust. As such they have special duties and special rights. They are uniformed. They operate within a formal chain of command. They have access to private property under a variety of circumstances and may be called upon to assist police. Their conduct and appearance while on duty or off-duty is specifically regulated. . . .

. . . [T]he particular crime involved, theft, or possession and sale of stolen property, renders the grievant particularly unsuited for fire fighting.

The late dean of the Yale Law School, Harry Shulman, while umpire for Ford Motor Company and the United Auto Workers, observed that management cannot regulate the lives and conduct of its employees outside of their employment relation and "[w]hat the employee does outside of the plant after working hours is normally no concern of the employer."[11] Dean Shulman went on to note that the jurisdictional line which separates the cases with which the employer may be concerned from those with which it may not, is not always a "physical line which bounds [its] property on which [its] plant is located."[12] The problem is determining when an employee's off-duty conduct or lifestyle (generally the employee's sexual, health, criminal, or other conduct that the employer disapproves of) can

[11]Opinion A-132, Ford Motor Co. and UAW-CIO (N.Y. State Sch. Indus. & Lab. Rels. 1944).
[12]*Id.*

result in discipline or even termination by management. Like most areas of the law, there are more questions than black-letter answers. What is clear from the cases, however, is that there are numerous traps that management can fall into when attempting to effect discipline or discharge because of disagreements with the employee's lifestyle or off-duty conduct. Familiarity with the criteria that arbitrators use in ruling on grievances will assist management in making sound personnel decisions and, at the same time, help companies avoid costly back pay awards.

I. JUST CAUSE CRITERIA

An examination of published and unpublished awards reveals a number of standards or criteria arbitrators use to evaluate discharge or discipline in off-duty conduct cases. These include (1) injury to the employer's business, (2) inability to report for work, (3) unsuitability for continued employment, and (4) co-employee refusal to work with the off-duty offender or danger to other employees. Also considered in separate categories is what action management may take on the basis of arrests and indictments; whether guilty and nolo pleas are viewed as equal to convictions after a trial on the merits; the effect of an expungement of a criminal offense; whether court-ordered probation is a mitigating factor; and whether public sector criteria relating to off-duty misconduct differ significantly from those applied in the private sector. Attention is also directed to off-duty considerations and employee loyalty to the employer and falsification of employment applications when employees withhold off-duty lifestyle information from management. While there is overlap between the cited categories, consideration of the topic within these areas is conceptually useful.

A. Injury to Employer's Business

Employers often assert that an employee's conduct should be subject to management's jurisdiction when the conduct causes an

actual or potential economic loss or, alternatively, the company's reputation is injured or is likely to be injured by retaining the employee.
As a general rule, where actual business loss or injury to reputation
is not established or is not apparent from the misconduct itself,
arbitrators are reluctant to sustain a discharge based on this argument,
although exceptions are found.

1. Actual or Potential Business Loss

Discharge for an employee's off-duty misconduct is most likely
to be upheld where an employer can link the employee's off-duty
conduct to an actual, as opposed to a potential or speculative, economic loss. But not always. Frequently a discharge has been upheld
where the arbitrator determined that a business loss was only a possibility. In the often-cited *Baltimore Transit Co.* decision,[13] a bus operator was publicly identified as the acting grand dragon of the state
branch of the Ku Klux Klan. In upholding the discharge, Arbitrator
Clair Duff acknowledged that, unless the discharge was sustained,
there existed a clear and present danger of physical violence and an
inevitable economic boycott against the company. In finding that
there was just cause for dismissal, the arbitrator also pointed out that
there was considerable support for a wildcat strike by the grievant's
fellow employees. Arbitrator Duff reasoned that the grievant's conduct, not his beliefs, were at issue in the case. The employee's "public
utterances were widely publicized and the admitted aims and objectives of the Klan made it eminently clear that the target of his activities
was not mere words but action contrary to the rights of a large
segment of the population . . . at least 50% of patrons of the Company's
bus lines."[14]

Likewise, in *Gas Service Co.*,[15] Arbitrator A.J. Granoff held that
a criminal conviction, coupled with numerous arrests, a known habit
of consorting with criminals and prostitutes, and a job requiring the
employee to work alone in customer homes reading meters amounted
to enough "potential" harm to a utility that discharge was justified
even though no actual business loss was demonstrated. Arbitrator

---

[13]47 LA 62 (1966) (Duff, Arb.).
[14]*Id.* at 66.
[15]39 LA 1025 (1962) (Granoff, Arb.).

Granoff noted that "an employment relationship imposes some responsibilities upon an employee which, as has been well stated, 'transcend the time and place of employment.' "[16] Granoff found that "Grievant's manner of living during leisure hours defies scavenging."[17]

Arbitrator Marcia Greenbaum, in an unpublished decision (November 18, 1985), considered the case of a commission salesman for a small producer and distributor of phonograph records. The salesman had been discharged after Postal Service inspectors, equipped with a search warrant, found several carts of pornography, including child pornography, in the salesman's home. The event received considerable local publicity on television and in the press. Inspection of the affidavit by the company indicated that the employee had been trading in child pornography, although no indictment had yet been issued against him. Even though the grievant had not yet been convicted of any crime, Arbitrator Greenbaum sustained the discharge. In so doing, she referred not only to the adverse reaction that had already taken place but also to probable future hazards for the company:

> [T]he next [flurry of information], if indictment and a trial with full disclosure, might bring further reactions, including reprisals of no longer dealing with the Company, if it were known that [the Company] had continued to employ [the grievant] after knowing what was contained in the affidavit. A company should not be subjected to such a possible consequence, nor its employees risk the loss of work, because one of their number had continued amongst them under these circumstances. . . .

An example of a dismissal that was reversed when management was unable to demonstrate some, but not significant, business damage was an unpublished decision reported by Arbitrator Benjamin Aaron (June 4, 1987). At issue was the dismissal of a male flight attendant who had pleaded guilty to soliciting an undercover male police officer for prostitution, a misdemeanor, and lying about it to his supervisors (significantly for the grievant, his supervisors were two women). The offense occurred while the employee was on layover. Because of his arrest, the employee missed his trip, causing the flight to be understaffed, resulting in diminished service to passengers. In finding

---

[16]*Id.* at 1028.
[17]*Id.*

the penalty excessive, the arbitrator focused on the consequences of the employee's offense:

> It is true that the flight he missed was understaffed and that the Company had to pay understaffing pay to those flight attendants who made the trip. That in itself, however, hardly seems to justify so severe a penalty as discharge. The Company suffered no adverse publicity; its business has not been affected by the incident. . . [Grievant's] offense. . .is not one likely to be repeated on the job, if at all.

Management often asserts that dress, grooming, and weight restrictions are necessary because of the image that the company is trying to project to its market.[18] In an effort to present a businesslike image and maintain revenues, employees are disciplined or even dismissed when they fail to observe grooming and weight restrictions. When the employer's rules regarding dress, grooming, and weight restrictions are based on health, safety, or legitimate business interests, and are administered in a nondiscriminatory manner, the regulation can be expected to be upheld by an arbitrator if challenged in an arbitral proceeding. A dress, grooming, or weight standard that is based only on the personal preference of a particular individual within the organization will, in all probability, not survive a "reasonableness" challenge in the grievance procedure.[19] Perhaps the best summary of current arbitral standards regarding grooming is provided by Arbitrator Peter Maniscalco, in *Missouri Public Service Co.*,[20] where he applied what appears to be a rational-basis-plus test and observed:

> The prevailing theory is that the Company has a right to require its employees to cut their hair and shave, when long hair and beards can reasonably threaten the Company's relations with its customers or other employees, or a real question of safety is involved, and an employer should be able to expect that his employees will practice personal hygiene and will clothe themselves in a neat manner, at least when the employee meets the public.
>
> However, there must be a showing of reasonable relationship between the Company's image or health and safety considerations and the need to regulate employee appearance. Therefore, management's right to

---

[18]See also *supra* Chapter 2 notes 79–83 and accompanying text.

[19]*See* the discussion of Arbitrator George Fleischli in Arrow Redi-Mix Concrete, Inc., 56 LA 597, 602 (1971) (Fleischli, Arb.) ("The arbitrator does not consider such personal likes or dislikes to be a legitimate basis for the establishment of a rule that impinges on the conduct of employees both on and off the job.").

[20]77 LA 973 (1981) (Maniscalso, Arb.).

regulate in this area is not absolute. Its exercise in any specific manner may be challenged as arbitrary, capricious or inconsistent with the objective for which the right is being exercised.[21]

While Arbitrator Maniscalco's case applied only to grooming standards, the same analysis applies to weight and dress regulations. Management is most successful in regulating an employee's appearance when the company can demonstrate a relationship between the standard and protecting the work force from injury.[22] When the issue is excessive weight, management may be required to allow the "offensive" employee the opportunity to undertake a weight loss program before the employee is adversely affected.

Where the concern of management is "public image," arbitrators have generally accorded great deference to the employer's standards in balancing the interests of management with the off-duty privacy interests of the employee.[23] Management is not always successful. When grooming regulations are struck down, it is usually because the standard is unreasonable as applied to a particular employee and not because the rule is per se unreasonable.[24] Laxity in enforcement may also preclude management from disciplining an employee for not observing the rule.[25]

---

[21]*Id.* at 976.

[22]*See, e.g,* Man Roland, Inc., 97 LA 175, 179 (1991) (Speroff, Arb.) ("Realistically and practically speaking, the Company's interest in protecting the grievant and possibly other employees from injuries is a legitimate concern. It is quite another matter however when it posits, as in this instant matter, that the grievant's excessive weight is instrumental with his injury record.").

[23]Albertson's, Inc., 77 LA 705 (1981) (Hulsey, Arb.) (delivery persons); Lloyd Ketcham Oldsmobile, 77 LA 953 (1981) (Hilgert, Arb.) (body-fender repairman); City of Cincinnati, 75 LA 1261 (1980) (Seifer, Arb.) (meter enforcement officials); Arkansas Glass Container Corp., 76 LA 841 (1981) (Teple, Arb.) (tank maintenance workers); *cf.* Safeway Stores, Inc., 75 LA 798 (1980) (Madden, Arb.) (grocery clerks).

[24]Frito-Lay, Inc., 81-2 Lab. Arb. Awards (CCH) ¶8562 (1981) (Forsythe, Arb.) (finding no-beard rule unreasonable for route salesman operating in rural community near college where beards were regularly worn in the community).
See generally Rolf Valtin, *Changing Life Styles and Problems of Authority in the Plant, in* LABOR ARBITRATION AT THE QUARTER-CENTURY MARK, PROC. OF THE 25TH ANN. MEETING, NAT'L. ACADEMY OF ARBITRATORS 235 (1973).

[25]*See, e.g.,* Rosauer's, Inc., 82-2 Lab. Arb. Awards (CCH) ¶8594 (1981) (LaCugna, Arb.) (allowing management to enforce grooming code prohibiting beards against all new employees but not against the grievant); Beatrice Foods Co., Butterkrust Bakeries Div., 77 LA 44 (1981) (Kulkis, Arb.) (employer not permitted to reinstate policy requiring employees to wear uniforms when they had been permitted to wear blue denims); Unites States Dep't of Justice, 81-2 Lab. Arb.

Another theme arbitrators often find persuasive when upholding management's regulation of employees' off-duty lifestyles is the potential civil liability that may result if the employee is retained. In *College of St. Scholastica*,[26] a decision with far-reaching implications for employers attempting to fend off lawsuits alleging negligent hiring, Arbitrator William Berquist upheld a Catholic college's dismissal of a part-time maintenanceman/janitor who had been arrested on a domestic sexual abuse charge (subsequently dismissed) and had a prior conviction of sexual misconduct (unknown to the college at the time of his hire). The arbitrator found that "the College would be adversely affected if the grievant is reinstated and retained because of the potential civil liability of the College if the grievant should commit misconduct of the nature disclosed by the prior conviction."[27] Reviewing case law on the nature of liability, Arbitrator Berquist stated that while the law is not clear as to liability, in his opinion "the Employer would be held civilly liable for damages for the conduct of the grievant primarily on the basis of negligent hiring and retention. The risk is too great for this arbitrator to expect the Employer to assume."[28]

2. Injury to the Company's Reputation

Damage to the employer's reputation is an often-cited standard because it connotes embarrassment to the company and a potential loss in business. Determining whether an employee's conduct or lifestyle has injured the company's reputation is difficult and is often highly subjective in the absence of any objective measurement of actual harm. Where it is argued that a company's reputation is injured, arbitrators look at the source and degree of adverse publicity,[29] the

---

Awards (CCH) ¶8607 (1981) (Meiners, Arb.); *cf.* Valtin, *supra* note 24, at 251 ("Hair and beard rules must be capable of uniform application and must, in fact, be uniformly applied. Discriminatory treatment may become the ground for reversal of disciplinary action.").

[26]96 LA 245 (1991) (Berquist, Arb.).

[27]*Id.* at 253.

[28]*Id.* at 253–54; *see also* Pepsi-Cola San Joaquin Bottling Co., 93 LA 58, 63 (1989) (Lange III, Arb.) (sustaining dismissal of service technician who pleaded guilty to sexual offense involving stepdaughter, noting potential financial liability should there be similar incident involving the grievant).

[29]*See, e.g.,* Haskell of Pittsburgh, 96 LA 1208, 1211 (1991) (Sergent, Arb.)

type of misconduct,[30] and the position held by the employee[31] in determining the extent of "injured reputation." Where certain felonies are committed (murder or sexual assault) it may not matter what position the employee holds. In these cases it is the *potential* for adverse public opinion that may be deemed sufficient to warrant a dismissal, even without an objective showing that the company's reputation has indeed been affected. The more public the position and the more serious the crime, the easier it becomes for management to sustain a dismissal. Arbitrator Berquist, in *College of St. Scholastica*,[32] provided the following analysis of the problem:

> As to the effect of reinstatement and retention of the grievant upon the reputation and business of the College, I realize that the Employer has not adduced any specific substantive evidence of loss of reputation or adverse effect upon the business, such as the declining of enrollment or complaints and comments from students as well as the public. At this point, and when the grievant was terminated, it was virtually impossible for the Employer to adduce evidence of this nature because it acted responsibly and as soon as it could after it became aware of the prior misconduct of the grievant. In other words, the College is not obligated to continue the employment of the grievant on a wait and see basis, that is to see if there is any adverse effect upon the reputation and actual business loss as a consequence. In my opinion such an adverse effect is reasonably foreseeable and consequently the College was not obligated to wait it out for such a determination.

> The status of an institution of higher learning causes it to be held up to closer scrutiny in reference to safety and care of its students than other companies such as manufacturing, or retail. There is no question that to retain the grievant would, in my opinion, be to affect detrimentally the high reputation accorded the College and would adversely affect its business in the future.

> The Employer in this instance is obviously in the best position and most qualified to assess the impact which might and probably would

---

(noting that customers, distributors, and sales representatives of company expressed concerns about grievant's drug dealings); Fairmont Gen. Hosp., 58 LA 1293 (1972) (Dybeck, Arb.); Baltimore Transit Co., 47 LA 62 (1966) (Duff, Arb.); Martin Oil Co., 29 LA 54 (1957) (Brown, Arb.).

[30]*See, e.g.,* Gas Serv. Co., 39 LA 1025 (1962) (Granoff, Arb.); Consolidated Badger Coop., 36 LA 965 (Mueller, Arb.); Quaker Oats Co., 15 LA 42 (1950) (Abrahams, Arb.).

[31]*See, e.g.,* Fairmont Gen. Hosp., 58 LA 1293 (1972) (Dybeck, Arb.); Gas Serv. Co., 39 LA 1025 (1962) (Granoff, Arb.); Consolidated Badger Coop., 36 LA 965 (1961) (Mueller, Arb.).

[32]96 LA 245 (1991) (Berquist, Arb.).

occur on its reputation. It indicates that it will be adverse. Its continuation as a viable college of higher learning is dependent upon its maintenance of a high degree of public confidence in it as an institution of higher learning and that it will protect and secure to the best of its reasonable ability, the interest and safety of its students.[33]

Arbitrators have often upheld discharge for the commission of off-duty felonies such as assault, drug possession, theft, firearm violations, and so on, concluding that the company's image and reputations would be negatively affected by an order of reinstatement. An unpublished decision by Arbitrator Donald Crane (February 27, 1985) concerned an employee who was arrested and charged with murder. While in jail, she sent a letter to her supervisor requesting a leave of absence or a vacation. Both requests were denied and she was discharged for an unexcused absence of more than three days. She had entered a plea of guilty to the lesser offense of manslaughter by the time the case was heard in arbitration. Upholding the dismissal, Arbitrator Crane considered (among other factors) the impact on her employer's reputation:

> In this case, we have no testimonial evidence that [the grievant] would damage the Company's image or create a potential danger to other employees. But none would be appropriate for it would only at best be an assumption or prediction. Until the Company had experiences with reinstated felons who committed crimes similar to [grievant's] there would be no way of demonstrating the results of their return to work. We have no such experience, but none is needed here. It is intuitively obvious that the Company's image would be tarnished by her reinstatement. C-- is a small town and [grievant's] crime was headlined in the local press. Literally, every citizen was aware of the incident and it would be naive to assume that the public would fail to associate her with the Company should she return to her job.

The Arbitrator also expressed concern about potential risks, especially in light of the specifics of grievant's crime:

> In addition, reinstating [the grievant] would pose a potential liability for the Company. It is clear that she left the house of the victim and deliberately secured a lethal weapon at her home. She had time to contemplate her action; it was not impulsive nor in the heat of passion. Remote as it may appear, it is possible that her behavior could be

---

[33]*Id.* at 254; *see also* Motor Cargo, Inc., 96 LA 181 (1990) (E. Jones, Jr., Arb.) (upholding dismissal for off-duty cocaine use while in possession of company truck, reasoning that employer was liable for injury for grievant's usage of truck).

repeated at work. Under the circumstances, employees could feel endangered. Even though one Union witness testified that he knew of no one who expressed concern about her reinstatement, there well may have been someone who feared her return. I do not want to be responsible for exposing employees to a potential danger [by ordering reinstatement of the grievant].

At times, the employer's plant or work rules will address the issue. For example, American Airlines' Rule No. 34 provides in part, "[a]ny action constituting a criminal offense, whether committed on duty or off duty, will be grounds for dismissal."[34] But in most cases it is left to the arbitrator to determine the effect or nexus between the conduct and the company's reputation.

In *Trailways Southeastern Lines, Inc.*,[35] Arbitrator Robert Gibson considered the discharge of a driver for violating the following rule: "Words or acts hostile to the Company, or words or acts which result in damage to the Company's reputation, property or service, are cause for disciplinary action."[36] The grievant had entered a guilty plea to breaking and entering his estranged wife's house with intent to commit murder, as well as trying to burn down another house belonging to his wife.[37] In sustaining the discharge, the arbitrator reasoned that the employee's conduct "could not help but result in damage to the reputation of the Company . . . because of the notoriety Grievant received in the newspaper reports."[38]

Arbitrator Robert Mueller, in *Cashton Cooperative Creamery*,[39] considered the discharge of an employee who had entered a plea of *nolo contendere*[40] to taking indecent liberties with his 14-year-old daughter. In sustaining the discharge the arbitrator noted that the

---

[34]American Airlines and Flight Attendants (APFA), Case No. SS-165-80 LA (1981) (Kagel, Arb.) (unpubl.).

[35]81 LA 712 (1983) (Gibson, Arb.).

[36]*Id.* at 713–14.

[37]*Id.* at 713.

[38]*Id.* at 716; *see also* Allied Materials Corp., 78 LA 1049 (1982) (Allen, Arb.) (rule prohibiting "conduct that violates common decency or morality"); Eastern Air Lines, 76 LA 961, 963 (1981) (Turkus, Arb.) ("conduct on or off the job which was in conflict with the Company's interest"); Air Canada, 75 LA 301, 302 (1980) (Brown, Arb.) (rule prohibiting "violations of a public law or commission of a criminal offence").

[39]61-1 Lab. Arb. Awards (CCH) ¶8008 (1960) (Mueller, Arb.).

[40]For a discussion of the implications of a nolo plea, *see infra* notes 165–82 and accompanying text.

conviction resulted in widespread publicity throughout the small community where the employer operated in a highly competitive industry. Moreover, the arbitrator also recognized the importance of the views of the grievant's colleagues by pointing out that, at the hearing, the employer presented a signed statement by 13 out of 18 employees to the effect that they did not want the grievant back as a co-worker. Arbitrator Elvis Stephens, in *Gulf Oil Co.*,[41] likewise ruled that management could terminate a 31-year employee who pleaded guilty to having sexual intercourse with a retarded 12-year-old girl. The arbitrator found the felony morally reprehensible, the community close-knit, and few employees willing to work with the grievant.[42]

Arbitrator Mark L. Kahn, in an unpublished decision (February 18, 1986), sustained the discharge of a female flight attendant based on her guilty plea to felony charges of lewd and lascivious acts with a 12-year-old boy who was living with his mother and brother in the grievant's home. The 36-year-old flight attendant was an employee with 17 years of service and a good work history. The record indicated that the grievant's arrest, indictment, conviction, referral to the state medical facility, and sentencing were each reported in the local newspapers, with the grievant identified by name and described as an "airline stewardess" but with no mention of the name of her employer. Although finding that her return to duty would not place unaccompanied children at risk nor give rise to an in-flight problem with co-workers, Kahn held that the critical factor for sustaining the dismissal was the effect of the grievant's conviction on the company's reputation. Kahn noted that flight attendant is among those job classifications with duties that involve substantial firsthand customer relations and, accordingly, the employer was entitled to greater concern about the adverse impact of unfavorable publicity relating to off-duty behavior. Explaining the basis of his decision, the arbitrator had this to say:

> I reach this conclusion [that just cause existed for the discharge] based on the gravity of this kind of misconduct as perceived by the traveling public; the fact that it involved the abuse of a youngster who was a boarder in grievant's home and who has been placed in grievant's care, for tutoring, by his mother; the fact that the misconduct was not a

---

[41]85-1 Lab. Arb. Awards (CCH) ¶8234 (1984) (Stephens, Arb.); *accord* Northwest Airlines, 53 LA 203 (1969) (Sembower, Arb.) (sustaining dismissal of employee for taking photo of nude teenage boy).

[42]Gulf Oil Co., 85-1 Lab. Arb. Awards at ¶8234.

single thoughtless act but continued over a period of many [eight] months; the fact that the affair received substantial local newspaper publicity over a period of time, identifying grievant by name and as an "airline stewardess" although her employer was not named; because there is a high risk of additional publicity adverse to the Company that could be generated by her reinstatement; and because there also remains a risk, of unknown dimension, that such off-duty misconduct might reoccur: an event that could subject the Company to the probability of substantial adverse public notice compounded by grievant's previous identification as a felony sex offender. The Company is not obligated, in my judgment, to assume such risks because of grievant's off-duty misconduct.

Another flight attendant removed a picture from its frame in her motel room while on layover, placed it in her suitcase, and took it with her from the motel. Her prior 13-year record with the company was unblemished. Arbitrator Richard Block, in an unpublished decision (February 17, 1981), concluded that the discharge was overly severe even though the airline was paying for the room and the motel had called the airline about the loss. Finding that the company did not suffer in any real way, Arbitrator Block addressed the reputation issue as follows:

> [T]here is some justification in the Company's claim that it was involved in a sensitive situation. The Company responded with a letter of apology and restitution—about $55.00—for a picture. But while there was misconduct on the Grievant's part, it was neither so open, notorious or scandalous as to warrant the finding that the Company suffered in any real way. Even granting the difficulty of showing hard evidence as to a damaged reputation, one may not conclude that [grievant's] actions brought discredit to anyone but herself. The Company may properly be concerned when the private actions of employees inevitably involve it in an unflattering light. At the same time, the Employer is neither the guardian nor the monitor of its employees' off-duty actions. Basic precepts of privacy require that, unless a demonstrable link may be established between off-duty activities and the employment relationship, the employee's private life, for better or for worse, remain his or her own.

Arbitrator Block reduced the penalty to a disciplinary suspension of 60 days.

In *Quaker Oats Co.*,[43] discharge was not sustained for an employee who pleaded guilty to contributing to the delinquency of

---

[43]15 LA 42 (1950) (Abrahams, Arb.).

a minor. The arbitrator noted that the employee's position did not place him in direct contact with the public and no complaints were received as a result of the incident.[44] Similarly, another arbitrator refused to allow discharge of an employee with 19 years' seniority who faced an assault charge for shooting his wife.[45] Even though adverse publicity resulted from the incident, the arbitrator commented: "If [the employee] has lost his acceptability to customers that fact, too, will quickly appear and the Company will have concrete evidence, rather than speculation, on which to base its decision."[46]

Likewise, in *Vulcan Asphalt Refining Co.,*[47] Arbitrator Henry Welch reversed the discharge of an employee for selling a former classmate (working as an undercover narcotics agent) a small amount of marijuana.[48] The arbitrator pointed out that while the incident was common knowledge in the small town and had been the subject of newspaper reports, it did not in any noticeable degree harm the company's reputation or product.[49] He also noted that the misconduct did not render the employee unable to perform his duties, and that his arrest and conviction could not be expected to cause refusal, reluctance, or inability on the part of other employees to work with the grievant.[50]

Proving injury to the company's reputation is more difficult than demonstrating that the employer's business suffered a financial loss due to the grievant's conduct. Indeed, some arbitrators have viewed "business reputation" as too nebulous a concept to be useful,[51] although these arbitrators are in the minority. When confronted with

---

[44]*Id.* at 43.
[45]Martin Oil Co., 29 LA 54 (1957) (Brown, Arb.). *See also* Iowa Public Serv. Co., 95 LA 319 (1990) (Murphy, Arb.) (reversing discharge of 10-year employee who pleaded guilty to off-duty assault against ex-wife and others, where employee had little contact with public or employer's customers, conduct was not widely known and did not affect employee's relationship with co-workers).
[46]*Id.* at 56.
[47]78 LA 1311 (1982) (Welch, Arb.).
[48]*Id.* at 1312.
[49]*Id.*
[50]*Id.* at 1313.
[51]Movielab, Inc., 50 LA 632, 633 (1968) (McMahon, Arb.) ("violation of the criminal law and having charges filed against him or even being convicted of a criminal offense for acts committed outside working hours and while off employer's premises, does not necessarily constitute a proper basis for disciplinary action unless there is an adverse effect upon the employer-employee relationship").

arguments that a grievant's off-duty misconduct damaged the company's reputation, most arbitrators have required a clear showing before sustaining discharges. This may be accomplished by reference to adverse media coverage or, in selected cases, by direct reference to the conduct itself. As a note of caution to employers, it may be difficult for an employer to argue that the off-duty criminal conduct of a grievant adversely affects its reputation where the company has in the past hired ex-convicts who have proved to be able and trustworthy employees.

B. Inability to Report for Work

Many discharges are effected because an incarcerated employee is unavailable for work. When an employee's off-duty conduct or lifestyle results in a jail sentence, he or she may have little recourse if dismissed by management. Such discharges are usually upheld by arbitrators who tend to reason that employees who commit crimes, and thus cause the public authorities to place them in jail, should not complain about a condition they have created.[52] However, arbitrators

---

[52]Besides the cases discussed in this section, *see* Ralphs-Pugh Co., 79 LA 6 (1982) (McKay, Arb.) (sustaining discharge for failing to report to work due to incarceration; no contractual obligation to grant leave to serve jail term); Rock Island Ref. Corp., 84-1 Lab. Arb. Awards (CCH) ¶8264 at 4183 (1984) (Schwartz, Arb.) (employee justified in refusal to grant leave of absence for jail term, stating that "the employee would have no 'right' to a leave of absence unless it could be shown that the Company denied a leave request for reasons that were wholly arbitrary or capricious"); Louisville Gas & Elec. Co., 85-1 Lab. Arb. Awards (CCH) ¶9018 (1984) (Fledman, Arb.) (ruling that company may properly deny leave of absence to incarcerated employee); Ohio Seamless Tube Div., 46 LA 947 (1966) (Dworkin, Arb.) ("An absence resulting from a violation of law, and confinement in jail, does not serve to exonerate the employee from blame, or to release him from his obligation to report to work as scheduled."). *See also* Westvaco, U.S., Envelope Div., 85-2 Lab. Arb. Awards (CCH) ¶8455 at ¶4839 (1985) (Koven, Arb.), where Arbitrator Adolph Koven pointed out that "sentences of 30 days [Sperry Rand Corp., 60 LA 220 (Murphy, 1973)], 60 days [Oren Roanoke Corp., 70 LA 942 (Boyd, 1978)], two months [Southwestern Ohio Steel Co., 1975 ARB ¶8391 (Dworkin, 1975)], ten weeks [Firestone Tire & Rubber Co., 83-2 Lab. Arb. Awards (CCH) ¶8462 (Van Pelt, 1983)], six months [Ralphs-Pugh Co., 79 LA 6 (McKay, 1982)], one and one-half years [Muncie Stone Co., 80-2 Lab. Arb. Awards (CCH) ¶8443 (Cox, 1980)], and 'an indefinite period' [Bush Beryllium Co., 55 LA 709 (Dworkin, 1970)], have all been long enough sentences to justify termination."

generally look for a violation of a specific provision of the collective bargaining agreement before sustaining discharge. This principle was expressed by Arbitrator George Roumell in *McInerny Springs and Wire Co.*:[53]

> [W]hen an employee is incarcerated, a company has the right to discharge him since he is, for that period of time, unable to work. The reason a discharge is proper in such cases is not because of the crime the employee has committed but rather it is simply that through the employee's own actions, he has made it impossible to fulfill his obligation to report to work. Therefore, in such cases, a company has "just cause" to terminate the employee since he is no benefit to the company.[54]

In *Dorsey Trailers, Inc.*,[55] an employee was jailed for armed robbery. The company had a plant rule that any employee failing to report for work without giving notice to the employer within three days lost all employment rights under the agreement. The arbitrator sustained the discharge.[56] But in *Metropolitan Transit Authority*,[57] Arbitrator A. Dale Allen, Jr., reversed the dismissal of a nine-year bus operator with a good work record who requested sick leave after failing to report to work because he was in jail approximately two and one-half weeks. Arbitrator Allen reasoned that the jail sentence (the only one in his life) was related to the employee's inability to accept his divorce and separation from his wife. The incarceration was not caused by alcohol or drug problems, and thus had no impact on his ability to perform his job and was in no way related to the company.[58] Back pay was denied.

In *Oxford Chemicals, Inc.*,[59] a decision reported by Arbitrator William Holley, the grievant—a packer in a chemical company with 16 years of seniority—was convicted of involuntary manslaughter and, in March 1981, sentenced to five years. The grievant was released on bond, and, after filing a motion for a new trial, returned to work. On June 16, 1983, the state filed a motion to dismiss the grievant's motion and to revoke bond. An order was then issued by the court for the grievant's arrest, and he was properly incarcerated. On June

---

[53]72 LA 1262 (1979) (Roumell, Arb.).
[54]*Id.* at 1265.
[55]73 LA 196 (1979) (Hamby, Arb.).
[56]*Id.* at 198.
[57]98 LA 793 (1992) (Allen, Jr., Arb.).
[58]*Id.* at 795.
[59]84-1 Lab. Arb. Awards (CCH) ¶8277 (1984) (Holley, Arb.).

18, 1983, the grievant spent a previously scheduled one-week vacation in jail. Unable to return to work on July 25, 1983, the grievant called management to explain the situation. The grievant told the company that he was being held by mistake and that his lawyer was trying to correct the matter. On July 27th, the grievant requested that he be allowed to use his three remaining weeks of vacation. His request was denied. The company, choosing not to accept the grievant's incarceration as an excuse, discharged the grievant on July 29, 1983, for four unexcused absences (under the company's rules, a total of four unexcused absences meant automatic discharge).

The arbitration hearing took place on February 15, 1984. After the hearing, but prior to the award, the union's brief and a motion to reopen the record was received by the arbitrator. The basis of the union's motion was that the grievant's conviction for involuntary manslaughter had been reversed on February 27, 1984. The company's brief was received in the afternoon mail. Ruling that the record is not officially closed until both briefs are received, the arbitrator decided to accept the information concerning the grievant's successful appeal as part of the record. His award was that the grievant should be reinstated.

Arbitrator Holley used the approach of Arbitrator John Murphy, in *Sperry Rand Corp.*,[60] in which Murphy declared:

> Whether or not confinement of an employee in jail will authorize his employer to take some sort of disciplinary action depends upon all the circumstances, including, among other things:
> a. The language of their contract.
> b. The length of confinement.
> c. The nature of the cause for confinement; i.e., whether as the result of an arrest and inability to post bond, or as the result of a sentence.
> d. The nature of the conduct resulting in confinement, i.e., its degree of seriousness and impropriety.
> e. The nature of the disciplinary action to be taken or which results.
> f. The employee's previous work and disciplinary record.
> g. The extent to which the absence affected the employer's production, etc.
> h. The effect upon plant morale.
> i. Whether or not the conduct occurred on plant property or during working hours.[61]

---

[60]60 LA 220 (Murphy, Arb.).
[61]*Id.* at 222–23; *see also* Bethlehem Steel Co., 32 LA 543, 544–45 (1959) (Seward, Arb.).

Arbitrator Holley pointed out that although the contract allowed the company to discharge for four unexcused absences, "The nature of the cause for confinement did not adversely affect the Company" and "no evidence was introduced to show that the Company had been adversely affected."[62] The arbitrator also observed that although the District Attorney was appealing the appellate court's reversal of the grievant's conviction, the grievant at that time did not stand convicted of involuntary manslaughter. The award directed that the grievant be reinstated effective on the date he could have returned to work following the reversal of his conviction.[63] The grievant was not entitled to any back pay, however, for the period between his discharge and the date on which the conviction was reversed.

The cases indicate that employers will fare better if the dismissal is based on the employee's unavailability for work and not simply on the jail sentence or the specific crime warranting the jail term. Black letter law in this area holds that, in general, management is not required to grant a leave of absence in order to allow an employee to serve out a jail sentence. Management has a right to expect its employees to be at work, and if an employee is absent during a period when he or she is required to be at work, absent a specific contractual right to a leave of absence, management can terminate an employee for not being at work.

C. Unsuitability for Continued Employment

What makes an employee unsuitable for continued employment? Mere lack of trust by management? When does conviction of a crime, for example, impair the employee's usefulness to the employer? May an employee's usefulness be impaired even though there is no media publicity of the off-duty misconduct? A major consideration is always the employee's job and how the misconduct affects his or her job responsibility or relates to the employee's duties. Similar to the reasoning of the courts in constitutional cases involving the privacy claims of police, arbitrators appear to give greater deference to management in cases involving guards and the protective services than nonmilitary-

---

[62]Oxford Chemicals, 84-1 Lab. Arb. Awards, at 4244.
[63]*Id.* at 4245.

type positions.[64] Also, public sector employees are frequently held to a higher standard relative to their private sector counterparts.[65]

An individual may possess the physical capacity to perform a job but, because of the nature of the off-duty misconduct and the particular job at issue, may be considered unsuitable for continued employment. Arbitrator Alfred Dybeck, in *Fairmont General Hospital*,[66] considered the discharge of a hospital maid for shoplifting at a local department store. Because the hospital had experienced a recent problem of theft, and even though the maid was not accused of stealing from the hospital, the arbitrator upheld discharge because her actions created a serious doubt as to her trustworthiness as an employee.[67] In a 1988 case involving this same hospital,[68] Arbitrator J. Ross Hunter, Jr., ruled that dismissal was too severe for a licensed nurse who pleaded guilty to an off-duty shoplifting charge. The arbitrator, applying a hard nexus requirement, reasoned that the record contained "no proof of actual detriment or harm, or convincing proof from which detriment or harm can be readily or reasonably discerned."[69] Still, the arbitrator ruled that the employee breached her duty of good faith and fair dealing, implied in her employment contract with the hospital. The dismissal was converted to a suspension.

The question of an employee's honesty in dealing with the employer forced the arbitrator, in *Southern California Edison Co.*,[70] to sustain a discharge. The employee failed to give notice of his absence and lied to the employer about his off-duty arrest for possession of marijuana (the employee said that he had been arrested for drunk driving). The employee did not attempt to make alternative arrangements and was away from work for several days to take care of legal matters. His failure to tell the truth led the arbitrator to conclude that the discharge was for cause.[71]

---

[64]*See, e.g.,* Hamilton County Sheriff's Dep't, 99 LA 6 (1992) (Duff, Arb.) (upholding dismissal of corrections officer for conduct unbecoming deputy sheriff for lying about theft of service revolver and associating with persons of questionable character, where officer on notice that higher standard of truthfulness was expected of police officer).

[65]See *infra* notes 121–64 and accompanying text.

[66]58 LA 1293 (1972) (Dybeck, Arb.).

[67]*Id.* at 1295–96.

[68]Fairmont Gen. Hosp., 91 LA 930 (1988) (Hunter, Jr., Arb.).

[69]*Id.* at 934.

[70]59 LA 529 (1972) (Helbing, Arb.).

[71]*Id.* at 533.

Similarly, in *Safeway Stores, Inc.*,[72] Arbitrator James Doyle ruled the company had just cause to discharge an employee for "proven dishonesty" after he was convicted for stealing a vacuum cleaner at another store. In so ruling, the arbitrator rejected the argument that the words "proven dishonesty" in the contract[73] meant only dishonesty relating to the grievant's employment.[74]

In *American Airlines*,[75] however, an employee was given a "second chance" after being convicted of shoplifting while off duty and not in uniform. The arbitrator reasoned that the employee had not given the employer any reason to question her honesty during her previous four years of employment and should be given the benefit of the doubt. No publicity was given the incident.[76]

Arbitrator Jonathan Liebowitz, in an unpublished decision (February 24, 1986) involving the off-duty misconduct of a nurse, quoted with approval the following discussion of Arbitrator Tia Denenberg (also unpublished):

> [The right of an employer to discipline an employee for off-duty misconduct] is indeed recognized by "arbitral common law," even when the off-duty employee is away from the employer's premises. But it is a narrow exception to the rule that off-duty conduct is beyond the disciplinary powers of the employer.
>
> Discipline for off-duty conduct is typically upheld only where the employee's actions amount to such a grave offense that they impugn the employee's competence or integrity, or bring community opprobrium upon the employer. . . . The off-duty misconduct must be so serious that there is a palpable nexus to the employment relationship:

---

[72]74 LA 1293 (1980) (Doyle, Arb.).

[73]*Id.* at 1294. The agreement stated, "[e]mployer shall not discharge any employee without just cause" and "[a]n employee shall have at least two (2) written warning notices of the specific complaint against the employee before discharge except in cases of proven dishonesty. . . ." *Id.*

[74]*See also* CSX Hotels Inc., 93 LA 1037 (1989) (Zobrak, Arb.) (sustaining discharge of maintenance employee who pleaded guilty to charge of stealing 4 tires from service station near hotel, even though media reported nothing but sentence; employee demonstrated lack of trustworthiness where he had access to hotel rooms in guests' absence); Corn Belt Elec. Coop., 79 LA 1045 (1982) (O'Grady, Arb.) (discharge by electric cooperative of journeyman-lineman for "theft" of electricity); Hilton Hawaiian Village, 76 LA 347 (1981) (Tanaka, Arb.) (discharge of bellman for sale of stolen handgun); Southern Bell Tel. & Tel. Co., 75 LA 409 (1980) (Seibel, Arb.) (upholding discharge of outside repair technician for making obscene telephone calls).

[75]68 LA 1245 (1977) (Harkless, Arb.).

[76]*Id.* at 1248.

the misconduct must give ample grounds for doubting the employee's ability to perform satisfactorily while on duty. Certainly, if an off-duty nurse commits an act which gives the employer reason to doubt her trustworthiness in caring for the sick, the employer might feel compelled to discharge her. A nurse who abuses a patient, for example, while serving as an independent contractor could be deemed unfit to continue her regular employment regardless of where or when the abuse occurred.

No discipline is warranted, however, for off-duty misconduct which does not impugn the intrinsic competence or character of the employee.

Arbitrator Liebowitz applied the above principle in a case where a supervisor of nurses secured a pacifier in the mouth of a 28-day-old infant with adhesive tape. The union argued that the grievant's regular employer lacked jurisdiction to impose discipline because the grievant was not working directly for that employer at the time the infraction occurred but for an independent contractor, although on her regular employer's premises. In finding that there was a "palpable nexus to the employment relationship," the arbitrator held that the infraction does "impugn the employee's competence." In his words, "It is hard to picture a closer nexus than is present in this case; all that is lacking is employment by the Corporation itself."

Arbitrator Richard Mittenthal considered the "suitability" standard in an unpublished case (May 4, 1983) where a security officer working for a major auto manufacturer was discharged upon his arraignment for drug trafficking. The Company had two of its officers at the preliminary examination, where a judge found that the evidence was sufficient to arraign the grievant on two felony counts: possession of cocaine and marijuana "with intent to deliver." The grievant eventually pleaded guilty to a reduced charge, namely attempted possession of less than 50 grams of cocaine. Arbitrator Mittenthal quoted at length from an early General Motors–UAW Umpire decision by Ralph Seward in which Seward eloquently characterized the problem this way:

> [I]t should be emphasized that the mere fact that an event takes place off the Plant premises and outside of working hours does not necessarily deprive Management of all disciplinary authority to deal with it. Previous decisions of this Officer have already established that events outside of a Plant which have a demonstrable injurious effect upon employer-employee relationships within the Plant may rightly be the subject of disciplinary action. It is true, of course, that the right of a Corporation

to discharge or discipline for cause stems from its position and function *as an employer* and thus ordinarily extends only over actions of its employees which take place on Plant property during working hours or in the course of their employment. There are no hard and fast geographic and temporal limitations, however, upon the employer-employee relationship. It is not terminated when an employee's shift ends and he leaves the Plant. Even while sitting with his family at home he is still on the payroll and still maintains with the Corporation a series of mutual rights and obligations *which no one not* an employee possesses. The reason why the Corporation, under the Agreement, may not usually penalize him for his actions away from the Plant and on his own time is not because the Corporation is no longer his employer but because ordinarily such actions do not have a sufficiently direct effect upon the efficient performance of Plant operations to be reasonably considered good cause for discipline.

The initial judgment as to whether or not an incident occurring off its property sufficiently affects Plant operations to justify discipline must obviously be made by the Corporation. Before the Umpire, however, such judgments are not entitled to the same presumption in favor as supports its judgments concerning events within the Plant and the necessity for particular Shop Rules. Employee morale may be affected to a greater or lesser degree by all sorts of events in the surrounding community—by the private quarrels of employees, their love affairs, their illnesses, their debts, their minor or major infractions of law, their marriages, and the smooth or stormy course of their family lives. Yet the mere fact that such events have repercussions within a Plant gives Management no general right to act as guardian of its employees' morals or supervisor of their private conduct. Only in exceptional cases, where the impact upon Plant operations is shown to be clear, serious and direct, may Management intervene. And in each contested case Management must satisfy the Umpire of the reasonableness of its judgment—must show that the effect of the incident upon working relationships within the Plant was so immediate and so upsetting as to justify the abnormal extension of its disciplinary authority.

The company argued that the grievant—a long-term employee with a spotless record—was no longer suitable for employment because he held a "position of trust" with respect to the enforcement of shop rules, plant regulations, and inspections of vehicles and packages. According to the company, the drug-trafficking conviction would render him ineffective in the security area because it could no longer rely on the "honesty, integrity, and trustworthiness" of the grievant as a security guard. Noting the absence of any indication that the grievant ever brought drugs into the plant or sold drugs to employees within or outside the plant, Arbitrator Mittenthal concluded that no hard evidence demonstrated that the grievant's off-duty conduct affected in any way his performance as a security officer. In the arbitrator's view:

> The root problem here is the Company's loss of trust in [the grievant]. If that were the controlling test, then the Company could discharge any security officer whom it no longer trusted because of the commission of an off duty crime. Such a subjective test is inappropriate. The issue must be, as stated by Umpire Seward, whether the off duty misconduct has "a sufficient direct effect upon the efficient performance of Plant operations to be reasonably considered good cause for discipline." Again, to use Seward's words, the Company "must show that the effect of the incident upon working relationships in the Plant was so immediate and so upsetting as to justify the abnormal extension of its disciplinary authority." I find that the Company has not made such a showing.

The arbitrator accordingly reinstated the grievant with full seniority and back pay.

Illustrative of the view of arbitrators involving unsuitability in the protective services[77] is *City of Stamford*,[78] where a State Board of Mediation ruled that just cause existed to terminate the employment of a police officer who apparently provided his insurance company with false information on a claim for damage to his boat. What is particularly interesting is that the grievant, whose personnel file was "replete with letters of reprimand," invoked the Fifth Amendment when asked questions at the hearing about the insurance incident and, in the words of the Board, "did nothing prior to the hearing to attempt to make restitution for his actions."[79]

In general, while off-duty convictions will not always warrant a termination, especially when the employee is long-term and does not falsely report his or her situation to management,[80] arbitrators are

---

[77] See also *infra* notes 106–46 and accompanying text.

[78] 97 LA 261 (1991) (Pittocco (Chair)).

[79] *Id.* at 262.

[80] *See also* City of Springfield, 92 LA 515 (1992) (Erbs, Arb.) (ruling for grievant where off-duty conduct (theft of railroad ties) did not generate publicity and nexus to job slight); W.R. Grace & Co., 93 LA 1210 (1989) (Odom, Arb.) (no just cause for dismissal of 21-year employee for off-duty, off-premises possession with intent to sell cocaine, concluding that danger to plant's operations no greater than those in most industrial plants and management failed to prove that grievant was threat to company as potential seller of drugs to co-workers or threat to safety because of his own drug use); Lockheed Aeronautical Sys. Co., 92 LA 669 (1989) (Jewett, Arb.)

particularly receptive to the views of management when the grievant's job requires trust by the public, especially the case in the protective services.

D. Objectionability or Danger to Other Employees

In some cases an employee's off-duty misconduct will cause co-employees to refuse to work with the grievant. To what extent do arbitrators consider the objections of the grievant's co-workers in off-duty conduct cases? If, for example, the union produces statements from fellow employees that they have no objection to working with the grievant, should this evidence mitigate the employer's argument

---

(defense contractor lacked just cause to dismiss employee indicted for off-duty, off-premises sale of marijuana, absent nexus between job and off-duty conduct); Union Oil Co. of Cal., 85-1 Lab. Arb. Awards (CCH) (1985) ¶8161 (Nicholas, Arb.) (reversing dismissal of refinery pipefitter for off-duty possession of drugs); Armstrong World Indus., 85-1 Lab. Arb. Awards (CCH) ¶8004 (1984) (Aronin, Arb.) (overturning dismissal reasoning "no nexus has been established between Grievant's conviction for a conspiracy to sell cocaine and Grievant's employment relationship"); Means Servs. Co., 81 LA 1213, 1216 (1983) (Slade, Arb.) ("connection between the facts of this case [off-duty theft] and the extent to which the business is affected must be reasonable and discernible"); Nugent Sand Co., 81 LA 988, 989 (1983) (Daniel, Arb.) (reinstating employee who entered guilty plea for growing marijuana notwithstanding rule subjecting employees to discharge for "[c]onviction of a felony involving honesty, death other than negligent homicide, morals, drugs or narcotics"); Maust Transfer Co., 78 LA 780 (1982) (LaCugna, Arb.) (discharge of truck driver for dishonesty after entering guilty plea of theft reversed absent showing of causal link between conduct and ability to perform job); Ralphs Grocery Co., 77 LA 867 (1981) (Kaufman, Arb.) (reversing discharge of employees who hosted party where "lesbian show" had taken place); PRC Sys. Serv. Co., 78-2 Lab. Arb. Awards (CCH) ¶8456 (1978) (Vadakin, Arb.) (reinstating engineering illustrator discharged upon a nolo plea to charges of possession and delivery of cocaine, citing the non–work-related character of offense).

But see Trane Co., 96 LA 435, 438 (1991) (Reynolds, Arb.) (distinguishing between drug use and drug sales, concluding that management is not required to retain a "panderer in its midst"); Eagle-Picher Indus., Inc., 86-1 Lab. Arb. Awards (CCH) ¶8222 (1986) (Canestraight, Arb.) (upholding discharge of employees of company with Defense Department contracts where employees made arrangements for sale on company premises and employer had reason to believe that conduct caused cancellation of contracts); Phillip Morris U.S.A., 78-2 Lab. Arb. Awards (CCH) ¶8434 (1978) (Coburn, Arb.) (sustaining dismissal of employee for off-duty cocaine use notwithstanding plant rule that authorized discipline only when employee carried drugs on plant premises where employer consistently terminated employees for on- and off-duty possession); Arco-Polymers, Inc., 69 LA 379 (1977) (Milentz, Arb.) (heroin); Wheaton Indus., 64 LA 826 (1975) (Kerrison, Arb.) (involving "hard drugs").

that reinstatement of the grievant will cause ill feelings at the workplace? Arbitrators do consider the impact that reinstatement will have on the grievant's co-workers, although mere objections by fellow employees will rarely, if ever, be dispositive of the ultimate issue of just cause. When confronted with such a claim concerning objections of co-employees, arbitrators generally require a clear demonstration that this is true.

Refusal to work with a fellow employee may stem from an employee's conviction of a serious crime. This was the case in *Robertshaw Controls Co.*,[81] where an employee pleaded guilty to sodomy and corrupting the morals of children. The employee was a scoutmaster in the community where he worked with parents, friends, and relatives of the victimized children. Arbitrator Clair Duff restated the principle set forth in *Chicago Pneumatic Tool Co.*:[82]

> Arbitrators are reluctant to sustain discharges based on off-duty conduct of employees unless a direct relationship between off-duty conduct and employment is proved. Discretion must be exercised lest Employers become censors of community morals. However, where socially reprehensible conduct and employment duties and risks are substantially related, conviction for certain types of crimes may justify discharge.[83]

Arbitrator Duff, in sustaining the discharge, noted that the misconduct could not be kept separate from the activities of the workplace because so many families were involved. As the arbitrator stated, "[a] business enterprise by its nature requires collaboration, accord and reasonable harmony among employees. The technical and administrative sides of an enterprise cannot function correctly if the human side of the business is disrupted with conflict."[84] Arbitrator Duff reasoned that families do not want their sons to seek or retain employment in a company where they would be subjected to the possible influence of a convicted sodomist. It is of note that the arbitrator made this finding notwithstanding the fact that employees signed a statement that they had no objection to working with the grievant.

In *Lone Star Gas Co.*,[85] an employee of a public utility was indicted and later found guilty of incest. The arbitrator found it was impossible to reinstate the employee when there was testimony by

---

[81]64-2 Lab. Arb. Awards (CCH) ¶8748 (1964) (Duff, Arb.).
[82]38 LA 891, 893 (1961) (Duff, Arb.).
[83]Robertshaw Controls Co., 64-2 Lab. Arb. Awards, at ¶5613.
[84]*Id.*
[85]56 LA 1221 (1971) (Johannes, Arb.).

the grievant's fellow workers that they were reluctant to continue working with him.

The same reasoning in *Robertshaw Controls Co.*, however, was not controlling in *Kentile Floors, Inc.*,[86] where an employee was convicted of possession of narcotics (amphetamines). Even though the company had a rule stating that employees convicted of crimes were subject to discharge, the arbitrator held that the discharge was inappropriate because the conviction had no discernible effect upon the employee's relationship with fellow workers.[87] It is of special note that Arbitrator Howard Block reasoned that the employer's rule was overbroad since it failed to take into account the relationship between the crime and the employment situation. The discharge was thus seen as arbitrary and capricious.[88] Similarly, in *International Paper Co.*,[89] discharge was reversed for an employee convicted of an off-duty assault and battery against his foreman. (The employee, in an apparent argument over a woman in a tavern, had slashed his foreman with a knife.) Though the arbitrator viewed the knifing as a serious act of misconduct, he believed that it would not disrupt plant operations by creating fear among fellow employees.[90]

In another case,[91] an employee was offered $20 by co-employees to "streak" in front of a baggage terminal at the airport where he worked. The employee accepted the offer and later, wearing nothing but a ski mask, tee shirt, and cowboy boots, streaked in front of the terminal.[92] When news of the incident reached management, the employee was discharged for irresponsibility.[93] In overturning the discharge, the arbitrator reasoned, in part, that the misconduct was not viewed negatively by co-workers. In fact, because some had even encouraged it, they had little, if any, reluctance to work with the grievant.[94]

When it is believed that the off-duty misconduct poses a threat to the safety of fellow workers, however, arbitrators are not reluctant

---

[86]57 LA 919 (1971) (Block, Arb.).
[87]*Id.* at 921.
[88]*Id.* at 923.
[89]52 LA 1266 (1969) (Jenkins, Arb.).
[90]*Id.* at 1266–67.
[91]Air California, 63 LA 350 (1974) (Kaufman, Arb.).
[92]*Id.* at 351–52.
[93]*Id.* at 354.
[94]*Id.*

to sustain discharge. In *Central Packing Co.*,[95] an employee convicted for attacking his wife and mother-in-law with a knife was subsequently discharged. At work, the employee had easy access to knives, cleavers, and other instruments. Even though the employee's numerous arrests and convictions were all unrelated to work, the board of arbitration upheld discharge for the protection of other employees.

Even when the off-duty conduct does not involve acts of violence, discharges have been sustained where a showing has been made that the safety or health of workers would be threatened by reinstating the grievant. In *Martin-Marietta Aerospace, Baltimore Division*,[96] Arbitrator Louis Aronin, in sustaining a discharge upon the employer's discovery that an employee had been convicted of selling cocaine to an undercover agent, found that this conduct had an impact on the employer's product, reputation, employee safety, plant security, production, and discipline.[97] The company established that the grievant had a history of drug abuse and, at times, was even under the influence of cocaine while at work.[98] The arbitrator, concluding that the employee was a "pusher," found that the evidence established more than mere "social use" of drugs by the grievant and determined that the employer could conclude that the grievant might attempt to sell drugs to other employees.[99]

Any time management can demonstrate that there may be risk to the enterprise and its employees by similar misconduct of the grievant on the job its case is strengthened. Arbitrator Eva Robins, in an unpublished case (April 17, 1984), considered the case of a flight attendant who was charged with second-degree murder for allegedly setting fire to a house he owned jointly with his wife. His sister had been killed because of the fire. The grievant pleaded guilty to a reduced charge of voluntary manslaughter and was sentenced

---

[95]24 LA 603 (1955) (Granoff, Arb.).

[96]81 LA 695 (1983) (Aronin, Arb.).

[97]*Id.* at 696.

[98]*Id.* at 696–98.

[99]*Id.* at 698–99; *see also* New York City Health & Hosps. Corp., 76 LA 387 (1981) (Simons, Arb.) (discharge of probationary ambulance corpsman for sale of cocaine); Eastern Air Lines, 76 LA 961 (1981) (Turkus, Arb.) (discharge sustained when stewardess while at airport and in uniform sold marijuana to co-employee); Chicago Pneumatic Tool Co., 38 LA 891, 893 (1961) (Duff, Arb.) (commenting, "[d]egeneration of the addict could at any time reach a point where it would seriously endanger the health and safety of fellow employees and Company equipment").

to six years of detention suspended under prescribed conditions of probation. These conditions included a ban on narcotic drugs and alcohol consumption and submission to alcohol treatment. There was no claim of adverse publicity or other harm suffered by the employer. Because the grievant had not stopped drinking, and there was evidence of "angry incidents and uncontrolled temper," Arbitrator Robins concluded that it would not be prudent to return grievant to his job. In her words, "The risks involved are simply too great." Arbitrator Crane acted on a similar concern when he stated that he "d[id] not want to be responsible for exposing employees to a potential danger. . . ."[100]

In *Union Oil Co. of California, Beaumont Refinery,*[101] the grievant, a pipefitter apprentice, had both been arrested while on sick leave and charged with the delivery of cocaine. On June 18, 1984, she received a 10-year unadjudicated probation for possession of prohibited drugs. The probation was to be removed from her record if successfully served.[102] After the grievant returned to work, the local newspaper erroneously reported the grievant's probation as a conviction for the delivery of cocaine. This publicity prompted the company to conduct an investigation that revealed the circumstances leading to her arrest, and on July 5, 1984, the grievant was dismissed.

Sustaining the grievance, Arbitrator Samuel Nicholas asserted that in order to extend the application of management's rights outside of the workplace, there must be a nexus between the employee's conduct and the company's operations. He found the company's justification for discharge—that the grievant was a safety risk and that the company had an obligation to prevent the spread of narcotic abuse among its employees—problematic because the company's focus was

---

[100]See unpublished case discussed *supra* this Chapter I.A.2. Injury to the Company's Reputation.

[101]85-1 Lab. Arb. Awards (CCH) ¶8161 (1985) (Nicholas, Arb.).

[102]One problem often encountered by labor-management practitioners is what an employee should do when confronted with the question on an employment application, "Have you ever been convicted of a crime?" Suppose an employee was convicted as a youth, but told by the court that if he stayed out of trouble for one year, the conviction would be expunged from his record. Can management dismiss the employee for executing a false employment application if it later learns of the conviction? After all, the application did not ask for convictions that were not expunged! The topic of false employment applications is discussed *infra* notes 277–304 and accompanying text.

on the employee's future conduct as opposed to her past misconduct. Citing Judge Learned Hand, the arbitrator stated that the risk to the company can be expressed in the following equation: "Total risk equals the *probability* of the occurrence of the hazard weighed with the *severity* of the hazard."[103] One point in the grievant's favor, said the arbitrator, is that she received an unadjudicated probation with heavy penalties facing her should she again become involved in a narcotics offense. The arbitrator also concluded that the grievant's reinstatement would not increase the chance of other employees being exposed to drugs.

In general, where co-employee concerns are at issue arbitrators will uphold discharge if management demonstrates that the safety of other workers is endangered by reinstatement. A clear showing that co-employees have already refused to work with the grievant will generally be sufficient to sustain a discharge, although there are exceptions. Evidence that employees will not work with the grievant if reinstated has also been credited by arbitrators.[104] Still, the better rule is that just cause should not be determined just on a popularity vote. The grievant may be helped, however, if co-employees come forth and declare that they have no objections to working with the employee.[105]

II. APPLICATION TO PUBLIC SECTOR

In the public sector, discharge for off-duty lifestyle infirmities may be restricted by contractual,[106] statutory,[107] or even constitutional

---

[103]Union Oil, 85-1 Lab. Arb. Awards, at 3674.

[104]Advocates have routinely conducted opinion polls in support of their clients. For example, in an unpublished case reported by Arbitrator Benjamin Aaron, discussed *supra* this chapter I.A.1., Actual or Potential Business Loss, the grievant submitted the following question to a random sample of flight attendants: "Would you be willing to work with a male flight attendant who had solicited for money an undercover police officer for sex and had been arrested, charged with the offense and paid a $72.00 fine?"

[105]*See, e.g.,* Virgin Islands Dep't of Health, 97 LA 500, 503 (1991) (Watkins, Arb.) (noting that more than 100 employees, a majority of whom were women, signed petitions in favor of a male hospital security guard who pleaded guilty to unlawful sexual contact with a female driver in the course of a second job).

[106]*See, e.g.,* City of Okmulgee, 91 LA 259, 260 (1988) (Harr, Arb.) (sustaining

mandates.[108] In general, just cause precedents and standards established by private sector labor arbitrators have also been applied in the public sector, although in off-duty cases there appears to be a greater sensitivity (relative to the private sector employer) to the criteria of the reputation and mission of the employer (state, local, or federal government) on the part of both arbitrators and courts. It may accordingly be easier for the public employer to sustain a dismissal based on off-duty infirmities where arbitrators recognize and credit "public trust" considerations as a major part of a nexus requirement.[109]

As in the private sector, the overriding principle in the public sector is that discipline for off-duty conduct is appropriate only when

---

dismissal for assistant fire chief for "conduct unbecoming an officer" because of work in recreational center that sold beer and featured topless dancers, where employer's work rule prohibited "working in or owning a bar, a night club, a lounge, a liquor store or other establishments that might discredit a member of the Fire Department").

[107]5 U.S.C. §7513(a) (1988) of the Civil Service Reform Act of 1978 permits removal of an employee "only for such cause as will promote the efficiency of the service." To dismiss a federal employee for off-duty conduct the government must make at least 2 separate determinations: (1) did the employee commit the act(s) allegedly responsible for his removal; and (2) is there a nexus between the employee's misconduct and the efficiency of the service. Cooper v. United States, 639 F.2d 727, 729 (1980). The Merit Systems Protection Board (MSPB) has, at times, interpreted §7513(a) to mean that, where the misconduct is egregious, a nexus is presumed. Abrams v. Department of the Navy, 714 F.2d 1219, 1221 (3d Cir. 1983) ("employee may rebut this presumption by showing an absence of adverse effect upon the efficiency of the service, thereby shifting the burden of going forward with evidence to the agency to establish, by a preponderance of the evidence, a nexus between the off-duty misconduct and the efficiency of the service"); Borsari v. FAA, 699 F.2d 106 (2d Cir. 1983), *cert denied,* 464 U.S. 833 (1983); Masino v. United States, 589 F.2d 1048 (1978). Note, however, that not all courts have embraced the MSPB's application of a "presumption of a nexus."

[108]See *supra* Chapter 4.

[109]*See, e.g.,* Borough of Baldwin, 95 LA 851, 853 (1990) (Duff, Arb.) (upholding dismissal of laborer on basis of conviction for possession and sale of marijuana to a minor, "even though it is conceded that the nexus between the sale of marijuana to a minor and the duties the Grievant performed as a Laborer is attenuated"); Westlake City School Dist., 94 LA 373, 376 (1990) (Graham, Arb.) (sustaining discharge of high school vice-principal's secretary upon grand-theft plea in connection with receipt of automobile illegally diverted from new-car dealer, where incident was widely publicized, secretary had contact with students, and state law requiring teacher convicted of felony to surrender teaching certificate demonstrates high standard expected of school personnel, stating that "the Employer's reputation must be above reproach" and "the good name of the District would be called into question by continued employment of the Grievant").

such conduct has a *demonstrable* adverse effect upon the employer's business or the overall employment relationship. Illustrative is *United States Internal Revenue Service*,[110] in which two male employees were suspended for "mooning" a woman in a parking garage. While discharge was not involved, the reasoning and analysis articulated by Arbitrator Samuel Edes are consistent with holdings of arbitrators in private sector discharge cases.

> [The] applicable standard to be applied in judging the conduct of employees in public service takes into realistic account the fallible nature of the human condition which results, with substantial frequency, in conduct which is less than exemplary by commandment of both moral and legal codes. It recognizes, quite properly, that, however much an employer may be wont to enforce such codes and condemn their transgression, [the employer] is entitled to do so only to the degree that there is a direct and demonstrable relationship between the illicit conduct and the performance of the employee's job or the job of others.[111]

Arbitrator Edes further noted that because one employee's off-duty actions may be subject to disciplinary penalty and another's may not, determination of the propriety of disciplinary penalty can only be made on a case-by-case basis.[112] Furthermore, an employer's power to discipline is restricted even where misconduct results in substantial embarrassment to the employer. In discussing this aspect, he commented that "[i]t is not unworthy of an employer to hope that all of his employees conduct themselves in a manner which . . . is above suspicion . . . [the employer] can only exercise his authority in respect to conduct which affects the work of his employees and, accordingly, the efficiency of his enterprise."[113]

The declarations by Arbitrator Edes highlight a principle used by many arbitrators in regard to off-duty misconduct. Again, arbitrators generally look for a nexus between the conduct of the employee and the employment setting. Absent a nexus, the discipline is overturned.

A paradigm case in the public sector is *United States Customs Service*,[114] in which Arbitrator Joseph Rocha considered the discharge

---

[110]77 LA 19 (1981) (Edes, Arb.).
[111]*Id.* at 21–22.
[112]*Id.* at 23.
[113]*Id.* at 22.
[114]77 LA 1113 (1981) (Rocha, Arb.).

of a customs inspector for homosexual behavior. In holding that the agency did not have just cause to effect the termination, the arbitrator focused on the grievant's off-duty private conduct and the grievant's on-the-job activities:

> If any fact has been firmly established by the evidence, it is that the grievant separated his homosexual practices from his activities as a Customs Inspector. He succeeded so well in this respect that no one associated with his employment knew of his homosexuality until he was discharged. Also critical is the fact that no traveler ever complained about [grievant] for any valid reason. Certainly, [grievant's] homosexual behavior did not manifest itself in any way that resulted in notoriety or public censure which would reflect unfavorably on Customs. . . .[115]

Customs relied for precedent on a 1970 "sanitized" case arising in Buffalo in which a Customs Inspector was discharged because he had been arrested and convicted for engaging in homosexual conduct in a public toilet.[116] That case is easily distinguished. In the 1970 case, the homosexual activity occurred in a public place; the arrest and conviction became a matter of public record. As a consequence, Customs was identified with notoriety and public censure and was exposed to an erosion of public confidence. The arbitrator found these elements absent from the 1981 case.[117]

This nexus requirement was again applied in *Social Security Administration*,[118] where an arbitrator was forced to determine if a nexus existed between an employee's conviction for sexual offenses against a minor, for which he served a six-month sentence, and his employment with satisfactory performance as a clerk-typist. The arbitrator was particularly concerned with possible adverse public reaction, for which the employer offered no supporting evidence. In overturning the discharge, the arbitrator held that, absent any demonstrable loss of public confidence in the employer, there could be no impairment in the efficiency of the agency.[119] His reasoning is cited at length:

> Under 5 U.S.C. §7701(c) (1) (B) [of the Civil Service Reform Act], Management has the burden of proof under the preponderance of

---

[115]*Id.* at 1114–15.
[116]*Id.* at 116–17.
[117]*Id.* at 1117 [footnote omitted].
[118]80 LA 725 (1983) (Lubic, Arb.).
[119]*Id.* at 726–27.

evidence test. In this respect, the Agency has a two-fold burden. It must first prove that a wrongful act has occurred and then that the discharge for the wrongful act would promote the Agency's efficiency. Since the Grievant's removal, as stated aforesaid, was based upon two actions, the sexual offense and impeding the operations of the SSA, they will be discussed separately. The sexual offense will be considered first.

Although H_____ denied in his testimony that he committed the sexual offense as charged, a copy of his conviction was entered into the record. Copies of court records are acceptable evidence and may be received by an arbitrator as such. *Maroon v. Immigration and Naturalization Service,* 364 F.2d 982 (8th Cir. 1966), *U.S. v. Verlinsky,* 459 F.2d 1085 (5th Cir. 1972). Thus Management has met its burden in proving the commission of a wrongful act by the Grievant.

It next must be determined whether, due to the Grievant's wrongful act, his removal from employment will promote efficiency of the SSA. This must be accomplished by proving a logical connection (nexus) between H_____'s off-duty misconduct and his employment with SSA. As stated in *Doe v. Hampton,* 566 F.2d 265, 272 (D.C. Cir. 1977),

> [T]here must be a clear and direct relationship demonstrated between the articulated grounds for an adverse personnel action and either the employee's ability to accomplish his or her duties satisfactorily or some other legitimate government interest promoting the efficiency of the service.

Although, in the case of "certain egregious circumstances a presumption of nexus may arise from the nature and gravity of the misconduct" *(Merritt v. Department of Justice,* MSPB Docket No. PH075209058 (1981)) the Agency specifically states that it does not intend to rely upon any such presumption. Thus the SSA must directly prove by a preponderance of evidence the nexus between the Grievant's off-duty sexual activities and [their effect] upon the efficiency of the service.

The testimony by various supervisors of H_____ upon which the Agency relies for this purpose, involved the concern for disabled employees, as well as student aides, working around the Grievant, the effect of disclosure and possible contact work with the public and the possibility that H_____ could become a physical threat. All of this is speculative. In order to engage in public contact work the Grievant would have to be transferred to a field office which under the circumstances appears highly unlikely. The fact that H_____ has made sexual advances to minors does not necessarily imply that he would while on duty attempt to engage in similar activities with disabled employees or student aides, especially since nothing even slightly similar to this has occurred over the past eight years. There was also no evidence that the public was even aware of H_____'s conviction. Thus the foregoing evidence is not sufficient to prove the necessary nexus.[120]

Referring further to federal law, the arbitrator concluded:

> As reprehensible as H_____'s misconduct is to this Arbitrator, I must hold that the recent decision of the Court of Appeals in *Bonet v. United States Postal Service,* 661 F.2d 1071 (5th Cir. 1981) is controlling in this matter. The employee in that case appealed from a decision of the Merit Systems Protection Board affirming his discharge from his job with the Post Office for alleged grossly immoral and indecent off-duty conduct with a child. As stated therein:
>
> > The Agency cannot satisfy the statutory requirement that an employee's removal promote the efficiency of the service by use of unsupported, general assertions that such action is necessary to maintain the public confidence. To permit otherwise would be to render nugatory the protections afforded the federal employee by the imposition of a standard for removal which requires a connection between employee misconduct (especially when off-duty and non-work related) and the job. The agency must demonstrate, therefore, a relationship between this employee's misconduct and the specter that *public confidence will be undermined.* (emphasis added)
> >
> > Despite our reflective revulsion for the type of off-duty misconduct in question, whether resulting from a now-cured mental disability or not, the 1978 (Civil Service Reform) Act does not permit this court nor an employing agency to characterize off-duty conduct as so obnoxious as to show, per se, a nexus between it and the efficiency of the service. The 1978 Act prohibits the discharge of a federal employee for conduct that does not adversely affect the performance of that employee or his co-employees. . . .

Although the Agency attempts to differentiate Bonet on the grounds that the employee in that matter was not actually convicted of a crime as here and that the employer therein relied solely upon the grossly immoral nature of the off-duty conduct as establishing a nexus per se, this argument is specious to say the least. The Bonet decision appears to be on all fours with the facts in the present matter and just because the criminal indictment against the employee therein was dismissed due to the unwillingness of the mother of the child to prosecute, this should not control the reliance thereon. Other than proof of the commission of the subject sexual act, the Agency here has failed to

---

[120]*Id.* [citations omitted] (quoting Doe v. Hampton, 566 F.2d 265, 272 (D.C. Cir. 1977), quoting Merritt v. Department of Justice, MSPB Docket No. PH075209058 (1981)).

prove any relationship between that act and the undermining of public confidence.[121]

Similarly, the arbitrator in *City of Wilkes-Barre*[122] refused to allow discharge of a blue-collar employee who pleaded guilty to possession of drugs. In so ruling, the arbitrator examined the employee's job performance, possible injury to the city's image and reputation, and the existence of a drug problem among other city employees.[123] In all three instances, the arbitrator concluded there was no evidence that indicated any injury to the employer.[124]

Goddard Space Flight Center[125] highlights the procedural rights that government must accord its employees with respect to dismissals for off-duty behavior. In *Goddard* an electrician pleaded guilty to one count of off-duty possession of cocaine with intent to distribute. He paid a $5,000 fine and received a suspended prison sentence. Approximately six months later the employee, in response to a request for information, informed the agency of his conviction. The employee was subsequently removed from the service for the off-duty criminal misconduct. After issuing a letter of removal, the agency conducted a further investigation and a report was generated linking the grievant to a "drug culture." Arbitrator Arthur Berkeley ruled that since the division chief's letter of proposed removal cited only facts relating to the grievant's arrest, charges, and disposition of the criminal case, *without mention of a nexus between the off-duty cocaine guilty plea and employment,* the dismissal should be reversed.[126] Referring to the *Merritt* decision,[127] Arbitrator Berkeley applied a hard nexus requirement. Citing *Merritt,* the arbitrator declared that " 'a nexus determination must be based on evidence linking the employee's off-

---

[121]*Id.* at 728–29 [footnotes omitted] (citing and quoting Bonet v. United States Postal Serv., 661 F.2d 1071, 108 LRRM 3158 (5th Cir. 1981) (alteration in original)).

[122]74 LA 33 (1980) (Dunn, Arb.).

[123]*Id.* at 34–36.

[124]*See also* County of Cass, 79 LA 686 (1982) (Gallagher, Arb.) (discharge of deputy sheriffs after their illegal taking of game fish held improper absent showing of direct threat to security of employer); Cuyahoga County Welfare Dep't, 76 LA 729 (1981) (Siegal, Arb.) (discharge improper for county clerical worker who, while away from work on her own time, swore and threatened assistant supervisor).

[125]91 LA 1105 (1988) (Berkeley, Arb.).

[126]Id. at 1112.

[127]Merritt v. Department of Justice, MSPB Docket No. PH075209058 (1981), discussed *supra* note 120 and accompanying text.

duty misconduct with the efficiency of the service or, in 'certain egregious circumstances,' on a presumption of nexus which may arise from the nature and gravity of the misconduct.' "[128] There was no obvious nexus in the Goddard case, and accordingly, it was improper for the agency to effect the dismissal based on a postdischarge report alleging grievant's connection to a "drug culture," a report that was not available until after the proposed removal. Also of note, the arbitrator ruled inadmissible testimony from one of grievant's co-workers that grievant introduced him to cocaine use and together they tried the drug frequently because the information came to light well after the decision to terminate the grievant was made.[129] The arbitrator reasoned that "[o]ne cannot seek to bulwark a decision by subsequent events or matters which come to light after the decision has been made."[130] Even if credible, the co-employee's testimony was inadmissible.

Arbitrator Louis Imundo, in *Lucas County Commissioners*,[131] reversed the dismissal of an agent (project inspector) of the county sanitary engineer for "failure of good behavior and immoral conduct." Finding a total lack of due process by the employer, the arbitrator pointed out that the grievant was dismissed before he entered a nolo plea to charges of dissemination of harmful materials to juveniles. Arbitrator Imundo ruled that the no contest plea could be admitted in evidence, although he conceded that it was not an admission of guilt. In the arbitrator's words, "failure [to admit the plea] could have disastrous consequences," especially for government organizations that "have to be more sensitive to the communities' reactions to employee conduct than private sector organizations."[132] Declaring that the "heavy burden" becomes "even heavier when the employee charged with criminal misconduct pleads no contest,"[133] management was required to prove any one or possibly some combination of the following:

> The Grievant's misconduct significantly damaged the County Sanitary Engineer Department's image, reputation, or ability to effectively conduct its business in the community.

---

[128]Goddard at 1110.
[129]*Id.* at 1112.
[130]*Id.*
[131]91-2 Lab. Arb. Awards (CCH) ¶5269 (1991) (Imundo, Arb.).
[132]*Id.* at 5275.
[133]*Id.*

The Grievant's misconduct was so repugnant, or so reprehensible that a substantial number of the Grievant's co-workers find it incredibly difficult or impossible to effectively conduct [the Department's] business in the community.

The Grievant in carrying out his normal job duties poses a serious risk to the safety and welfare of others, i.e., customers, employees, the community at large, for which serious adverse consequences could result.

The Grievant's misconduct has rendered him incapable of being able to perform his regular or customary job duties in a satisfactory manner, or appear at work.

The Grievant's reinstatement would pose a grave risk for his physical safety, and Management cannot in any way, take prudent steps to keep him from serious physical harm.[134]

Unable to demonstrate any relationship between disseminating harmful material to juveniles and the employee's job (the arbitrator pointed out that most of the time the grievant worked alone and did not come in contact with children),[135] the employee was reinstated with full seniority and benefits.

However, in *Commonwealth of Pennsylvania*,[136] discharge was sustained for a state liquor store employee for "conduct unbecoming a State employee."[137] In that case, the employee fatally injured a 71-year-old woman who asked him to stop beating his wife. News of the incident was widely reported in the media, which prompted his termination.[138] In recognizing that an employer may take appropriate disciplinary action when off-duty misconduct affects or is likely to affect the employment relationship, the arbitrator concluded that the publicity would cause fellow workers to fear the grievant and make customers hesitant to deal with him.[139]

Discharge was also justified for a police officer in *City of Taylor*.[140] The officer gave drugs to a female citizen who was also an informant

---

[134]*Id.* at 5275.

[135]*Id.* at 5276.

[136]65 LA 280 (1975) (Stonehouse, Arb.).

[137]*Id.* at 281.

[138]*Id.* at 282–83.

[139]*See also* Polk County, 80 LA 639 (1983) (Madden, Arb.) (suspension proper for correctional facility counselor whose duties included administering breathalyzer tests after grievant entered guilty plea to charge of operating vehicle while intoxicated); New York Div. of Criminal Justice Servs., 79 LA 65 (1982) (Sabghir, Arb.) (upholding discharge of senior identification clerk in division of criminal justice services for sale of methadone to undercover police officer).

[140]65 LA 147 (1975) (Keefe, Arb.).

for the city. The arbitrator determined that the incident would negatively reflect upon the police force and would further give rise to the distinct possibility of adverse publicity against the city and lowered police force morale.[141] Arbitrator Calvin Sharpe, in *State of Ohio*,[142] similarly sustained the dismissal of a state trooper convicted of driving under the influence following an off-duty accident. Concluding that management established a "nexus," Arbitrator Sharpe found persuasive that television and newspaper comments attended the grievant's arrest, conviction, and sentence. In response to the union's argument that the state must do more than produce newspaper articles to show that the grievant's conduct impaired the ability of the Highway Patrol to carry out its mission, Sharpe noted that "an actual adverse impact of employee off-duty conduct need not be shown in order to establish the proper nexus."[143] Police officers who sell cocaine in their spare time can look forward to a similar fate.[144] The same may not be said for mere marijuana possession.[145]

In a decision with far-reaching implications for individuals with tax problems, Arbitrator Peter Feuille, in *Lawrenceville Unit School District No. 20 and William McCullogh*, an unpublished (November 3, 1987) decision, sustained the dismissal of a tenured teacher who had been indicted, arrested, and incarcerated for three misdemeanor counts of income tax evasion. In sustaining the dismissal, the arbitrator reasoned that the teacher attempted the functional equivalent of renouncing his citizenship by claiming that the federal and state government had no authority over him. He also noted that the teacher was hospitalized for psychological evaluation and treatment and that "most of the events were widely publicized in the community." Indeed, "there was considerable awareness of the Teacher's behaviors among students, teachers, administrators, Board members, and parents. . . . Further, the Teacher offered no persuasive evidence to show that

---

[141]*Id.* at 149–50.

[142]94 LA 533 (1990) (Sharpe, Arb.).

[143]*Id.* at 538.

[144]City of Miami, 92 LA 175 (1989) (Abrams, Arb.) (sustaining discharge, ruling that results of polygraph test voluntarily taken by accused police officer admissible in determining credibility of witness).

[145]U.S. Penitentiary, 96 LA 126 (1990) (Hendrix, Arb.) (removal of federal corrections officer arrested for off-duty possession of marijuana in violation of agency's code of conduct excessive; discharge converted to 30-day suspension and reinstatement to former position).

the media reporting of his conduct was noticeably inaccurate." The emphasis of the arbitrator was that the teacher could not be an effective role model for students "because he can no longer credibly teach or demonstrate such virtues as honesty and patriotism."[146]

III. EMPLOYER ACTIONS PRIOR TO TRIAL

Employers sometimes take action against an employee after they learn about the employee's arrest and/or indictment for the kind of off-duty offenses that they believe would justify discharge before an arbitrator. When is a pretrial suspension or discharge justified if the employer has no independent evidence of guilt other than the mere fact of arrest or indictment? If the employer suspends without pay and the employee is acquitted, is the employer ever obligated to make the employee whole, even though management believes that the employee is guilty and has independent evidence of guilt? If the employer permits the employee to work for several months pending the outcome of the criminal proceeding, and the employee's work record remains a good one, does this weaken management's case if the employee is found guilty? And what effect should appeals have? Sometimes there are pertinent contract provisions or published employer policies in this area. The collective bargaining agreements with the United States Postal Service, for example, provide for immediate suspension when the employer "has reasonable cause to believe an employee is guilty of a crime for which a sentence of imprisonment can be imposed." The State of Illinois provides for the revocation of a teaching certificate upon conviction of a felony. Most of the time, however, the complexities in the area are resolved by arbitrators.

Arbitrator Marvin Feldman, in *Louisville Gas & Electric Co.*,[147] ruled proper the indefinite suspension of a utility worker after he

---

[146]*See also* Las Vegas Bldg. Materials, Inc., 83 LA 998 (1984) (Richman, Arb.) (sustaining discharge for employee who, as part of organized tax protest claimed 14 dependents, had wages garnished by IRS); Shawnee Plastics, 71 LA 832 (1978) (Goldstein, Arb.) (sustaining discharge for 2 instances of garnishment, holding Consumer Credit Protection Act not applicable). *But see* Delta Concrete Prod. Co., 71 LA 538 (1978) (Bailey, Arb.) (ordering reinstatement where garnishments resulted from debts grievant co-signed).

[147]85-1 Lab. Arb. Awards (CCH) ¶8018 (1984) (Feldman, Arb.).

was charged with a murder that was not connected with his employment. The grievant was also advised that "the Company does not consider incarceration as a legitimate reason for requesting a personal leave of absence."[148] He was later convicted of manslaughter and then discharged, but the arbitration concerned only the validity of the indefinite suspension prior to conviction. Feldman found that "an allegation and arrest for a serious crime may well trigger immediate discipline. . . . If that were not so, then, in the event the Company would be unable to maintain safety for its employees for which it is charged."[149]

In an unpublished decision by Arbitrator Mark Kahn (December 2, 1983), a flight attendant with five years of service was suspended on November 9, 1981, pending the outcome of a trial (scheduled for January 25, 1982) for the sale of cocaine to an undercover police officer. In January 1982, prior to that trial, the company learned that the grievant had pleaded guilty on April 13, 1978, to the offense of "sale of marijuana" and had been sentenced to a jail term of two and one-half years. Execution of this sentence was stayed, however, in favor of a comparable period of probation and a fine of $1,500. The grievant had lost no work time because of these events and the company was not aware, until January 1982, that they had occurred. The company decided to dismiss the grievant on January 21, 1982, on the basis of the 1978 marijuana conviction.

Two grievances were filed, one challenging the January 1982, dismissal based on the 1978 conviction, and one alleging that the November 1981 suspension, based solely on the indictment, was improper. As to the former, Arbitrator Kahn found "that the substantial passage of time involved, during which grievant's job performance was satisfactory and the Company suffered no detriment of any kind because of the 1978 conviction, would militate against the termination of grievant's employment in January 1982." Kahn pointed out that the grievant had functioned satisfactorily as a flight attendant before and after the marijuana conviction and concluded: "There is no evidence of any kind of nexus between grievant's illegal conduct in 1978 and his employment as a Flight Attendant."

The arbitrator also ruled, however, that it was permissible for the company to remove the grievant from flight status in November

---

[148]*Id.*
[149]*Id.* at 3081.

of 1981 pending the outcome of his cocaine trial. The allegations were found to be serious, and, in the words of Kahn, "[such] allegations provided a reasonable basis for a Company decision that grievant should not be on duty until the criminal charges against him were decided by a court."

In an unpublished decision (December 1991), Arbitrator Marvin Hill, Jr., ruled that a public utility (a telephone company) could suspend an employee, charged with delivery of a controlled substance (cocaine) to an undercover agent, pending the outcome of the criminal proceeding. Arbitrator Hill found that "case law indicates that management can suspend an employee for a reasonable period of time pending the outcome of a criminal proceeding when a nexus is established, although there are arbitrators who rule to the contrary." Hill did note that management must conduct some kind of independent investigation indicating that there is reason to believe that the employee is guilty of wrongdoing. Hill reasoned that the grievant worked in customer homes and businesses without supervision and drove a company vehicle. The grievant was also able to monitor communications including police communications. Hill stated that "it is not unreasonable that management would not want to turn over its service cables and switching systems to an employee currently under a state attorney's information (the equivalent of an indictment) for cocaine distribution." Finally, Hill pointed out that at issue "is not the legal concept of 'innocent until proven guilty' but, rather, the Company's ability to protect its reputation, business interests, and the public safety and welfare of its workforce."

In *Trane Company*,[150] Arbitrator James Reynolds recognized drug misconduct as an important exception to the general rule that an employee's activities while off-duty are outside of the employer's legitimate concerns. Arbitrator Reynolds stated that "[t]he Employer has the duty to attempt to protect its employees from the individual who would sell them illicit drugs for profit"[151] and that "[t]here is no basis for the position that the Employer should be tolerant of such a panderer in its midst. . . ."[152] Similarly, in *C & A Wallcoverings, Inc.*,[153] Arbitrator Avins upheld the dismissal of an employee initially

---

[150]96 LA 435 (1991) (Reynolds, Arb.).
[151]*Id.* at 438.
[152]*Id.*
[153]90-1 Lab. Arb. Awards (CCH) ¶8110 (1990) (Avins, Arb.).

charged with possession of cocaine with the intent to deliver, even though the incident took place off company premises and the employer could not show specific proof of injury to its image or production. Arbitrator Avins stated that "[d]rug vendors are commonly considered a menace to society, and the company's desire to eliminate an employee it reasonably fears is one is understandable."[154]

In *Brown & Williamson Tobacco Co.*,[155] Arbitrator Pearce Davis rejected the legitimacy of a company rule which called for immediate suspension without pay for any employee arrested for a serious off-duty crime. Arbitrator Davis ruled that suspension solely on the basis of indictment is contrary to the basic tenets of our code of justice. Further, in *General Portland Cement Co.*,[156] Arbitrator Leonard Davidson held that absent proof that the company or any of its employees have been or would be damaged or that the employees's ability to do his work would be impaired, the suspension of the employee following a criminal charge for possession of narcotics violated the employee's rights under the collective bargaining agreement.

Where the employer's rule authorized discharge only for "conviction," Arbitrator Jonathan Dworkin ruled that the City of Cleveland improperly discharged a construction superintendent who had been indicted, but not yet tried, under the federal Racketeer Influenced and Corrupt Organizations Act for gambling, where reports of his conduct did not threaten public confidence and the city's treatment of employees under indictment was inconsistent.[157] The arbitrator rejected the argument that the indictment alone placed the employee within the scope of the city's rule that an employee's tenure may be canceled for "failure of good behavior which is detrimental to good service."[158] Similarly, in *Clair Pendar Co.*,[159] Arbitrator Robert Burke held that the employer did not have the right to place an employee on indefinite, unpaid suspension while he awaited trial on the charge of second-degree murder of his wife. Arbitrator Burke's caution against equating an arrest with a finding of guilt is applicable in most situations facing arbitrators.

---

[154]*Id.*
[155]62 LA 1211 (1974) (Davis, Arb.).
[156]62 LA 377 (1974) (Davidson, Arb.).
[157]City of Cleveland, 91 LA 265 (1988) (Dworkin, Arb.).
[158]*Id.* at 269.
[159]63 LA 173 (1974) (Burke, Arb.).

In *Florida Power & Light Co.*,[160] Arbitrator Fred Kindig ruled that management had just cause for suspending an employee after the company learned of his arrest and indictment for possession of illegal firearms, despite the grievant's excellent work record. The arbitrator pointed out, however, that the grievant was not in a public relations job or directly involved with the company's customers. Rather, the employee worked in a plant with other employees. Similarly, in *Pearl Brewing Co.*,[161] Arbitrator Robert Howard held that management was justified in imposing an indefinite suspension pending the outcome of criminal proceedings for burglary and assault with intent to rape. While Arbitrator Howard recognized that the accused is presumed to be innocent until proven guilty, he nevertheless ruled that management may suspend when the criminal charges against the employee could reasonably be expected to affect the employer's affairs. In *Group Cable, Inc.*,[162] Arbitrator Joseph Chandler upheld a limited suspension for an employee who admitted to being in a company vehicle used to transport cocaine. What is particularly interesting in that case is the arbitrator's discussion of how long management can effect a suspension. In the arbitrator's words:

> There is basis for a brief indeterminate and summary suspension when an investigation is required to determine the facts which may lead to discipline and any mitigation thereof. Two major issues are those of how lengthy a disciplinary action delay is permissible and the potential court proceedings and the relationship of those proceedings to the Company based discipline. In *Air France* [71 LA 1113, 1116 (1978) (Turkus, Arb.)] the arbitrator stated[:]
>
>> . . . [T]he question then, of whether the suspension of the Grievant was proper, is to be answered in the affirmative . . . however . . . a suspension is a temporary act only, and at some point it must end by either reinstatement of the employee or his termination. To decide whether an employee has been unjustly dealt with the Board must necessarily consider the indefinite suspension as part of an overall discipline, including its underlying basis. . . .

In *Indiana Bell Telephone*,[163] Arbitrator Elliott Goldstein ruled that just cause existed for a suspension, but not discharge (criminal charges were subsequently dismissed), for an employee's off-duty

---

[160]88 LA 1136 (1987) (Kindig, Arb.).
[161]48 LA 379 (1967) (Howard, Arb.).
[162]80 LA 205 (1983) (Chandler, Arb.).
[163]93 LA 981 (1989) (Goldstein, Arb.).

drug arrest, reasoning that the employer has the right to protect its business from the adverse effects arising from public accusation and arrest. The grievant was awarded back pay from the point of his discharge, but not during his suspension. In that decision the employer produced the testimony of the undercover agent and the grievant's tape-recorded conversation concerning receipt of marijuana. The arbitrator concluded that the evidence record provided clear and convincing proof that the grievant was, to some extent, involved in illegal drug activity.

A case particularly relevant to the resolution of back pay grievances relating to suspensions is *Electrical Refractors Co.*[164] In that decision the arbitrator ruled that management may suspend an employee accused of criminal conduct without liability for back pay if: (a) the employee is subsequently found guilty or pleads guilty, or (b) even if guilt is not subsequently established, if (1) the suspected criminal conduct is of a nature which carries with it a serious threat to the safety or welfare of the business enterprise, including employees and customers, and (2) the circumstances are promptly and carefully investigated in a fair and impartial manner, and (3) the results of the investigation are as such to persuade reasonable minds, acting in good faith but not necessarily skilled in the law, that the employee is guilty and may continue or repeat his criminal acts.

IV. GUILTY AND NOLO PLEAS VERSUS CONVICTIONS AFTER TRIAL

Should a guilty plea have preclusive effect in a subsequent arbitration even though the issue of guilt had never been litigated? Is a guilty plea more than an ordinary admission? If management has a rule establishing immediate termination for off-duty possession of illegal drugs resulting in a criminal conviction and the court accepts the grievant's guilty plea, has the employee been "convicted" under the rule?[165] What about a "nolo" plea? Should it be considered the

---

[164]77-4695 Lab. Arb. Awards (CCH) ¶8397 (1977) (Strasshofer, Arb.).
[165]*See* Washington Area Transit Auth., 94 LA 1172 (1990) (Garrett, Chair) (holding that management's rule violated when court accepted grievant's guilty plea, even though judgment was stayed and grievant eligible for expungement of criminal record).

same as a guilty plea?[166] Professor Allen Vestal has argued that in a subsequent civil action a plea of guilty, at least in a serious crime, should normally be preclusive against the person who entered the plea, unless that person could show that, when the plea was entered, there was no opportunity or incentive to litigate the matter.[167] Black letter law on the matter provides that preclusion applies only when the issue is "actually litigated and determined by a final and valid judgment."[168] Those who argue that a guilty plea should not have preclusive effect point out that there is a difference between a conviction following an adversary trial and a plea of guilty. Others have submitted that a guilty plea should carry more weight than a conviction because it constitutes a solemn admission of the elements of the crime in open court and the Constitution requires that a guilty plea is made voluntarily. Moreover, many jurisdictions require an independent factual basis for all guilty pleas. Still, guilty and nolo pleas are often the product of plea bargains and their reliability can be subject to question.[169]

Our review of the cases suggests that some arbitrators have been reluctant to consider going behind a guilty plea. For example, Arbitrator John Sembower, in *Northwest Airlines and Transport Workers Union,*[170] wrote:

> Although the grievant testified that he pleaded guilty only upon advice of an attorney that it would be the easiest way out of a not-too-serious charge and the way to obtain a suspended sentence, it is not

---

[166]In City of Shawnee, 91 LA 93, 99 (1988) (Allen, Jr., Arb.). Arbitrator A. Dale Allen, Jr., had this to say regarding nolo pleas:

> Acting on advice of legal counsel, [grievant] plead "nolo contendere" to a charge of second degree manslaughter. Ballentine's Law Dictionary defines "nolo contendere" as:
>
> > Literally, "I do not wish to contend." Substantially, though not technically, a plea of guilty; an implied confession. . . . It is difficult to define the exact nature of a plea of nolo contendere . . . the plea for practical purposes is a plea of guilty.
>
> Assuredly, the undersigned will not attempt to assess the degree of guilt of [grievant] in the boating accident. The court undoubtedly had better and more complete evidence than was presented to the undersigned.

[167]Allen Vestal, *The Restatement (Second) of Judgments: A Modest Dissent,* 60 CORNELL L. REV. 464, 471, 478–83 (1981).

[168]RESTATEMENT (SECOND) OF JUDGMENTS §27 (1982).

[169]*See, e.g,* Means Servs., Inc., 81 LA 1213, 1216 (1983) (Slade, Arb.), where the arbitrator, in reinstating an employee for an off-duty theft, concluded that the grievant's guilty plea may have been the result of a plea bargain.

[170]69-2 Lab. Arb. Awards (CCH) ¶8867 (1969) (Sembower, Arb.).

possible to go behind such a plea. Unfortunately quite a few defendants appear to be counselled thus, and as a consequence have seriously blemished records, for in 14 American Jurisprudence 952, Criminal Law, 272 "Force and Effect of Plea," it is bluntly stated:

> A plea of guilty accepted and entered by the court is a conviction of the highest order. . . .[171]

It does not appear to be disputed that a guilty plea should be admitted by the arbitrator as valid evidence against the grievant. It is, after all, an admission against interest and should be accorded whatever weight is justified.[172] The authors believe, however, that the arbitrator should also accept evidence pertaining to the circumstances surrounding the plea. There can be a difference between legal guilt and guilt in fact. An individual may not be guilty of the precise crime to which he or she had pleaded but, in fact, of a lesser or greater crime. Arbitrator David Feller has stated that, when admitting into evidence a nolo or guilty plea, he would recognize that "many times people plead guilty in a plea bargain when they really think they are innocent" and that he would therefore "allow the grievant to explain her plea if she wanted to."[173]

An example of going beyond a guilty plea and considering the overall evidence record is *Nugent Sand Co.*,[174] a case reported by Arbitrator William Daniel. The grievant entered a plea of guilty to the felony of manufacture of a controlled substance (grievant apparently had been growing a substantial amount of marijuana in his backyard). Rejecting the company's argument that the plea constituted a conviction that automatically justified his termination under the company's rules, Arbitrator Daniel reasoned that the grievant, in deciding to enter a plea, relied upon assurances from the company's vice president that he would not be fired over the matter, although the arbitrator found that the record did not support the assertion that it was the promise of the vice president that caused the grievant to act in this respect.[175] The arbitrator reduced the discharge

---

[171]*Id.* at ¶5944.

[172]*See, e.g.,* Department of Air Force, 74 LA 949 (1980) (Ward, Arb.); Washington Area Transit Auth., 94 LA 1172 (1990) (Garrett (Chair)).

[173]ARBITRATION 1982: CONDUCT OF THE HEARING, PROC. OF THE 35TH ANN. MEETING, NAT'L ACADEMY OF ARBITRATORS 119 (eds. James Stern and Barbara Dennis 1983).

[174]81 LA 988 (1983) (Daniel, Arb.).

[175]*Id.* at 992.

penalty to reinstatement without back pay and without any seniority credit for the time that the grievant was off work.

While we agree with the proposition that an arbitrator can accept a nolo plea into evidence and give it what weight it deserves, we are unsure what weight it does deserve. Moreover, in the event that an arbitration hearing is considered a civil proceeding, state statutes may preclude introduction and use of the plea by the arbitrator.[176]

V. EXPUNGEMENT OF CRIMINAL RECORDS

What about a grievant who satisfies all the requirements for expungement of his or her criminal record prior to the arbitration? An employee who has a conviction expunged has no safe harbor if management elects to proceed with discipline and the evidence record otherwise supports the penalty. Illustrative of the thinking of arbitrators is *U.S. Air, Inc.,*[177] a decision reported by Arbitrator Robert Ables. The grievant, a flight attendant, was convicted of purchasing 20 tablets of Percocet (a "narcotic" whose effects are similar to heroin and cocaine) from an undercover police detective and placed on probation for 30 days. Completing the probation, no judgment was entered, the criminal proceeding was dismissed, and the grievant's record expunged.[178] One month later, the company terminated the grievant because he had been found guilty of possession of a controlled narcotic substance. In sustaining the dismissal, Arbitrator Ables reasoned that the company's work rules allowed discharge for serious misdemeanors, the employee did not use the employer's employee assistance program, and the current grand jury and Federal Aviation Administration investigations into drug use by airline employees created a sufficient "nexus"[179] between the off-duty conviction and

---

[176]*See* U.S. Postal Serv., 89 LA 495, 499 (1987) (Nolan, Arb.) (noting that "[i]n return for making possible a speedy disposition of the charge, the accused who pleads nolo contendre gets the protection of an evidentiary rule banning admission of the plea in subsequent civil proceedings, a rule applicable both to federal and to Florida courts").

[177]91 LA 6 (1988) (Ables, Arb.).

[178]*Id.* at 7.

[179]In the arbitrator's words, "This is the buzz word on the question whether

the company's business. Whatever nexus was required was supplied the prosecuting attorney when he called company officials to report the arrest and pending trial of the grievant. In the arbitrator's words, "He did so, according to reports from security officials, because: 'I fly US Air.' "[180] The expungement of grievant's record did not work to salvage his employment.[181] Other arbitrators have similarly concluded that an expunged conviction carries little weight in a grievance arbitration.[182]

VI. PROBATION AND WORK RELEASE PROGRAMS

Does management have an obligation to cooperate with a prison work release program or with a probation officer who is anxious to have the grievant gainfully employed? Do arbitrators have any obligation to reinstate when the judicial system sees fit to order probation (as opposed to jail) for the grievant? An affirmative view was expressed by Arbitrator Florian Bartosic in an unpublished decision: "There is substantial authority for the proposition that a grant of probation by a court 'represents a determination that Grievant is a safe and useful member of society with the assistance of the probation department.' "[183] Accordingly, in reinstating a flight attendant who had entered a plea of guilty to committing forgery involving the use of stolen credit cards, the arbitrator focused on the treatment of the grievant by the court:

> Here, the Court granted Grievant's request to participate in a work release program to serve his 30-day confinement [which grievant was unable to do because of his prior discharge] and placed him on probation for the remainder of his sentence. Thus, not only did the court conclude ‗

---

bad, off duty, conduct reflects badly on the employer, sufficient to hurt its business significantly." *Id.* at 8.

[180]*Id.* at 9.

[181]*See also* Transit Mgmt. of Sw. La., 95 LA 74 (1990) (Allen, Jr.) (holding company improperly withdrew offer of reinstatement where 20-year driver changed plea from guilty to not guilty citing, among other considerations, that grievant satisfied conditions of reinstatement and conviction of theft was expunged by court).

[182]See cases cited *infra* note 313 and accompanying text.

[183]Citing Linde Co., 37 LA 1040, 1043 (1962) (Wyckoff, Arb.).

that the Grievant was a safe and useful member of society; the Court concluded that the grievant was particularly safe and useful to the Company. This determination was presumptively based upon a comprehensive investigation conducted by the probation department, which recommended grievant for the work release program. Under these circumstances, to sustain the Company's decision to discharge grievant would, in effect, be at odds with the court's decision. Like the Court, the Board of Adjustment is of the view that the Grievant is capable of making a valuable contribution to the Company.

Of particular interest was the arbitrator's reasoning in regard to the question of back pay.

> For the Board to order reinstatement yet deny back pay would require the Board to assume logically incompatible positions, namely (1) absent a connection between an employee's off-duty misconduct and the employment relationship, no discipline may be imposed and (2) despite the fact that no such connection exists, the misconduct warrants discipline.

Arbitrator Bartosic, accordingly, concluded that the grievant should be reinstated and made whole for "all wages and benefits that he would have received but for the discharge."

Arbitrator John C. Shearer reinstated the young employee of a chemical plant who had been discharged in connection with a guilty plea to the misdemeanor of marijuana possession. His offense had been off-duty and did not involve other employees. The grievant had been fined $500 and sentenced to two years on probation, with the understanding that if he met the terms of the probation the conviction would be expunged from his record. In crediting the results of the court the arbitrator commented:

> It was clearly the intention of the court *not* to brand Grievant as a convicted criminal if he successfully met the terms and conditions of his probation and paid the $500 fine. The court thereby clearly sought to protect society while at the same time protecting Grievant against the stigma and its consequences, such as reduced unemployment opportunities, which often accompany criminal conviction. Although the manner in which a court may handle a case does not necessarily determine what an employer may do in disciplining an employee for the same offense, in the present set of circumstances the Company's considerable emphasis on the "criminal conviction" as the main reason for the discharge is largely invalidated by the court's decision. . . .[184]

---

[184]Vulcan Materials Co., 56 LA 469, 473 (1971) (Shearer, Arb.).

As noted in *Union Oil,* Arbitrator Samuel Nicholas regarded the fact that the grievant had been sentenced to an unadjudicated probation, during which she faced heavy penalties should she again become involved in another narcotics offense, as "one point which runs in Grievant's favor."[185]

Arbitrator A. Dale Allen, Jr., in *City of Shawnee,* [186] found that a critical factor weighing in favor of a firefighter's reinstatement was the court's relatively lenient sentence, in this case 160 hours of community service, a directive to stay out of a boat for two years, and a sentence of two days and one night in jail. The grievant had entered a nolo plea to second-degree manslaughter arising from a boating accident involving the death of a passenger in another boat. He could have been sentenced to four years in prison. Arbitrator Allen found it persuasive that the court did not consider grievant a "menace to society." The arbitrator converted the dismissal to a 90-day unpaid suspension.

Suppose an employee, having been convicted of an off-duty criminal offense, agrees to a sentence which includes a probationary release program to which the employer was not consulted. After the sentence the grievant, since discharged, notifies management and expects it to participate in the agreement he made with the court. Must management honor the agreement? In *Brockway Pressed Metals,*[187] Arbitrator Len Mayer ruled that a manufacturer of metal parts in a small community was required to reinstate a 22-year employee convicted of delivery of a controlled substance. Applying a nexus requirement, Arbitrator Mayer reasoned that the employee's conduct was on his own time and off premises, the conduct did not adversely affect the employer's business or its employees (the union pointed out that a majority of employees voted to take the case to arbitration), the act at issue did not constitute a violation of the parties' collective bargaining agreement or the company's work rules, and the employee had a good work record. The neutral rejected the company's argument that, as a government contractor, management was obligated to run a drug-free workplace, and having a known deliverer of drugs in its

---

[185]Union Oil Co., 85-1 Lab. Arb. Awards, at ¶3674, discussed *supra* notes 101–103 and accompanying text.
[186]91 LA 92 (1988) (Allen, Jr., Arb.).
[187]98 LA 1211 (1992) (Mayer, Arb.).

employ could possibly cause the company to lose future orders. The arbitrator denied any back pay (but granted other benefits including seniority) because the grievant did not secure management's consent to a work release program prior to an agreement with the court. In the words of the arbitrator: "To do so [grant back pay] would be tantamount to a fine on the Employer for a circumstance over which it had no control."[188]

Case law in this area indicates that if an employee is placed on probation it does not necessarily mean that a dismissal was improper. It is clear, however, that probational status, including work release programs, merits consideration by the arbitrator as an element in determining whether just cause did exist.

VII. EMPLOYEE LOYALTY

One aspect of employee misconduct involves employee "loyalty," often demanded by management of its employees.[189] The thoughts of Arbitrator Edgar Jones, Jr., in the often-cited *Los Angeles Herald-Examiner* decision, reflect the complexity of formulating a useful definition of loyalty:

> "Loyalty" is indeed a nebulous psychological phenomenon. As a state of mind, it varies widely both among individuals, in their capacity to experience it, and again, in relation to the nature of the various groups with which a particular individual has significant contact—his family, his country, his community, his church, his schools, his friends, his employer, his clubs and professional associations. Because it is so individual a matter it would be impossible to exhaust all the various clusters of interests and people with which in some way each of us forms social contact and generates aspects of attachment and support which may properly be describable as "loyalty."[190]

---

[188]*Id.* at 1215.

[189]This section is taken, in part, from MARVIN F. HILL, JR., & ANTHONY V. SINICROPI, MANAGEMENT RIGHTS: A LEGAL AND ARBITRAL ANALYSIS 234–54 (BNA Books, 1986). *See generally* Howard G. Foster, *Disloyalty to the Employer: A Study of Arbitration Awards,* 20 ARB. J. 157 ("any attempt to fit disloyalty cases into a unified theoretical framework is destined for futility" *Id.* at 167).

[190]Los Angeles Herald-Examiner, 49 LA 453, 464 (1967) (Jones, Jr., Arb.).

Loyalty is more than a state of mind. Similar to the legal concept of negligence, loyalty concerns conduct. Arbitrator Jones recognized this when he went on to argue that a "legally cognizable duty" to act in a loyal fashion may arise in the employer-employee relationship which "must certainly be reckoned as an important aspect of the common enterprise." In the words of Jones, "[a]s marked out in decisions in cases in which an employee has been disciplined or terminated for allegedly violating it, it is a practical command subject to a rule of reason."[191] Another arbitrator put it this way: "The duty of loyalty is inherent in every employer-employee relationship."[192]

Although loyalty defies precise definition, its parameters in the context of off-duty considerations may be revealed through the following problem areas: (1) competing with the company; (2) maintaining or failing to disclose a conflict of interest; and (3) making injurious remarks against an employer.[193] In general, arbitrators who conclude that an employee's actions either impact the company's business or have the potential to do so, will sustain some form of discipline, although many arbitrators may require that management publish a rule or policy regarding the employee's outside interests.[194]

A. Competing With the Company

Holding another job while working for an employer, commonly known as "moonlighting," does not by itself constitute employee misconduct. In fact, many collective bargaining agreements specifically provide unit employees with the right to hold a second job free of punishment. However, when the nature of an employee's outside interests closely resembles the work done by the primary employer, an employee's loyalty can be questioned, especially where the

---

[191]*Id.* at 464.

[192]Swift-Eckrich Inc., 98 LA 361 (1991) (Wolff, Arb.).

[193]One arbitrator, deciding a case involving competition with the company, observed that in the literature these cases fall under general categories known as "conduct away from the plant," "employee loyalty," "moonlighting," "conflict of interest" and "impairment of customer relations." Brauer Supply Co., 97 LA 526 (1991) (Cipolla, Arb.).

[194]Continental Tel. Co., 86 LA 274, 281 (1985) (Rothschild, Arb.) ("it is quite clear from the cases cited by the Company that Grievant's knowledge that he is violating a rule is a condition precedent to discharge").

employer has a limited customer base and depends upon repetitive business from those customers.[195] An employee's work performance may not suffer, but employees with divided interests are suspect. Similar to most off-duty cases, the element that arbitrators find most significant is the economic impact on the primary employer. For example, Arbitrator James Stern, in *Phillips Brothers, Inc.*[196] upheld the discharge of a cigarette salesman who, while working for a cigarette wholesaler on a commission basis, had been running his own vending machine company that also supplied cigarettes. Arbitrator Stern found that so long as the grievant refused to terminate his closely related activities that caused economic harm to the company, the legitimate business interests of the employer compelled dismissal.[197]

Similarly, in *Jacksonville Shipyards, Inc.*,[198] Arbitrator Richard Taylor sustained the discharge of two hourly paid supervisors who had started a company to do ship-decking work. The employees were found to have violated a rule that prohibited "[d]isloyalty to the Government or law, the Company, the foreman or other supervisor."[199] The grievants apparently formed a company in competition with the employer and contracted to perform work for a competitor that had been the successful bidder on work their employer had lost in the bidding process. Further, the grievants were actively soliciting decking jobs from among the employer's customers.[200]

In *City of Rockville*,[201] a city plumber, who had been doing plumbing work on his own time (but without a required license), was reinstated by an arbitrator, despite work rules prohibiting outside work. Arbitrator Levitan found that the employee had not been warned and, furthermore, other employees who had violated the city's rules regarding outside employment and working without licenses

---

[195]*See, e.g.,* Brauer Supply Co., 97 LA 526 (1991) (Cipolla, Arb.) (supply company rule prohibiting employees from working for companies or operating businesses that install heating and air conditioning equipment reasonable where rule narrow in scope and allowed employees to purchase and install equipment for themselves, other employees, or immediate families).

[196]63 LA 328 (1974) (Stern, Arb.).

[197]*Id.* at 331.

[198]74 LA 1066 (1980) (Taylor, Arb.).

[199]*Id.* at 1067.

[200]*But see* Heinrich Motors, Inc., 68 LA 1224 (1977) (Hildebrand, Arb.) (soliciting business in employer's paint shop on employee's own behalf).

[201]76 LA 140 (1981) (Levitan, Arb.).

were reinstated after a period of suspension. Arbitrator Richard Kanner, in *Northern Rebuilders Co.*,[202] reversed the dismissal of an employee terminated both for competing with his employer (both grievant and his employer were in the business of remanufacturing or overhauling automobile engines) and for refusing to answer questions about his outside activities. Arbitrator Kanner, while recognizing that some types of misconduct (insubordination, theft, drinking on the job) do not require notice before termination can be imposed, agreed with the union's defense that the company had no rule prohibiting competition by employees and, for this reason, the grievant should be returned to work. The arbitrator's reasoning with respect to off-duty conduct and notice to the employee is particularly instructive:

> In my view, grievant's conduct in arguably competing with the Company falls within the purview of the category of rules which must be clearly articulated by the Company to the employees.
>
> It is well recognized, as a general proposition, that off-duty conduct such as inebriation, theft, etc. cannot be the basis for employer discipline. The only exception is where it can be clearly shown by the employer that the employee's off-duty conduct directly and derogatorily affects his working relationship with fellow employees, the employer's reputation, and/or with his ability to perform his job. . . .
>
> The Employer asserts that the element of loyalty is inherent in grievant's work relationship. Accordingly, since direct competition impacts on the financial health of the Employer, such conduct should be well understood by grievant as leading to discipline and even discharge without the necessity of the Employer promulgating a specific rule. But I am cited on arbitration authority standing for such proposition. To the contrary, the predominant arbitral precedent, with which I agree, supports the principle that there must be notice to employees of a specific rule prohibiting competition. As stated in *American Broadcasting Company*, 86 LA 1073 (1986):
>
>> The relationship of employer and employee is one of mutual trust and confidence. An employer in consideration of these duties and obligations which he owes to the employee is entitled to the assurance that the employee will not engage in interests damaging to the enterprise. The good faith that is implicit in and is an articulate premise of every contract, guaranties [sic] that. Such reasonable an assurance does not need expression in the contract. In its absence, it is reasonable and proper for an employer to promulgate a rule or regulation prohibiting 'conflict' of interest activities. Lacking any general rule, an employee may find other

---

[202]96 LA 1 (1991) (Kanner, Arb.).

appropriate means of bringing it home that his outside activities on behalf of a competing employer are detrimental to the enterprise and inconsistent with his duties as an employee.[203]

Arbitrator Kanner determined that "[t]he above quote denotes that a clear rule proscribing competition is required."[204]

With respect to the insubordination charge, the arbitrator reasoned that "where an employee violates a clear work-related rule, he has a duty to cooperate with the employer to the extent of answering questions relative to the violation."[205] In such a case, however, no back pay should be awarded because, in the arbitrator's eyes, the employer should not be penalized by an award of back pay by the employee's failure to answer questions. According to Arbitrator Kanner, "[t]he rationale underlying such principle is that, at least arguably, the employer might not have discharged the employee if he had cooperated and given the employer his version of the facts in dispute."[206] Where there is no rule, the no back pay principle for refusing to cooperate is not applicable because "in such a case the employee has no duty to answer questions of the employer since these questions do not pertain to any work-related rule violation."[207]

In *Country Club Markets,*[208] Arbitrator Mario Bognanno held that a retail meat store properly imposed an indefinite suspension of meat department managers who opened their own retail meat store, even though the employer had no written rule prohibiting this conduct. Rejecting the Union's argument that the lack of a rule prohibiting the grievants' conduct precluded the suspension, Arbitrator Bognanno reasoned that all employees implicitly agree not to compete with the employer and, as such, a written rule or provision is unnecessary. In the arbitrator's words:

> Within the employment relationship the quid pro quo for employment and subsequent wages is the duty of loyalty and an agreement not to compete with the Employer's business. These obligations are, in the opinion of the undersigned, so fundamental to the employment relationship that they need not be expressly stated.[209]

---

[203]*Id.* at 4.
[204]*Id.*
[205]*Id.*
[206]*Id.*
[207]*Id.*
[208]85 LA 286 (1985) (Bognanno, Arb.).
[209]*Id.* at 289. *See also* United Grocers Inc., 93 LA 1289 (1990) (Snow, Arb.)

While the arbitrator agreed with the general proposition that disloyalty or conflicting interests must be demonstrated with concrete or empirical evidence, he nevertheless reasoned that at some point the evidence must be evaluated on a subjective basis. Arbitrator Bognanno determined that it would be hard for the grievants to give full performance in the employer's meat departments while operating their own business.

One issue frequently litigated in the arbitration forum is the ability of an employee to keep working a second part-time or full-time job when the job is interfering with the employee's performance of, or attendance at, his primary job. In *Mercoid Corp.*,[210] an employee was charged with working a second job during his sick leave. The grievant had been working this job weekends for several years with the employer's knowledge. Arbitrator Sinclair Kossoff stated the general proposition on moonlighting as follows:

> Where, however, there is no rule against dual employment and the employee involved has held the second job for many years without its interfering with production or efficiency in any way, there is no reason to fear that an employee on a legitimate leave of absence, obtained without deceit, is abusing that leave by continuing on his second job during the period of his leave. This is especially true where the second job is a part-time job, performed only on weekends, and during hours when the employee would not be scheduled to work on his regular job.[211]

In *Aluminum Foundries, Inc.*,[212] an employee, while making an emergency trip to pick up a part, went out of his way to stop by a competitive foundry to inquire about position openings. In sustaining the discharge, Arbitrator Marshall Seidman focused, in part, on the lack of loyalty of the grievant:

> It seems to me that an employee who believes that he can take paid premium time off from his employer's business to engage in personal business, particularly when the main purpose of that business is to seek employment from a competitor of his employer, does not have either that sense of loyalty or understanding of the American economic system to continue in the employ of his employer.[213]

(holding that just cause existed to suspend employee under exception to progressive discipline requirements for "serious" misconduct when employee wrote letter containing vicious, unprovoked personal attacks, abusive language, and unjust criticisms of management).

[210]63 LA 941 (1974) (Kossoff, Arb.).

[211]*Id.* at 945.

[212]82 LA 1259 (1984) (Seidman, Arb.).

[213]*Id.* at 1261.

A final consideration in the area of competition and moonlighting concerns soliciting business from among an employer's customers. In *Dispatch Services, Inc.*,[214] Arbitrator Arthur Matten sustained the discharge of an employee who was charged with giving his employer's customers proposals dealing with the costs and viability of setting up their own dispatching offices. The purpose of this proposal was to enable these customers to cease using the grievant's employer. Further, the grievant had apparently recommended himself for the position of department head of the new office for one customer. While recognizing that it is perfectly acceptable for an employee to seek other employment, Arbitrator Matten found the grievant went beyond this. His reasoning is particularly instructive:

> In every contractual relationship, and employment is a contractual relationship, there is a "reasonable person" understanding as to what each party may expect from the other party. . . .
> When an individual agrees to accept employment, he knows there will be rewards in wages and fringe benefits in return for his properly carrying out his job duties. His efforts are necessary so the employer can meet its business responsibilities to customers and clients. If the employee does not perform well, he *indirectly* can cause the employer to fail.
> An employee is also responsible for his actions which may *directly* harm the employer. When an employee has contacts with a customer or customers, proposing that they can do without the services of the employer, his actions are a *direct* threat and detriment.[215]

In a similar case, *Arroyo Foods*,[216] an arbitrator upheld the discharge of a grievant who had been soliciting business for a competitor. The grievant had taken a trip to San Diego, which he claimed to be for pleasure only. Management later discovered he went with a friend, a sales manager for a competitive firm, and visited several long-standing customers of Arroyo, arguably to solicit business. In sustaining the discharge Arbitrator Melvin Darrow concluded that the grievant had been disloyal to his employer by soliciting for his friend

---

[214]67 LA 632 (1976) (Matten, Arb.).
[215]*Id.* at 634 (emphasis in original). *See also* Monarch Mach. Tool Co., 82 LA 880, 883 (1984) (Schedler, Arb.), where the arbitrator upheld the 20-day suspension of a grievant who wrote "America Builds Junk" on the bottom of a newspaper clipping displayed on a company bulletin board. Arbitrator Schedler stated: "The Grievant had a duty to do his job well and support the Company's efforts to remain a competitor in the machine tool industry. . . . In my opinion, the disparaging comment was malicious and almost reached the point of a disloyal act."
[216]67 LA 985 (1976) (Darrow, Arb.).

business that normally would have gone to grievant's employer. The arbitrator commented that "such an act tends to injure the interests of the employer and cannot be excused as an act of friendship."[217]

In *Quality Building Maintenance*,[218] an employee began seeking other employment following an incident that he believed resulted in his discharge. In the course of his search he solicited customers of his soon-to-be ex-employer. When the original incident, a meeting concerning his performance, did not result in discharge, the employer nevertheless discharged him for an act of disloyalty—recruiting customers from among the employer's customers. Arbitrator George Heliker found that the grievant had every reason to believe that he had been discharged, and therefore "was justified in seeking work anyplace he could find it, including with customers of his about-to-be ex-employer."[219]

B. Conflicts of Interest

Conflict of interest cases concern an employee's duty to avoid or disclose any actual or possible conflict of interest with the employer's business. In *Swift-Eckrich Inc.*,[220] the employer determined that a conflict of interest arises "when an employee for some reason feels an obligation or has a personal interest, which preclude[s] his ability to make objective decisions in the Company's interest." One part of the policy prohibited employees from engaging in personal business relationships with individuals or concerns with whom they do business, or with competitors of the company. The employee, a packaged meat salesman with several outside interests, purchased a 5,000-square-foot grocery store that was on his route. The store had averaged $250 to $300 in purchases of Eckrich products prior to the grievant's purchase. Purchases increased to more than $600 a week after the sale. Finding no evidence that the grievant violated a specific rule concerning the operation of his route, and that the grievant was a loyal and industrious employee for 22 years with an exemplary attendance

---

[217]*Id.* at 988.
[218]80 LA 302 (1983) (Heliker, Arb.).
[219]*Id.* at 315.
[220]98 LA 361 (1992) (Wolff, Arb.).

record, Arbitrator Aaron Wolff reversed the dismissal. The arbitrator also reasoned that there was no specific language in the company's conflict-of-interest policy that declares that a salesman may not own a grocery store or that such a relationship automatically gives rise to a conflict of interest. What is especially noteworthy is that after his discharge grievant bought a second store which was not then purchasing his former employer's products. After grievant bought the store he dropped the competitor's products and began buying the company's products. The arbitrator found that it showed that "Grievant's bent was to aid, not harm the company, even after it had fired him." More important, at his store, the grievant did not purchase meat from a competitor of the company. In the arbitrator's words, "[s]uch conduct on Grievant's part, if engaged in, would amount to disloyal acts which would sustain disciplinary action even if the Company did not have a [conflict of interest policy]."[221]

Often arbitrators find that it is not the conflict itself that results in discipline. Rather, it is the failure to disclose the conflict of interest, or to divest the interest when warned that it gives rise to some form of punishment. In an illustrative case, *University of California*,[222] Arbitrator Marshall Ross held that discharge was "reasonable" for an employee who had failed to disclose a conflict of interest to the university. The grievant, in charge of arranging video taping of workshops at the university, contracted with a firm in which her husband (under a fictitious name) has a substantial financial interest. At no time did she reveal this relationship to management. In upholding the discharge, Arbitrator Ross stated that it was not unreasonable for management to conclude that the employee knew her conduct was improper and that her failure to disclose her husband's involvement constituted an act of disloyalty to her employer. The arbitrator rejected the grievant's argument that she should not be disciplined because she had no prior notice of rules or policy on the matter at issue.

> Common sense dictates knowledge [that] there is "something improper about an employee participating in an action that makes it possible for an outside concern to do business with an employer and for an employee to obtain personal gain from that transaction without the employer's knowledge."[223]

---

[221]*Id.* at 367.

[222]78 LA 1032 (1982) (Ross, Arb.).

[223]*Id.* at 1037 (quoting the grievant). *See also* United States Medical Center,

The conflict of interest problem surfaced in *New York Post Corp.*,[224] a decision involving a sportswriter whose job was to pick favorites for horse races. The sportswriter, through an arrangement with one of the stable owners, became part-owner of a horse. Although the employee refrained from picking favorites when his horse was racing, management still believed that a substantial conflict of interest was present since horses of the same stable ran in other races. Arbitrator Milton Friedman rejected the writer's argument that he was above being influenced towards picking horses from his horse's stable. Arbitrator Friedman reasoned that conflicts, or apparent conflicts of interest, should be judged using a "reasonable person" standard, that is, a "standard of conduct which may properly be demanded of *everyone,* those of weaker moral fiber—or potentially weaker moral fiber—as well as those who may be generally regarded as possessing unimpeachable virtue."[225]

Arbitrator Richard Calhoon, in *Great Atlantic & Pacific Tea Co.*,[226] found that a conflict of interest must be proven before discipline can be sustained. The grievant, a butcher for A&P, was suspended following the discovery that he was teaching his son how to cut meat in the son's butcher shop. Since his son's shop also sold meat on a retail basis, management believed that a conflict of interest existed. Arbitrator Calhoon held otherwise. Finding that a conflict "is difficult to determine, contingent as it is on both the nature and volume of outside activities in relation to the principle occupation," the arbitrator determined that no effect on either job performance or competition with A&P was shown.[227]

C. Denigrating the Employer

The basic issue involved in an employee's denigrating his employer was summarized by Arbitrator Calvin McCoy, who asked,

---

80-1 Lab. Arb. Awards (CCH) ¶8134 (1980) (Bothwell, Arb.), where the arbitrator found that a correctional officer violated prison rules regarding contact with the families of inmates when he failed to inform management that he was renting a house to the divorced wife and son of an inmate.

[224]62 LA 225 (1973) (Friedman, Arb.).

[225]*Id.* at 226–27 (emphasis in original).

[226]75 LA 640 (1980) (Calhoon, Arb.).

[227]*Id.* at 641–42. *See also* Airport Ground Transp., 58 LA 1296 (1972) (Rohman,

"Can you bite the hand that feeds you, and insist on staying for future banquets?"[228] Reflecting the better weight of arbitral authority, Arbitrator McCoy answered the question in the negative. Arbitrator Robert Ables stated the rule this way:

> [I]t is in the fabric of American institutions, including the workplace, that if an employee, bargaining unit or not, effectively declares war against his employer about how the employer is conducting his business, he must do it from outside his job. . . . A certain loyalty to the employer must be presumed.[229]

Arbitrators uniformly hold that employees cannot make false, malicious, or disparaging remarks about their employers or their employers' products. As stated by another arbitrator, "As a general rule, injurious remarks against an employer that damage the employer's image or adversely affect employee discipline or morale are grounds for discharge or substantial discipline."[230] There is also indication that a significant consideration is whether the employer is in the public domain. To this effect Arbitrator David Borland, in *City of Charlotte*,[231] declared:

> Employers and employees in the public sector always have had expectations thrust upon them by society, because they are entrusted with particularly sensitive, personal situations. Even though such employers and employees often feel that such expectations are unjust, American society expects its police, teachers, and even custodians of mental health patients, among other groups, to exhibit strong and exemplary models of sensitive behavior to the inconsistencies among the people they serve.[232]

In the cited case, Arbitrator Borland upheld the discipline of a public works employee who at a City Council meeting stated that the City Manager told "a total lie" regarding the grievant's dissatisfaction with the replacement of his driveway during construction by the department.

Arbitrator Robert Johnson, in *San Diego Gas & Electric Co.*,[233] upheld a utility's issuance of a written reprimand for an employee

---

Arb.); Albertsons, Inc., 65 LA 1042 (1975) (Christopher, Arb.); Department of Justice, 72 LA 1095 (1979) (Kossoff, Arb.).

[228]Forest City Publishing Co., 58 LA 773, 783 (1972) (McCoy, Arb.).

[229]United Press Int'l Inc., 94 LA 841 (1990) (Ables, Arb.).

[230]United Grocers Inc., 93 LA 1289 (1990) (Snow, Arb.).

[231]97 LA 1065 (1991) (Borland, Arb.).

[232]*Id.* at 1072, quoting Michigan Dep't of Mental Health, 82 LA 1306, 1311 (1984) (Borland, Arb.).

[233]83 LA 1039 (1983) (Johnson, Arb.).

who had written a letter, containing substantial falsehoods, to a local newspaper opposed to the use of nuclear power. Arbitrator Johnson reaffirmed that the employment relationship imposes responsibilities on both the employer and employee. One obligation is loyalty to the employee's place of employment. It is of note that the arbitrator found inapplicable the grievant's argument that his conduct was protected by the First Amendment, correctly stating that "the right to be free of government interference does not extend to a private company."[234] Similarly, Arbitrator Edgar Jones, Jr., in *Los Angeles Herald-Examiner*,[235] upheld the discharge of a general assignment reporter for what Jones termed a "breach of his duty of loyalty to his employer." The facts are especially interesting. The grievant resigned due to an action of the newspaper he believed to be unethical. For modesty's sake the paper airbrushed the penis off the Infant Jesus in a reprint of a painting, Veronese's *Holy Family*, that was to be shown on the front page. In seeking other employment, the employee explained his reasons for leaving the *Herald* to a competitor, which made a headline story of the disclosure. As a consequence, the *Herald* discharged him immediately, before the end of his two-week notice period. The grievant then attempted to rescind his resignation. Arbitrator Jones let stand the original resignation and, further, ruled that during this two-week period the grievant was not released from his duty of loyalty to the company. Arbitrator Jones reasoned as follows:

> When Grievant tendered his written resignation on December 27 he gave two weeks' notice, agreeably to his employer, assuring himself a financial cushion while he found another job. During that time, he remained on the payroll, was entitled to all the benefits of an employee, and was subject to the normal duties of any employee. Included in that latter category throughout his employment, in those last few days as much as in his first days on the job, was his obligation to do his best to act or refrain from acting so as to enhance rather than to endanger the best interests of his employer. This is the duty of loyalty.[236]

An interesting aspect of releasing negative information is whether arbitrators recognize constitutional-type rights of employees to speak

---

[234]*Id.* at 1041.

[235]49 LA 453 (1967) (Jones, Jr., Arb.).

[236]*Id.* at 463–64. *See also* Forest City Publishing Co., 58 LA 773 (1972) (McCoy, Arb.); General Elec. Co., 40 LA 1126 (1963) (Davy, Arb.) (union business agent guilty of "indisputable disloyalty" for publishing article stating that employer was "insisting on bad parts" in production of military orders).

freely about their employers.[237] In *Washoe County*,[238] a county employee made public to the local elected board of health his views concerning public management and his employer's venereal disease program. He was subsequently dismissed, allegedly for making these statements to the board and the media. Arbitrator Patrick Boner, stating that the resolution of the grievance depended upon the balancing of the "free speech" rights of the employee and the right of the employer to conduct its business in an orderly fashion, ruled that the public statements were not sufficient to sustain the discharge under a just cause standard.

Arbitrator Leo Weiss, in *City of Los Angeles, Harbor Dept.*,[239] reports a decision involving a senior accountant suspended for writing a letter to a newspaper referring to the head of his employment group as "the head inquisitor for his section." Arbitrator Weiss reasoned that the grievant was not free to write such a letter under the ordinances and regulations of the City (the Employee Manual provided that "[n]o employee shall publicly disparage the Department, its policies or its personnel"). Applying a First Amendment analysis, the arbitrator ruled that calling the grievant's chief financial officer and his principal manager "the head inquisitor" does not rise to the level of "legitimate public concern" that was involved in the U.S. Supreme Court's *Pickering* and *Connick* decisions.

In *Town of Plainville*,[240] a public works employee was discharged for writing an anonymous letter to a town councilman. The grievant, who had admitted authorship, had charged the town with misappropriating tools, in this case a "rototiller." Arbitrator Howard Sacks, acting as a panel chairman, defined the issue as "whether a public-sector employee can be disciplined if his whistle-blowing proves to be mistaken." Balancing the interests of the employer with the rights of expression of the employee, Arbitrator Sacks applied the following standards:

> [W]e have formulated a set of standards for judging whistle blowing in the public sector. Our aim has been to balance the competing interests of employee and employer, and to give appropriate attention to the

---

[237]See *supra* Chapter 4 notes 107–66 and accompanying text.
[238]75 LA 1033 (1980) (Boner, Arb.).
[239]84 LA 860 (1985) (Weiss, Arb.).
[240]77 LA 161 (1981) (Sacks, Arb.).

public's interest in bringing to light instances of suspecting official wrongdoing or mismanagement.

1. The significance of the activity exposed by the act of whistleblowing. The more important such interest, the greater the protection that ought to be afforded the whistleblower. Compare the communication of information about (1) illegal acts; (2) the investment of municipal pension funds in corporations doing business in South Africa; and (3) a projected reorganization of a six-person clerical unit in a recreation department that would reduce the whistleblower's responsibilities.

2. The employee's motives in becoming a whistleblower. Are they purely personal, e.g. to protect or advance his own career? Or are they directed toward vindicating the public's interest in preventing fraud, waste or criminal activity?

3. Whether the information given by the employee is true, and if not, the employee's "state of mind" regarding the truth of such information. Thus, if it turns out the employee is mistaken, did he have reasonable grounds for believing the truth of his charges? Or was he guilty of knowing use of false information or of reckless indifference to the truth of such information? In this regard, we prefer the standard established by the Civil Service Reform Act, "reasonable belief," to the somewhat lower standard enunciated in *Pickering [Pickering v. Board of Education,* 391 U.S. 563 (1968)], any state of mind other than "knowledge of falsity or reckless disregard for truth or falsity of the information."

4. The means chosen by the employee to communicate his information or allegations. Ordinarily, internal channels should first be used, unless there are good reasons for not using them, such as a reasonable belief that his superiors will do a poor or dishonest job of investigating the matter. If special channels for whistleblowers are established, . . . the employee should use this channel. If the circumstances justify going outside of regular channels, does the employee write his legislator or the prosecutor, or does he arrange a media event? If he attempts to maintain his anonymity, is there a good reason for it, such as a legitimate fear of employer reprisal?

5. The potential or actual harm to the employer caused by the whistleblowing. Harm can take several forms: creation of disharmony within the enterprise; impairment of discipline of the whistleblower and others; other interference with efficiency; damage to the employer's relations with other government agencies, persons it services, taxpayers, or citizens generally. The employer's ability to defend itself must also be considered, such as its ability promptly and effectively to refute false charges of wrongdoing. . . .

6. The employee's right to engage in self-expression, that is, his freedom, as a citizen, to exercise his rights of free speech and the right to petition.[241]

---

[241]*Id.* at 166–67.

In reinstating the employee the arbitrator declared that while the award vindicated the right of whistleblowing by a public sector employee, it did not decide whether there is a duty on the part of employees to "blow the whistle" when wrongdoing or mismanagement is suspected.[242]

Sometimes the argument is made that the false or malicious statements are protected concerted activity under the Taft-Hartley Act. Illustrative is *United Cable Television Corp.*,[243] a decision reported by Arbitrator Adolph Koven. In that decision a shop steward was discharged for posting a letter to employees on the union bulletin board calling the employer's vice president a "liar" when the parties were committed to detente. Applying National Labor Relations Board precedent,[244] and other arbitral authority, Arbitrator Koven noted that conduct, although concerted, can be unprotected if it maliciously disparages an employer or otherwise unduly interferes with the employer's business interests. Further, and as held by the Board, such statements must be more than arguably false or malicious.[245] In this case—where the grievant was warned about misrepresenting or defaming the company or interfering with the conduct of its business—the arbitrator ordered reinstatement but without back pay. Arbitrator Koven correctly ruled that the First Amendment is not applicable to private employment disputes "since the Constitution guarantees free speech only against an abridgement by government."[246] He did note, however, that "the 'right' to speak freely may become a factor in establishing that 'just cause' was not present for disciplinary action in a particular case."[247]

---

[242]*See also* City of Detroit, 83-2 Lab. Arb. Awards (CCH) ¶8562 (1983) (McCormick, Arb.) (upholding 5-day suspension of city auditor for violating rule against discussing work-related matters with media).

[243]92 LA 3 (1989) (Koven, Arb.).

[244]*See* Dreis and Krump Mfg. Co., 221 NLRB 309, 90 LRRM 1647 (1975), where the administrative law judge stated:

Offensive, vulgar, defamatory or opprobrious remarks during the course of protected activities will not remove activities from the Act's protection unless they are so flagrant, violent, or extreme as to render the individual unfit for further service (citations omitted).

[245]Harris Corp., 269 NLRB 733, 116 LRRM 1415 (1984).

[246]United Cable, 92 LA at 12. *Cf.* United Grocers Inc., 93 LA 1289 (1990) (Snow, Arb.) (stating that "[f]ree speech rights are not lost in the work place, but there is also an obligation not to be a disruptive influence").

[247]92 LA at 11.

Unless otherwise protected by statute, such as the case where an employee files a workers' compensation charge or a complaint with the EEOC, employees who commence a lawsuit against their company risk dismissal for disloyalty. Such was the case in *Southwestern Electrical Power Co.*,[248] a decision reported by Arbitrator F. Jay Taylor. In that case a utility dismissed a troubleman for filing a lawsuit against the company and five management officials. The employee was claiming damages in the amount of $1.5 million for injuries sustained when an aerial bucket that was used to replace a street light malfunctioned causing him to be suspended in midair. Sustaining the discharge, Arbitrator Taylor found that the employee's actions constituted a direct affront to the authority of the company's managers which adversely affected the employer-employee relationship and "did so in a manner as to make the Grievant's continued employment harmful to the best interest of all concerned."[249] Persuaded that the lawsuit was filed to promote some "discernible adverse effect on the company's business," the arbitrator concluded that the company is entitled to "some measure of loyalty from its Employees and should not be required to continue the employment of an individual who has taken spiteful and vengeful action against Management in a public denouncement."[250]

What of an employee who solicits other employees to file a lawsuit against the company? In *Elyria Foundry Co.*,[251] Arbitrator Nicholas Duda ruled that discharge was excessive for a long-term employee (34 years) with a good work record who solicited a co-worker during working hours to consult an attorney who was also handling the grievant's lawsuit against the employer. The arbitrator reasoned that the solicitation was brief, not inherently disloyal or malicious, and had a minimal adverse impact on operations. The arbitrator also pointed out that the company did not dismiss the grievant for originally filing a lawsuit. It is of note that the arbitrator stated that "Grievant cannot be held accountable for the reaction of other employees to his legitimate exercise of legal rights."[252]

---

[248]84 LA 743 (1985) (Taylor, Arb.).
[249]*Id.* at 748.
[250]*Id.* at 749.
[251]87 LA 1129 (1986) (Duda, Arb.).
[252]*Id.* at 1135.

D. Factors Considered by Arbitrators in Disloyalty Cases: A Synthesis

Arbitrator Joe Gentile, in *Zellerbach Paper Co.*,[253] listed numerous factors considered by arbitrators in disloyalty cases. Factors that should be accorded controlling weight include:

1. Whether the act of conduct was expressed orally or in writing (if expressed in writing, it arguably has a greater impact on the outcome of the case);

2. Whether the act or conduct was directed toward persons within or outside the organization (if outside, the act is considered more serious; if within, the next inquiry is to whom it was directed and the person engaging in the act, such as a union representative);

3. If the act or conduct was directed toward a customer or a competitor of the organization, did it cause damage to the business? (if harm is found, and other considerations are equal, arbitrators will generally sustain some degree of discipline);

4. If the act or conduct was directed to a government enforcement agency, did the employee exhaust internal channels of redress? (if internal avenues are not followed, management's case is strengthened);

5. Were the statements known to be or reasonably held by the employees making them to be "true," "false," or "undetermined" at the time they were made? (if known to be false or undetermined, arbitrators find this to be a highly persuasive factor in support of the company's case);

6. Was the "tone" or actual language of the statements malicious, slanderous, inflammatory, or disruptive, with respect to the company? (inflammatory-type statements may support management's case against the grievant);

7. Were there "substantial personal rights of expression and citizenship" involved? (if so, this consideration can be a mitigating factor in favor of the employee); and

8. Did management condone the act in the past and did the company's policy adequately place the employee on notice of

---

[253]75 LA 868 (1980) (Gentile, Arb.).

the possible and probable consequences if the act or conduct were carried out? (if answered in the affirmative on either, arbitrators find this a factor in favor of the employee).[254]

In common with all off-duty decisions and the criteria advanced by Marvin Hill & Mark Kahn,[255] a combination of the above sufficient to sustain discharge will depend on the specific evidence record before the arbitrator.[256]

VIII. OFF-DUTY CONSIDERATIONS AND DRUG TESTS: DISCHARGE AND DISCIPLINE FOR EMPLOYEES HAVING DRUGS "IN THEIR SYSTEM"

Drug tests merely establish the presence of drugs in the employee's system.[257] They indicate that an employee ingested drugs in time past; they do not indicate whether an employee is "under the influence." Suppose an employee tests positive for drugs but there is no evidence that the employee used drugs while on duty? Does a positive test result, unaccompanied by any indication that the employee is "under the influence," automatically mean that the employee is subject to discipline or discharge? When a fire department administered a random drug test during a return-to-work physical, Arbitrator David Dilts ruled that just cause did not exist to dismiss a fire fighter, who had tested positive for cocaine, for "on duty" use of illegal drugs, at least in the case where there was no public knowledge of the matter. The employee then entered a rehabilitation center, prompting the arbitrator to conclude that there now exists reasonable suspicion of the grievant's use of cocaine, thus making him eligible for testing.[258]

---

[254]*Id.* at 875–77.

[255]*Infra* note 317 and accompanying text.

[256]An especially interesting case where once-in-a-lifetime mitigating factors were found in favor of an employee dismissed for making disparaging remarks to a customer is *Oklahoma Fixture Co.*, 98 LA 1178 (1992) (Allen, Jr., Arb.).

[257]*See* MARVIN F. HILL, JR., & ANTHONY V. SINICROPI, EVIDENCE IN ARBITRATION (2d ed.) 181–95 (BNA Books, 1987) for a discussion of alcohol- and drug-related evidence.

[258]City of Evanston, 95 LA 679, 689 (1990) (Dilts, Arb.).

Arbitrator Thomas Phelan, in *Maple Meadow Mining Co.,*[259] addressed the respective rights of management and its employees concerning drug use in a case where management enacted a rule prohibiting the "possession, use, sale or purchase of unauthorized or illegal drugs"[260] and made such possession, use, sale, or purchase grounds for termination regardless of whether it was on company property, or during working hours, or while on company business, and regardless of whether there was any showing of adverse impact upon an employee's ability to perform the job. Arbitrator Phelan found that the rule was overbroad and exceeded management's powers under the parties' labor agreement. Management was not free to regulate an employee's conduct away from the job site when there was no impact on either the employee's job or the employer's business.[261] The arbitrator had particular problems with the rule's prohibition against mere possession even though possession may be entirely legal or done unintentionally.

Arbitrator Jerry Fullmer, in *Stanadyne,*[262] reached a similar conclusion involving an employee who twice tested positive for marijuana in a medical exam pursuant to being recalled to active employment. The record indicated that grievant had used marijuana at various times before being recalled to work and at least once in his off-hours during the period he was in active employment after being recalled to work. Finding that there was no evidence that the grievant ever had drugs in his possession at the workplace, and that grievant was not "under the influence" while actually working at the plant, the arbitrator reversed the suspension and disqualification of grievant. The arbitrator's reasoning is particularly instructive with respect to outlining the problems for management:

> The more subtle question is beyond use as to what the two tests tell us as to whether the Grievant was *under the influence* while he was actually at the plant. The answer appears to be that there is no scientific basis upon which it can be established from a particular level of marijuana (THC) in the urine that the employee providing the sample is under the influence of marijuana (THC) at the time the sample is given.[263]

---

[259]90 LA 873 (1988) (Phelan, Arb.).
[260]*Id.* at 875.
[261]*Id.* at 879.
[262]91 LA 993 (1988) (Fullmer, Arb.).
[263]*Id.* at 1001.

Arbitrator Fullmer quoted at length a law review article on determining whether an individual is "under the influence" from a test result alone:

> But supporting an allegation of "under the influence" with a urinalysis result raises serious nexus issues, because a positive merely substantiates that the use occurred in the past, not that the grievant was impaired on the job. To that extent, marijuana analysis is quite unlike blood alcohol testing, which shows current effects; it fights the presumption that the employer is primarily concerned with on-the-job impairment.
>
> [T]he marijuana immunoassy, the most popular form of urinalysis, is based on inference: it detects not psychoactive substance itself but the excreted metabolites—that is the waste products into which the drug has been broken down by the body's physiological processes. Such a testing procedure is analogous to inferring—in the Sherlock tradition—that cigarette smoking has occurred by dicovering tobacco ashes. The inference is a fair one, so far as it goes. But it begs the question crucial to grievance arbitration: How recently did the grievant use marijuana? To what extent was the employee's ability to carry out his duties affected by the drug? Just as one could not tell exactly when the cigarette was smoked from the mere presence of ashes, urinalysis cannot demonstrate when an employee used marijuana or was impaired by it.[264]

The arbitrator concluded "that from a scientific standpoint the two positive drug tests do not provide any evidence that the grievant was under the *influence* of marijuana."[265]

Another arbitrator likewise rejected management's argument that marijuana usage should itself be a basis for sustaining a discharge. Such a rule would not be reasonable without considering its effect on job performance.[266]

To many arbitrators the significance of finding impairment on the job appears crucial, especially when the drug is "soft" (marijuana) and the employer's work rules do not prohibit off-duty use.[267] Even

---

[264]*Id.*, quoting Tia Schneider Denenberg & R.V. Denenberg, *Drug Testing From an Arbitrator's Perspective,* 11 Nova L. Rev. 371, 399–400 (1987).

[265]*Id.* at 1002.

[266]Southern Cal. Gas Co., 89 LA 393 (1987) (Acosta, Arb.).

[267]*See, e.g.,* Southern Cal. Rapid Transit Dist., 93 LA 20 (1989) (Christopher, Arb.) (reinstating 18-year driver who tested positive for marijuana following accident, where driver never accused of being "impaired" or "under influence"); United Technologies Carrier, 92 LA 829 (1989) (Williams, Arb.) (traces of marijuana insufficient to show affect on grievant or that employee had consumed marijuana on job); Union Oil Co. of Cal., 88 LA 91 (1986) (Weiss, Arb.) (reversing suspension

an admission by the grievant that he smokes marijuana daily and has done so for years may not be enough to sustain a dismissal absent some demonstrable nexus to the job, meaning "impairment."[268] Management will increase its chances of sustaining a dismissal when its rules clearly provide that off-duty illegal drug use constitutes discharge (as opposed to simply a dischargeable offense) and the employee's job is one that affects the safety of co-employees or the public (air traffic controllers, for example).[269] Uniform enforcement of the rule is imperative.[270] Management's case is further strengthened if such a rule is implemented with union input.[271]

A grievant whose blood-alcohol level exceeds state alcohol intoxication standards can properly be presumed to be under the influence.[272] In arbitration, as in the legal forum, the "game is over" for such an employee who argues nonimpairment. An employee who

---

of 4 employees who tested positive—3 for marijuana and 1 for cocaine—absent showing that employees were unable to perform job duties and absent published work rule prohibiting mere presence of illegal drug in employee's system while at work); Trailways, Inc., 88 LA 1073 (1987) (Goodman, Arb.) (holding management did not have just cause to terminate bus driver whose urine tested positive for marijuana; arbitrator credited testimony of toxicologist who argued that urinalysis does not reveal frequency of use, most recent use, or present effect of drug, and scientific data do not prove connection between job performance and positive test result).

[268]Crucible Materials Corp., 94 LA 540 (1989) (Harkness, Arb.) (reversing dismissal for autoclave operator for refusing to agree to conditions for continued employment, including completion of in-patient drug rehabilitation program, following disclosure during annual physical examination that he smoked marijuana daily, off-duty, for 15 years, where plant had no rule against off-duty drug use and no evidence of job impairment).

[269]See, e.g., Duquesne Light Co., 92 LA 907 (1989) (Sergent, Arb.) (sustaining discharge for marijuana and cocaine positive test, rejecting postdischarge rehabilitation argument); Indianapolis Power & Light, 87 LA 826, 827 (1986) (Volz, Arb.) (upholding discharge of groundskeeper where urine showed heavy use of marijuana and company rule declared that "off-the-job alcohol and/or drug use adversely affect an employee's job performance and could jeopardize the safety of other employees, the public or Company equipment").

[270]MacMillan Bloedel Containers, 92 LA 592 (1989) (Nicholas, Arb.) (converting discharge to suspension where management had been lax in enforcing rules).

[271]See, e.g., Texas City Refining, 89 LA 1159, 1163 (1987) (Milentz, Arb.) (sustaining dismissal for second positive marijuana test of maintenance electrician, noting that drug-testing program was in effect for 6-month period and survived labor agreement negotiations without union challenge).

[272]See, e.g., Pittsburgh & Midway Coal Mining Co., 91 LA 431 (1988) (Cohen, Arb.) (upholding dismissal of mine worker whose blood-alcohol level exceeded state standards in test administered 3 hours after reporting for work).

tests under the legal limit may be presumed to be unimpaired. As such, the burden is on management to show impairment.[273] Where management has reasonable suspicion that the employee is under the influence, and the employee refuses to submit to fitness-for-work medical evaluation, the employee can be presumed to be under the influence or, alternatively, can be disciplined for insubordination.[274] In this respect Hill and Sinicropi conclude:

> [M]ost arbitrators will uphold discipline or even dismissal when an employee refuses to take an examination so long as management can establish a reasonable basis in fact (probable cause in the public sector) for believing that the employee was under the influence. Alternatively, when a test is refused, an arbitrator may simply conclude that the employee was under the influence and not bother to rule on the question of whether discipline was proper for refusing the examination. Whichever alternative is chosen, the end result is the same. The suspected drug user is disciplined or terminated from employment.[275]

An off-duty, off-premises arrest for drug or alcohol use may be insufficient basis to order an employee to submit to testing.[276]

IX. FALSIFICATION OF EMPLOYMENT APPLICATIONS: WITHHOLDING OFF-DUTY OR LIFESTYLE INFORMATION

As part of the hiring process employers frequently ask applicants questions about past misconduct, past employers, health considerations, or otherwise request information that an employee may want to keep private (a live-in relationship, for example). Suppose

---

[273]United States Steel Corp., 95 LA 7, 10 (1990) (Talarico, Arb.) (employer failed to prove grievant "under the influence" where grievant tested .062% blood alcohol content, stating that there is a difference between the mere consumption of alcohol and being under the influence).

[274]*See* Marvin F. Hill, Jr., & James A. Wright, *Employee Refusals to Cooperate in Internal Investigations: "Into The Woods" With Employers, Courts, and Labor Arbitrators,* 56 MISSOURI L. REV. 869, 908–12 (1991).

[275]MARVIN F. HILL, JR., & ANTHONY V. SINICROPI, REMEDIES IN ARBITRATION (2d ed.) 189 (BNA Books, 1991). *See also* Harry A. Flannery, *Termination of Employment for Refusal to Take a Drug Test,* 40 LAB. LAW. J. 293–301 (1989).

[276]Philips Indus. Inc., 93 LA 1133 (1989) (Dilts, Arb.).

an employee withholds information about his or her past and is later discovered by management? Does it matter whether the employment application warns the employee that withholding information or falsification is ground for dismissal? What about an employee who makes an "honest" mistake? Do arbitrators recognize a "statute of limitations"? Are there some areas of inquiry that are off-limits to management?

In the selection and appointment process management has consistently asserted its right to truthful and accurate information from a prospective employee. Arbitrators have regularly found that a fraudulent entry of a fact material to the hiring decision is grounds for discharge, although no hard and fast rules are applied.[277] The

---

[277]Besides the cases discussed in this section, *see, e.g.,* Noranda Aluminum Inc., 94 LA 690 (1990) (Pratte, Arb.) (sustaining dismissal for failure to disclose incident of acute heat exhaustion, where company had sought to avoid problems with heat-related illness); St. Marie's Gopher News, 93 LA 738 (1989) (Eisele, Arb.) (upholding dismissal for failure to disclose arrest for assault of live-in girlfriend, rejecting argument that domestic problems are private and irrelevant to employment decision); Braniff Inc., 93 LA 124, 126 (1989) (Gentile, Arb.) (sustaining dismissal of customer service agent who indicated on application that he was then working for another company and that there were "no gaps in my employment"); Owens-Illinois Forest Prods., 83 LA 1265 (1984) (Cantor, Arb.) (sustaining dismissal of employee for failing to "fully disclose" to physician at time of preemployment physical past medical history relating to back injury); Wine Cellar, 81 LA 158 (1983) (Ray, Arb.) (upholding dismissal of waiter for failure to disclose most recent employment on job application); Armco Composites, 79 LA 1157 (1982) (House, Arb.) (falsification of grievant's identity); Brink's, Inc., 79 LA 816 (1982) (Briggs, Arb.) (dismissal proper for failing to disclose neck injury sustained in auto accident); United States Steel Corp., 74 LA 354 (1980) (Dybeck, Arb.) (upholding termination for falsification of employment application regarding psychiatric problems although grievant was permitted to work for 1 month after examination by company medical director); Huntington Alloys, Inc., 74 LA 176 (1980) (Katz, Arb.) (criminal conviction); I.E. Prods., Inc., 72 LA 351 (1979) (Brooks, Arb.) (upholding discharge of employee for intentionally failing to disclose on employment application workers' compensation award for back injury suffered in prior employment, reasoning that collective bargaining agreement did not limit management's right to determine criteria for hiring, including establishment of health standards for applicants); Indianapolis Power & Light Co., 73 LA 512, 516 (1979) (Kossoff, Arb.) (sustaining discharge for employee who answered "no" to question whether she had relatives employed by employer, where rule provided for discipline or discharge for dishonesty, including falsification of employment application, and "management rights clause expressly reserved to the Company the right to 'manage and operate its property and business according to its best judgment' "); Gardner-Denver Co., 71 LA 1126 (1978) (Dunn, Arb.) (criminal record); Eaton Corp., 73 LA 367 (1979) (Atwood, Arb.); Farmland Foods, Inc., 64 LA 1260 (1975) (McKenna, Arb.) (withholding information on medical condition);

reported decisions indicate that the following factors may be considered by arbitrators in deciding whether just cause exists for the dismissal of an employee: (1) the nature of the fact or item falsified; (2) the number of items concealed; (3) the time between the occurrence and falsification; (4) whether disclosure would have precluded hiring; (5) the time between falsification and disclosure; (6) the employee's overall job performance; (7) the reason or factor that triggered the discharge; (8) the employer's motivation (was it punitive in nature?); (9) special safety or security considerations involved in the employee's job or the employer's business; and (10) mitigating factors, such as the employee's marital status or age, or the motivation of the employee (was there an intent to deceive?).[278]

When an employee is found to have falsified relevant information on an employment application, some arbitrators have not sustained discharge, especially when a long period of time has elapsed since the hiring and the employee's work record is good. The leading and perhaps most quoted decision in favor of a limitations period was reported by the late Dean Shulman while an umpire for Ford Motor Company. Dean Shulman stated that some time limitation should be implied, even if the falsification was deliberate and material:

> The question remains, however, of how long an employee's false statement in securing employment can continue to hang over him as a ground for discharge. Is he subject to discharge for time without limit so long as he remains in the employ of the Company? That would surely be a harsh and unjust rule. The notions of waiver and conditions are as well established in law and morals as is that of rescission for fraud. If, after learning of the false statement, the employer does not promptly discharge the employee but continues his employment, the continuance after knowledge may properly be considered as

---

Price Bros., 62 LA 389 (1974) (High, Arb.) (prior employer); Chanslor-Western Oil Co., 61 LA 1113 (1973) (Meiners, Arb.) (back injury).

But see Firestone Tire & Rubber Co., 93 LA 381 (1989) (Cohen, Arb.) (reversing discharge for falsification of medical history where no intent to deceive or defraud employer); Gold Kist, Inc., 77 LA 569 (1981) (Statham, Arb.) (employee reinstated where evidence established that individual in personnel department helped grievant fill out employment application); United States Postal Serv., 71 LA 100 (1978) (Krimsly, Arb.) (discharge improper where employee held belief that criminal charges had been expunged); Commonwealth of Pa., 66 LA 96 (1976) (LeWinter, Arb.) (12-year-old criminal indictment); Kaiser Steel Corp., 64 LA 194 (1975) (Roberts, Arb.) (discharge improper where grievant told that misdemeanor was dismissed).

[278]*See* Brink's, Inc., 79 LA 816 (1982) (Briggs, Arb.), which applied the criteria outlined by Arbitrator Burton Turkus in Kraft Foods, 50 LA 161 (1967) (Turkus. Arb.).

employment in the first instance with knowledge, and the falsification of itself cannot thereafter be deemed a proper ground for discharge.

But a rule that the employee guilty of such falsification is subject to discharge for a reasonable period after the employer first learns of the falsification, whenever that may be, would also be unduly harsh and capricious. It, too, would provide for no definite time limit. In addition, it would put a premium on the employer's failure to ascertain the truth. And the fate of employees similarly situated would depend entirely upon the pure chance of when the employer happened to learn of the falsification.

Again, in law and morals generally, the principle of a statute of limitations is well recognized, even though it means that the mere lapse of time thus enables a guilty person to escape what otherwise would be regarded as just punishment. The principle is recognized not merely in order to encourage diligence on the part of the aggrieved persons and to direct energies to the relative present rather then to the remote past, but also as a measure of justice to the guilty person whose offense, it is believed, should not render him permanently insecure.[279]

The concept of a "statute of limitations," apparently introduced by Dean Shulman, has not found a great deal of support in the reported decisions,[280] particularly when the parties' agreement or the

---

[279]Case No. A-184 (1945), cited in Opinions of the Umpire (New York State School of Indus. and Lab. Rels.).

[280]*But cf.* Labor Mgmt. Servs. Admin., 80 LA 250 (1983) (Dworkin, Arb.) (discharge improper for probationary investigator who failed to reveal misdemeanor shoplifting charge 10 years prior to applying for employment where employment application required any *felony* convictions; nothing in grievant's work history as probationary investigator suggests negative effect upon ability to serve as agency employee).

In Wine Cellar, 81 LA 158 (1983) (Ray, Arb.), Arbitrator Douglas Ray had this to say on the issue of false statements on employment applications and time limits:

The published arbitration reports contain dozens, if not hundreds, of cases involving alleged false statements on employment application forms. Most such cases involve alleged misrepresentation on questions involving physical condition and prior injuries, arrest records and, as in the instant case, employment history. Numerous cases have recognized that an employee may be discharged for his failure to mention prior employment in [an] application where such information is material for the assessment of qualifications. Here, however, there has been a lapse of time between the misrepresentation and the discharge. In such cases, many arbitrators will not automatically uphold a discharge, but rather apply safeguards in the form of a four point test. The test consists of the following questions:
 (1) was the misrepresentation willful?
 (2) was the misrepresentation material to the hiring?
 (3) was it material at the time of discharge?
 (4) has the employer acted promptly upon discovery?
Id. at 163 (citations omitted).

employer's work rules provide that falsification of an application or dishonesty is grounds for discharge.[281] Arbitrator Jonas Katz, in *Huntington Alloys, Inc.*,[282] rejected the "statute of limitations" theory, and reasoned as follows:

> This Board of Arbitration is not willing to conclude that an employer who is deliberately misled by an employee loses its right to invoke reasonable disciplinary actions simply because it had not discovered the employee's fraud for a period of time, provided the falsification would have borne on the employee's initial employment.
>
> ... [T]here is a substantial line of cases which uphold the discharge of persons filing false employment applications even after a substantial period of time under certain facts and circumstances.... These cases upholding discharges are based upon one of two theories: the punishment theory and the annulment theory. The first theory is that, where certain facts exist, a penalty of discharge is appropriate even where several years elapse prior to discovery of the falsification of the employment application. The annulment theory holds that where the employment contract is obtained by the applicant upon the basis of a misrepresentation of a material fact, there is a voidable contract which the employer may void at its option upon learning of the material misrepresentation which was part of the basis of the employer's decision to hire the applicant.[283]

Arbitrator Richard Ross, in *Salt River Project*,[284] likewise found that management had just cause to dismiss a public utility lineman who failed to list a drug-dealing conviction on a "felony questionnaire" accompanying his original employment application. The fact that the conviction was eight years old was, in the arbitrator's words, "nothing more than one of the factors which must be considered under just cause standards."[285] Reflecting arbitrators' reasoning in similar cases, Ross found that the matter of time that must pass is a question of "reasonableness," and "it is the obligation of the arbitrator to factor in all of the facts and circumstances."[286]

---

[281]*See, e.g.,* the lengthy discussion of case authority by Arbitrators Burton Turkus in Kraft Foods, 50 LA 161, 165–66 (1967) (Turkus, Arb.), and Jonas Katz in Huntington Alloys, Inc., 74 LA 176, 179 (1980) (Katz, Arb.). *See also* United States Steel Corp., 74 LA 354 (1980) (Simpkins, Arb.) and the citations, *supra* note 1.

[282]74 LA 176 (1980) (Katz, Arb.).

[283]*Id.* at 179 (citations omitted).

[284]91 LA 1193 (1988) (Ross, Arb.).

[285]*Id.* at 1196.

[286]*Id.*

One concern voiced by arbitrators is the trend in holding management liable for damages from negligent hiring or retention of workers known to have committed criminal acts.[287] Once management knows that an employee has a checkered past, negligence may result from retention of that employee, especially when that employee deals with the public.[288]

Where individuals have failed to disclose prior convictions, courts have upheld dismissals for falsification of applications against charges that these policies violate Title VII[289] or other labor laws. The Fifth Circuit, in *NLRB v. Florida Steel Corp.*,[290] has stated:

> Any employer has the right to demand that its employees be honest and truthful in every facet of their employment. Absent an antiunion motivation, any employer has the right to discipline an employee for his dishonesty or untruthfulness.[291]

One arbitrator correctly observed that "[t]he problem with falsification of employment application cases is that discovery often occurs weeks, months or years after the event. By that time, the employee has established a work record and has a stake in the job."[292] This is an area where arbitrators are split, although more appear to subscribe to the "annulment" as opposed to the "punishment" theory

---

[287]*See, e.g.,* the discussion of Arbitrator Frederick Eisele in *St. Marie's Gopher News*, 93 LA 739 (1989) (Eisele, Arb.).

On the issue of negligent hiring and retention, *see generally* RONALD M. GREEN & RICHARD J. REIBSTEIN, EMPLOYER'S GUIDE TO WORKPLACE TORTS: NEGLIGENT HIRING, FRAUD, DEFAMATION, AND OTHER EMERGING AREAS OF EMPLOYER LIABILITY, 3–24 (BNA Books, 1992).

[288]*See, e.g.,* North Houston Pole Line Corp. v. McAllister, 667 S.W.2d 829 (Tex. Ct. App. 1983) (upholding jury verdict of $500,000 for negligent hiring of truck driver).

[289]Avant v. South Central Bell Tel. Co., 716 F.2d 1083, 32 FEP Cases 1853 (5th Cir. 1983); Jimerson v. Kisco Co., 542 F.2d 1008, 13 FEP Cases 977, 978 (8th Cir. 1976) (noting that "black persons are indisputably more likely to suffer arrest than white persons," but holding that plaintiff-employee was not discharged for having an arrest record, but for falsifying this record when applying for employment, stating, "[t]o establish a prima facie case of disproportionate racial impact under Green [Green v. Missouri Pac. R.R., 523 F.2d 1290, 10 FEP Cases 1409 (8th Cir. 1975)], it was necessary for [plaintiff] to show that blacks as a class were excluded for falsifying their arrest records at a higher rate than whites"); Trapp v. State Univ. College at Buffalo, 30 FEP Cases 1499 (W.D.N.Y. 1983).

[290]686 F.2d 436, 100 LRRM 2102 (5th Cir. 1978).

[291]100 LRRM at 2107, quoting NLRB v. Mueller Brass Co., 509 F.2d 704, 713, 88 LRRM 3236, 3243 (5th Cir. 1975).

[292]Wine Cellar, 81 LA 158, 164 (1983) (Ray, Arb.).

in upholding discharges for falsification of employment applications. The better rule in falsification is simply to avoid absolutes and to give consideration to all of the 10 factors noted above.

Should special consideration be accorded workers' compensation cases? In *Darnell, Inc. v. Impact Industries*,[293] plaintiff Norma Darnell was discharged on the second day of her job when Impact Industries learned that she had been hurt and filed a claim under the Illinois Workman's Compensation Act (now known as the Workers' Compensation Act) while in the employ of Federal-Huber, a former employer. Darnell, on her employment application, indicated that she had neither "had a serious illness or injury in the past 5 years" nor "received compensation for injuries."[294] The appellate court held that the circuit court should not have granted a directed verdict for Impact Industries, but, rather, a jury should have been allowed to hear her evidence as to the reasons she was discharged.[295] The Illinois Supreme Court affirmed the appellate court decision and ruled that the case should have been submitted to a jury. The court reasoned that there is no distinction between the situation where an employee is discharged for filing a workers' compensation claim against a primary employer and one where the employer discharges an employee upon discovering that the employee had filed a claim against another *unrelated* employer. In the court's view, "in either situation a retaliatory discharge is equally offensive to the public policy of this State. . . ."[296] As the dissent pointed out, under *Darnell* a worker who has filed a suit under the Act may bring suit against any subsequent employer, regardless of the length of time that intervenes, if the employer considers the filing of that claim in making an employment decision.[297]

Arbitrators do not appear to track the public policy consideration when management discharges employees for withholding information about claims with former employers. Arbitrator Stanley Sergent, in

---

[293]473 N.E.2d 935, 117 LRRM 3371 (Ill. 1984).

[294]*Id.* 117 LRRM at 3372.

[295]Darnell v. Impact Indus., 457 N.E.2d 125, 115 LRRM 5012 (Ill. App. Ct. 1983). Darnell had testified that she was told she was discharged because she had filed a workers' compensation claim. Also, management's calls to former employers were made in order to determine whether she had filed a workers' compensation claim. 117 LRRM at 3372–73.

[296]117 LRRM at 3372.

[297]*Id.* at 3374 (Moran, dissenting).

Peoples Gas System Inc.,[298] ruled that management had just cause to discharge a serviceman who falsely stated that he never filed a claim for workers' compensation and failed to reveal prior employment, where the misrepresentation was deliberate, the facts were material to the hiring decision, the employee had been forewarned about the consequences of falsification (the application contained an entry that any falsification would be grounds for dismissal), and the employer acted promptly. Arbitrator Sergent stated that because employment applications and medical histories are a critical element of the hiring process, management has a fundamental right to truthful, accurate, and complete answers.[299] Arbitrator Samuel Nicholas, in *Friedrich Air Conditioning,*[300] reached a similar conclusion involving an employee who lied about a back injury while working for another employer.[301]

Are there any limits to what management can require employees to disclose? In *Southwestern Bell Telephone Co.,*[302] Arbitrator Diane Massey sustained the dismissal of a 12-year records clerk for listing her live-in boyfriend as her "husband" on medical and insurance forms. The arbitrator found unpersuasive the employee's argument that she believed that she was in a common-law marriage.[303] Clearly the issue in *Southwestern Bell* was not whether management could sustain a discharge because the employee, when asked, did not disclose her live-in relationship. Arbitrators who apply any kind of a nexus requirement are unlikely to sustain discipline when an employee fails to disclose personal relationships, such as their live-in partners, and other personal information,[304] although exceptions are likely.

---

[298]91 LA 951 (1988) (Sergent, Arb.).

[299]*Id.* at 953.

[300]94 LA 249 (1990) (Nicholas, Arb.).

[301]*See also* I.E. Prods., Inc., 72 LA 351 (1979) (Brooks, Arb.) (sustaining dismissal for failing to disclose receipt of workers' compensation for back injury in prior employment).

[302]95 LA 46 (1990) (Massey, Arb.).

[303]*See also* Arkansas Oklahoma Gas Corp., 96 LA 704 (1991) (Allen, Jr., Arb.) (reversing dismissal of divorced employee who attempted to receive medical payment for ex-wife, believing that divorced-but-living-together couples retained insurance coverage); Bi-State Dev. Agency, 96 LA 1090 (1991) (Cipolla, Arb.) (upholding dismissal where grievant designated fiancee and her children as his wife and stepchildren in order to claim health benefits).

[304]*See, e.g.,* Sharples Coal Corp., 91 LA 1065 (1988) (Stoltenberg, Arb.) (holding

X. VICARIOUS LIABILITY AND SPOUSAL RELATIONSHIPS

Can a spousal relationship ever result in an employee's discipline or dismissal on a vicarious liability theory? In *Indiana Bell Telephone*,[305] a 24-year utility employee (a facilities assigner) was discharged after accepting at her home a one-half pound package of marijuana that was addressed to her husband. Arbitrator Elliott Goldstein, while holding that management could suspend without pay the employee pending the disposition of criminal charges, ruled that the dismissal was improper. Declaring that the grievant's acceptance of a package containing marijuana does not elevate her to a drug dealer, Goldstein's comments regarding holding the grievant responsible for the actions of her spouse are noteworthy:

> [W]hatever her husband's activities may be, the mere fact of Grievant's spousal relationship does not, in my view, establish a detrimental impact on the Employer's reputation or product. Indeed, the Employer has not cited any precedent awards in which the misconduct of an employee's *spouse* is considered as the basis for discharge in a case involving off-duty, off-premises conduct.[306]

Management's claim—"that the acceptance of the marijuana automatically created a nexus and that the harm to the company can be injected by the conduct itself"—was rejected.[307]

Consistent with the thoughts of Arbitrator Goldstein, employers will have a difficult time demonstrating a nexus between the employee's off-duty misconduct and the employer's business when the basis of the liability is the conduct of a spouse.

XI. SUMMARY

Arbitrators are reluctant to sustain discipline or discharge based on off-duty misconduct (i.e., conduct that occurs off the premises

---

that requirement that employees on prescription drugs furnish signed prescription from licensed physician before undergoing drug test unreasonable).
[305]93 LA 981 (1989) (Goldstein, Arb.).
[306]*Id.* at 988.
[307]*Id.*

during nonworking time) absent some relationship or nexus to the job. Where off-duty misconduct results in the physical inability of an employee to properly perform work duties (jail, for example), arbitrators examine whether such conduct violates a specific provision of the agreement. If it does, discipline or discharge will normally be upheld, especially where the company can also demonstrate some injury to its operations. When it is argued that an employee's off-duty misconduct renders the employee unsuitable for employment, arbitrators in sustaining dismissals have focused on considerations of honesty and the overall character of the grievant as these traits relate to a specific job. Other considerations being equal, it will be difficult for an employer to sustain a discharge based merely upon the fact of a criminal conviction or that management finds the employee's lifestyle or off-duty conduct distasteful or embarrassing. In the "inability" and "unsuitability" cases, however, arbitrators may properly take into consideration mitigating circumstances such as the employee's prior work record and whether in similar situations progressive discipline had been applied. The fact that the company does not have a policy dealing with the alleged off-duty, off-premises infirmity does not always mean that management cannot discipline employees who engage in such conduct, especially when the conduct is criminal in nature. As stated by Arbitrator Sass, "just because the Company does not have a policy prohibiting bank robbery does not mean that it must continue to employ a known bank robber—particularly not in a position that requires the handling of money."[308] With respect to off-duty criminal activity, the arbitrator pointed out that "it is simply unnecessary for a company to recodify the state's criminal laws in its personnel policies manual."[309] Still, and as pointed out by Arbitrator Sass, "just because an employee violates some criminal law or another does not mean that the Company has just and sufficient cause to discharge [the employee]. Some violations are more serious than others and some are more related to the work relationship than others."[310] If management elects to condition

---

[308]United Food and Commercial Workers Union, Local No. 7 and King Shoppers, Inc., 1991 BNA Unp. Arb. LEXIS 110, at 19 (Sass, Arb.) ("In this Arbitrator's view, dealing cocaine is similar to robbing a bank which is subject to disciplinary action even though there is no specific Company policy prohibiting it." *Id.* at 20.).
[309]*Id.* at 20.
[310]*Id.*

a suspension or dismissal of an employee based on the outcome of a criminal or civil proceeding,[311] when the legal system is done with the case, absent independent justification for its actions management may have to live with that outcome.[312] Thus, when management

---

[311]*See, e.g.*, Group Cable, Inc., 80 LA 205 (1983) (Chandler, Arb.) (upholding limited suspension for employee who admitted being in company vehicle used to transport cocaine); Florida Power & Light, 88 LA 1136 (1987) (Kindig, Arb.) (discharge for conviction of firearms felonies overturned absent demonstration of job impairment; arbitrator notes that employee received suspended sentence and reduced probation as first-time offender); Great Atlantic & Pac. Tea Co., 45 LA 498, 499 (undated) (Livengood, Arb.) (holding that a suspension pending the outcome of a criminal proceeding is not disciplinary, stating "the question is whether management has the right to suspend an employee whose ability to provide the service for which he was hired has been substantially impaired, regardless of whether the impairment was due to any fault of the employee"); Pan American World Airways, 83 LA 732 (1984) (Dranzin, Arb.) (ruling that management can suspend pending outcome of trial, even though no jury had as yet heard the charges, at least in the situation where the probability of a capital conviction is likely); Continental Baking Co., 88 LA 1142, 1147 (1987) (Statham, Arb.) (suspension without pay for off-duty charge of drug trafficking proper, even though court placed case on dead docket; arbitrator notes that "the alleged crime did not involve the Company in any way other than the fact that the Grievant was an employee" and "once the indictment was dismissed against the Grievant, the Company was, in reality, in an untenable position, as it had to prove a criminal offense which the state had declined to prosecute"); Johnson & Johnson, 95 LA 409 (1990) (Allen, Jr., Arb.) (grievant properly suspended on basis of indictment for off-duty possession of marijuana and undercover agent's report of grievant's involvement with drugs; grievant not entitled to back pay where charges had adverse impact on work site, management acted reasonably in not contesting unemployment compensation and reinstating employee immediately upon dismissal of charges, and contract did not require back pay under such circumstances); Indiana Bell Tel., 93 LA 981 (1989) (Goldstein, Arb.) (holding just cause for suspension, but not discharge, for off-duty drug arrest, reasoning that employer has the right to protect its business from adverse effects arising from public accusation and arrest; grievant awarded back pay from point of discharge, but not during suspension); Latner Co., 87 LA 1300, 1302 (1986) (Thornell, Arb.) (stating that management "took some risk in suspending Grievant [who pleaded guilty to illegal sale of narcotics]. If he had been acquitted the Company may have been required to make Grievant whole for lost wages.").

[312]*See, e.g.*, Lucky Stores, 59 LA 559, 562 (1972) (Koven, Arb.) (ruling that employer that suspended 2 employees following arrest on drug charges is obligated, following dismissal of charges, to compensate employees for loss of earnings which they sustained during suspension); Air France, 71 LA 1113, 1116 (1978) (Turkus, Arb.) (ordering back pay for suspended fleet service clerk, stating: "The Company, having offered no other evidence to sustain [mail theft] charges—the indictment being no more that a set of charges, having no evidentiary value—there is a total absence in this proceeding of clear and convincing proof that Grievant was guilty of the charges for which he was originally suspended. . . . He is therefore entitled to the compensation which he would have received had he not been suspended for

suspends an employee for off-duty drug dealing pending the outcome of his trial, if the case is dropped by the state management will have to reinstate the employee, perhaps with full back pay, if it cannot convince an arbitrator that there are independent grounds for sustaining the discharge. When criminal charges are dropped or, alternatively, when the employee is adjudicated "not guilty," management may still sustain a dismissal based on the results of its own investigation,[313] although the arbitrator is likely to place considerable importance on an acquittal.[314] Accordingly, the dismissal of criminal

---

that period."); Brown & Williamson Tobacco Co., 61 LA 1211, 1213 (1974) (Davis, Arb.) (voiding plant rule providing for suspension without pay of employees accused of serious crime, where grievant acquitted of drug offense, reasoning that "the company rule here involved requires that an employee be punished before conviction and regardless of whether he is eventually proven to be guilty or innocent"); Electrical Refractors Co., 77-A Lab. Arb. Awards (CCH) ¶8397 at ¶4699 (1977) (Strasshofer, Arb.) ("management may suspend an employee accused of criminal conduct without liability for back pay if: a) The employee is subsequently found guilty or pleads guilty, or b) Even if guilt is not subsequently established, if 1) the suspected criminal conduct is of a nature which carries with it a serious threat to the safety or welfare of the business enterprise, including employees and customers, and 2) the circumstances are promptly and carefully investigated in a fair and impartial manner, and 3) the results of the investigation are as such to persuade reasonable minds, acting in good faith but not necessarily skilled in the law, that the employee is guilty and may continue or repeat his criminal acts"). *See generally* KOVEN & SMITH, JUST CAUSE: THE SEVEN TESTS (2d. ed.) 297–98 (BNA Books, 1992), where the authors, asserting the majority position, write: "If [management] decides to suspend an employee on the basis of arrest or indictment, leaving the job of establishing guilt or innocence to the court, management has elected to abide by what the court decides. So if the verdict is not guilty, the company would be required not only to reinstate the employee but in many cases to compensate him for his lost time."

[313]As was the case in Mobil Corp., 91-1 Lab. Arb. Awards (CCH) ¶8007 (1990) (Allen,Jr., Arb.) (sustaining dismissal even though criminal charges were dropped, reasoning that grievant was at least minimally involved in the manufacture of drugs). *See also* cases cited *supra* notes 177–182 and accompanying text.

[314]*See* Board of Educ., S. Hollard, Ill. v. Dorethy (1976) (Adelman, Arb.) (unpubl.). In *Dorethy,* an industrial arts teacher purchased from a student 3 citizen band radios with a value of $470 to $500. Dorethy paid $110, was charged with accessory to the theft, but was subsequently dismissed from the case. In ruling that Dorethy did not know that the radios were stolen, Hearing Officer David Adelman placed considerable weight on the teacher's acquittal from the criminal charges.

See also Board of Educ., Chicago School Dist. v. Gleason, 792 F.2d 76 (7th Cir. 1986) (holding that due process did not require reopening of dismissal hearing for teacher convicted of felony theft even though an appellate court overturned the conviction of diverting students' travel money when teacher made restitution; Hearing Officer Robert McAllister sustained dismissal because teacher's misuse of funds affected students).

charges against the grievant is not conclusive or res judicata of the grievance but is merely another piece of evidence to be considered in a just cause proceeding under a collective bargaining agreement. The better rule is that an arbitrator will not conclude that the grievant is not guilty of what management alleges based merely on what happens in the criminal forum.[315] This rule or principle followed by many arbitrators has been well stated by Arbitrator Joseph Bard:

> An arbitration proceeding is *de novo,* that is to say, the Arbitrator is entitled to arrive at his own conclusions from the facts of the incident; he is not bound by the conclusions of a court nor is he obligated to slavishly follow such conclusions or even a guilty plea. Arbitration proceedings involve alleged violations of one or more contractual provisions of a contract, the interpretation and application of these provisions, and other aspects of the employer-employee relationship. When the parties bargained for the arbitration process, they did not bargain for a jury of lay persons or for a conclusion based on a plea bargain. They bargained, instead, for an independent finder of fact who is charged with making a judgment not as the grievants appeared to a jury or a judge, but rather to someone whose training and experience qualifies him to make such judgments. While an arbitrator is prepared to take note of a jury's decision or a guilty plea in court, he nevertheless makes independent determinations both as to facts and applicable law.[316]

Still, is there a synthesis or theory to principles established by arbitrators? Because arbitrators often apply a balancing test, there is no black letter law, maxim, or rule that will lead practitioners to the dispositive consideration in a particular case. However, Marvin Hill and Mark Kahn, in an address before the National Academy of Arbitrators, have summarized most of the criteria arbitrators apply in off-duty cases as follows:

> The *characteristics of the employer* may be critical. If it is claimed that the off-duty misconduct had adversely affected or will harm the company's reputation or sales, or both, this may be of greater concern for firms that operate in highly competitive, consumer-oriented markets (e.g., airlines, retail stores, private schools, health clubs, day-care centers) than for oligopolistic firms with product-oriented markets.
>   The *location of the employer* may be a factor. A prominent employer in a small isolated town may be legitimately more sensitive to scandal

---

[315]An expanded discussion of the effect of collateral proceedings on the arbitral forum is found in HILL & SINICROPI, EVIDENCE IN ARBITRATION, *supra* note 257, at Chapter 18, *Weight of Other Proceedings.*
[316]King Co., 89 LA 681, 687 (1987) (Bard, Arb.).

based on off-duty misconduct than an anonymous employer in a large metropolitan area.

The *nature of the misconduct:* Violent, destructive, or perverted actions may reinforce the nexus more than crimes of the so-called white-collar variety (e.g. tax evasion). A misdemeanor (e.g., marijuana possession) is much less likely to be considered just cause for discharge than a felony (e.g., marijuana sales).

The *occupation of the offender.* Many decisions [in the off-duty area] have hinged on a link between the employee's job duties and obligations and the content of the misconduct. It is not hard to demonstrate a nexus when a police officer commits a felony off-duty, when a teacher molests a child off-duty, when a sales clerk is convicted of shoplifting (from someone else's store), or when a bank teller has embezzled funds from his church's treasury. The extent and nature of the grievant's customer contacts are important, especially if they relate to the type of misconduct. Committers of sex crimes or property thefts will probably not be retained in jobs that entail entering customers' homes.

Finally, there is the *extent and kind of publicity.* When the public's attention has focused on the misconduct and the miscreant has been clearly identified with the employer, the nexus is reinforced. Often, of course, it is the publicity that caused the employer to become aware of the off-duty misconduct.[317]

Hill and Kahn conclude by noting that, in this context, it is easy to see why so many of the cases have arisen in connection with government units that are concerned about their reputation for economic or political reasons, or both. What the labor-management practitioner should realize is that to say that there is a nexus between the off-duty conduct and some aspect of the job is a conclusion. The management practitioner can only focus on the "verbs," asserting that the conduct at issue causes sufficient injury to the employer's business or, alternatively, is so heinous as to render the grievant's continued employment untenable.

A final note in this area: What is often important in effecting dismissals (in some off-duty cases it may even be dispositive of the just cause determination) is the *process* management employs in accomplishing terminations. Numerous arbitrators have held that the concept of just cause encompasses a procedural as well as a substantive component.[318] A 1990 case reported by Arbitrator John Sands

---

[317]Hill & Kahn, *Discipline and Discharge for Off-Duty Misconduct, supra* note 1, at 121–54, 153–54 (emphasis supplied).

[318]These cases are discussed at length in HILL & SINICROPI, REMEDIES IN ARBITRATION, *supra* note 275, at 246–49.

highlights the pitfalls for management when it fails to conduct an adequate investigation of an off-premises incident. At issue in *Stroehmann Bakeries*,[319] was the dismissal of a 17-year male truck driver for an alleged sexual assault on a female receiving clerk at a customer's store. Finding that management had already decided to terminate the grievant before obtaining the grievant's side of the story (the company acted on the report of the manager of a customer's store), the arbitrator, calling the company's investigation "burlesque,"[320] held that the dismissal was not for just cause and ordered reinstatement with full back pay. While the case was reversed by a reviewing court applying its own sense of industrial justice, other arbitrators have likewise reversed decisions of management for investigative infirmities.[321] One arbitrator, considering the dismissal of a clerk on a night stocking crew who had been charged with auto theft, stated the rule that should be followed this way:

> In the interests of justice and fair play, arbitrators, as a rule, have also found that the discharge of any employee based merely upon the arrest of that employee and without investigation is neither just nor fair.[322]

The key word is "investigation." Employers, in effecting discipline, should communicate with the grievant and the union before making the decision to impose a penalty. To do otherwise is to risk having the decision overturned.

---

[319]98 LA 873 (1990) (Sands, Arb.), vacated and remanded to a different arbitrator, Stroehmann Bakeries v. Local 776, 762 F. Supp 1187, 136 LRRM 2874 (M.D. Pa. 1991), *aff'd* 969 F.2d 1436, 140 LRRM 2625 (3d Cir. 1992), *cert. denied*, 140 LRRM 2984 (1992).

[320]*Id.* at 876.

[321]*See also* King Co., 89 LA 681 (1987) (Bard, Arb.) (holding that employees were improperly suspended for vandalizing a co-worker's car and lying during the investigation, where the incident occurred off-duty and off-company premises, the incident had no impact on the company's operations, and the employer submitted no competent evidence, other than a hearsay account of the grievants' confession; the only reliable evidence submitted by management was a newspaper account of the grievants' guilty pleas to gross misconduct as the result of a plea bargain); Alpha Beta Co., 91 LA 1225, 1228 (1988) (Wilmouth, Arb.) (grievant who was discharged, without investigation, on basis of one missed shift and grand theft report, entitled to back pay from date of discharge to date 8 days later on which he had opportunity to discuss matter with employer; arbitrator noted that "[e]mployer made no effort to interview Grievant or communicate with the police department to discuss the charges against him").

[322]Alpha Beta Co., 91 LA 1225, 1227 (1988) (Wilmouth, Arb.).

Chapter 6

Conclusion

What is the rule or maxim management should follow when attempting to exercise jurisdiction over an employee because management does not like that employee's lifestyle or off-duty conduct? Management has an interest in regulating the private lifestyles of its employees to the extent, and only to the extent, that a nexus exists between the employee's job and the off-duty conduct or, alternatively, between the employer's product or reputation and the conduct at issue. Absent a clear showing that the private, off-duty, personal activities of the type that would otherwise be protected by the constitutional guarantee of privacy, speech, or association have a nexus or relationship to an employee's job performance or the employer's product or reputation, the decision should be in favor of the employee. The better rule was stated by Arbitrator Richard Bloch in an unpublished (February 17, 1981) decision. In reinstating a 13-year flight attendant who while on layover, removed a picture from its frame in a motel room, Arbitrator Bloch stated the rule this way:

> The Company may properly be concerned when the private actions of employees inevitably involve it in an unflattering light. At the same time, the Employer is neither the guardian nor the monitor of its employees' off-duty actions. Basic precepts of privacy require that, unless a demonstrable link may be established between the off-duty activities and the employment relationship, the employee's private life, for better or for worse, remains his or her own.

255

Saying a nexus exists will not make it so, although as the job in question becomes more public or customer-oriented the employer's burden in sustaining a discharge is easier than when the job does not involve dealing with the public. Indeed, in some public services (police, fire, and to a lesser extent, elementary and secondary education and the postal service) the test and corresponding burden sometimes have been little more than a mere declaration that the employee's activity is disgusting to management and any reasonable citizen.[1] The more unconventional the activity (a sixth-grade teacher dressing and undressing a mannequin in his backyard, for example), the easier it becomes for management to sustain a dismissal, although we believe that courts and arbitrators should proceed with caution before concluding that public or private hostility to the individual's conduct alone justifies actions against the individual.[2] Constitutional rights, as well as rights under a collective bargaining agreement, should not be determined by polling the public or the immediate work force. The views of co-workers and the public may be relevant, but rarely, if ever, should such considerations be dispositive of dismissal in any forum.

Public management will and should have a more difficult time regulating an employee's weight, dress, sexual preferences, and other "addictions" in nonmilitary-type organizations. However, paramilitary organizations, like police and fire, are arguably freer to do as they please when the employee does something unconventional, but not always. In the private sector, where constitutional restraints are absent,[3] management is accorded significant discretion and power to

---

[1]A case illustrating how balances may get resolved in favor of management because of an unconventional lifestyle of an employee is *In re* Grossman, 316 A.2d 39, 9 FEP Cases 1291 (N.J. Super. Ct. App. Div. 1974), where a 55-year-old music teacher, otherwise found mentally and physically fit to teach, was nevertheless terminated as "incapacitated" after undergoing sex-reassignment surgery that changed his external anatomy to that of a female.

[2]*Cf.* Palmore v. Sidoti, 466 U.S. 429 (1984) (holding that private biases and the possible injury they may inflict could not be considered in deciding whether a child should be taken from white mother living with black man); Egger v. Phillips, 710 F.2d 292, 317 (7th Cir.), *cert. denied,* 464 U.S. 918 (1983) ("the unpopularity of the issue surely does not mean that a voice crying out in the wilderness is entitled to less protection than a voice with a large, receptive audience").

[3]Hudgens v. NLRB, 424 U.S. 507, 513, 91 LRRM 2489 (1976) ("It is, of course, a commonplace that the constitutional guarantee of free speech is guaranteed only against abridgement by government, federal or state. [citation omitted] Thus, while

affect employees' lifestyles, although Title VII, the Rehabilitation and Americans with Disabilities Acts, and state statutes (where they exist) provide some restraint. To the extent the employer is organized and the union has negotiated a grievance arbitration provision in a collective bargaining agreement, arbitrators may provide greater protection to employees than the courts applying a mere rational basis test. Most arbitrators apply more than a rational basis test, especially in discharge cases that involve off-duty conduct issues. They may not announce they are doing this, but a fair reading of the cases supports this proposition. Whether arbitrators in general apply what would amount to a strict scrutiny test when fundamental rights are at issue is open to question. We believe that numerous arbitrators have taken the road in favor of employees when lifestyle issues are litigated before them.

Furthermore, because arbitrators often look to the law for guidance,[4] they may tend to accord more discretion to private sector

---

statutory or common law may in some situations extend the protection or provide redress against a private corporation or persons who seek to abridge the free expression of others, no such protection or redress is provided by the constitution itself.").

[4]Frequently, either at the parties' request or even on his own motion, an arbitrator will fashion an award patterned after external law. *See, e.g.,* City of San Antonio, 90 LA 159 (1987) (Williams, Arb.) (holding that order impermissibly restricted officer's constitutionally protected off-duty sexual conduct); Memphis Light, 98 LA 1123, 1126 (1991) (Goldman, Arb.) ("If the Employer is covered by the Vocational Rehabilitation Act, it would be proper to assume that the contractual standard of "just cause" encompasses the Act's requirement that the employer take affirmative action to employ and advance qualified handicapped individuals."). Indeed, in the federal sector, remedies must conform to the mandates of law and agency regulations. *See* Cornelius v. Nutt, 472 U.S. 648, 119 LRRM 2905 (1985) (holding that federal sector arbitrators are required to follow the "harmful error" rule contained in 5 U.S.C. §7701(c) (2) (A) (1988)).

The obligation and authority of a labor arbitrator to interpret and apply the law when resolving grievances have been the subject of much discussion and litigation, both in the legal and arbitral forum. *See generally* Archibald Cox, *The Place of Law in Labor Arbitration, in* THE PROFESSION OF LABOR ARBITRATION, SELECTED PAPERS FROM THE FIRST SEVEN ANNUAL MEETINGS OF THE NATIONAL ACADEMY OF ARBITRATORS, 1948–54 (BNA Books, 1957); Bernard Meltzer, *Ruminations About Ideology, Law, and Labor Arbitration, in* THE ARBITRATOR, THE NLRB, AND THE COURTS, PROC. OF THE TWENTIETH ANN. MEETING, NAT'L ACADEMY OF ARBITRATORS (1967); Richard Mittenhall, *The Role of Law in Arbitration, in* DEVELOPMENTS IN AMERICAN AND FOREIGN ARBITRATION, PROC. OF THE TWENTY-FIRST ANN. MEETING, NAT'L ACADEMY OF ARBITRATORS (1968); Mike Sovern, *When Should Arbitrators Follow Federal Law? in* ARBITRATION AND THE EXPANDING ROLE OF NEUTRALS, PROC. OF THE TWENTY-THIRD ANN. MEETING, NAT'L ACADEMY OF ARBITRATORS 29 (1970).

Scheinholtz and Miscimarra argue that is it not instructive to ask whether arbitrators

companies in regulating lifestyles where constitutional restraints are not operative, but this practice is questionable and there is no policy basis for the rule. Public and private sector management should adopt an objective nexus rule between the "misconduct" engendered by the employee's lifestyle and job performance. One court, rejecting the traditional approach of unquestioned deference to management, and applying a balancing approach to the problem, stated the better test this way:

> [N]o longer is there the unquestioned deference to the interests of the employer and the almost invariable dismissal of the contentions of the employee. . . . [T]his court [is] no longer willing to decide these questions without examining the underlying interests involved, both of the employer's and the employee's as well as the public interest, and to the extent to which our deference to one or the other serve[s] or disserv[es] the needs of society as presently understood.[5]

Hard evidence that an employee's lifestyle—be it heterosexual or homosexual affairs, sexual practices, dress, weight, religion, or other addictions—affects job performance should be the rule, not the exception, before an employee's discharge is effected.

The most difficult cases are those where the employer asserts that the employee may be mentally and physically capable of performing his or her job with the same degree of competency as before the "infirmity" came to light, but that the actions of the employee

---

should or should not consider statutory issues. Rather, if arbitration is to be preserved as a practical, expeditious, and final method of dispute resolution under the parties' labor agreement, the more helpful query is "whether and under what circumstances is the consideration of statutory issues appropriate." Leonard L. Scheinholtz & Philip Miscimarra, *The Arbitrator as Judge and Jury: Another Look at Statutory Law in Arbitration,* 40 ARB. J. 55 (June 1985). Noting that it is impossible to formulate a single answer to the question of whether statutory issues should be considered by an arbitrator, the authors maintain that 4 "guiding principles" should be considered when determining whether an arbitrator should consider external law: (1) the authority of the arbitrator (whether the parties explicitly indicate in their labor agreement that an arbitrator cannot consider issues of external law); (2) arbitral expertise (is the arbitrator competent to resolve the statutory issue?); (3) arbitration hearing procedures (will the parties' procedure enable a fair resolution of the issue?); and (4) the finality or "nonredundancy" of the procedure (does an arbitrator ever perform a service by handing down an award that from its inception is predestined not to be enforced?). *Id.* Consideration of statutory issues will vary depending on a balancing of these factors.

[5]Woolley v. Hoffmann-LaRouche, Inc., 491 A.2d 1257, 1260–61, 1 IER Cases 995 (N.J. 1985).

have harmed the employer's reputation and, if allowed to continue with the company, will significantly affect the company's business or even subject the employer to civil liability. How does management demonstrate that its reputation has been harmed, or is in danger of being harmed, if the employee is allowed to continue working? How can the City of Detroit, for example, ever demonstrate that its reputation has been damaged by an employee's lifestyle if the determining criterion is loss of business revenue?[6] The same question can be asked of any provider of services in an oligopolistic market. At a minimum, management should be allowed to submit evidence that the conduct was the subject of notoriety in the media or, alternatively, that the conduct was so outrageous (sexual relations with a retarded child, for example)[7] that no employer operating in its relevant labor market could permit the employee to continue working and, at the same time, value its reputation. Under this test, an off-duty drug offense may be found to have no effect on the company's reputation if the offense received little media coverage and the individual does nothing but take care of the grounds. A different result may be reached if the drug offense is reported in the media and the employee services customer accounts or repairs commercial airplanes.

Unless management has a deep pocket and is unconcerned with the potential liability of an improper dismissal, an individual who engages in a lifestyle privately, unobtrusively, and without publicity should not be subject to discipline simply because of that lifestyle. The decision makers within the system—employers, courts, agencies, and arbitrators—will presume that there are areas of an employee's private life that are beyond the scope of management's inquiry and regulation. The problem in the lifestyle area is that consensus as to what constitutes appropriate employer concern diminishes when one moves from the abstract to the specific. At one end of the spectrum we have a hard time believing that the Georgia Attorney General really has a legitimate interest in the sleeping partners of the lawyers

---

[6]*Cf. Big Problems and an Image to Match,* N.Y. TIMES, Oct. 1, 1992, at A8 (discussing image of Detroit: "She [a Florida woman visiting a downtown church] asked if we needed an armed guard to walk the guests to the hotel").

[7]Gulf Oil Co., Port Arthur Refinery, 85-1 Lab. Arb. Awards (CCH) ¶8234 (1984) (Stephens, Arb.) (sustaining discharge of grievant for having sex with retarded 12-year-old girl).

in his office[8] or that the Mad River School Board should be concerned that a high school guidance counselor, who never proselytized bisexuality, announces to her officious secretary one morning while in "a good mood" that "she was in love with a woman."[9] At the other end, a different result can be supported when the Assemblies of God, a sectarian employer, discovers that its popular evangelist is again having sexual relations with prostitutes,[10] or when a local school board learns that a secondary teacher is regularly having sex with her students in the faculty lounge,[11] or when middle-school teachers in North Kingstown, Rhode Island, start marrying their students.[12] We can also understand the concern of the administration at Phillips Exeter preparatory academy when its drama teacher is charged with distribution of child pornography.[13]

---

[8]*Lesbian Lawyer Who Wed Mate Is Denied a State Job by Georgia,* N.Y. TIMES, Oct. 6, 1991, at A18.

[9]Rowland v. Mad River Local Sch. Dist., 470 U.S. 1009, 1016 n.11 (1985), 37 FEP Cases 188 (Brennan, J., dissenting from denial of *certiorari.*).

[10]*Woman Says Swaggart Asked Her for Sex,* N.Y. TIMES, Oct. 13, 1991, at A17; *cf. Judge Cuts Baker's Prison Term, Making Parole Possible in 4 Years,* N.Y. TIMES, Aug. 24, 1991, at A10.

Any priest or chaplain will have a difficult time convincing a court that it should intervene in an employer's decision to terminate his services. *See* O'Connor Hosp. v. Superior Court, 240 Cal. Rptr. 766, 2 IER Cases (Cal. Ct. App. 1987) (opinion withdrawn); Miller v. Catholic Diocese of Great Falls, 728 P.2d 794, 1 IER Cases 1152 (Mont. 1986).

[11]*See, e.g.,* Chicago Bd. of Educ. vs. Shuey, No. 81-102-6 (Nov. 5, 1981) (Dunham, Arb.) (unpubl.) (upholding the dismissal of a tenured teacher for having sexual intercourse with a 17-year-old student "over five and under thirty times").

[12]*See* Michelle Green, *Outraging the Town He Taught In, a Rhode Island Teacher Marries His Former Sixth-Grade Student,* PEOPLE, Oct. 3, 1988, at 23.

After being dismissed from the teaching position at Wickford Middle School for marrying Kimberly Ryan, 17 (a little more than six years after they met at school when Ryan was 11), Frederick Hone, then 46, served a 3-month sentence for violating a court order that he stay away from Ms. Ryan. Hone is reported to have commented, "Since when do I need the permission of the Superintendent or the school committee before I marry?" *Id.* Responding to the allegation that he violated the trust placed in him as a teacher, Hone stated "I didn't violate any ethics. What do they think? That I'm going to marry all of their daughters or something?" *Id.*

The Hones are now in divorce proceedings with Mr. Hone facing felony charges of threatening the judge who jailed him. *Teacher Who Married Pupil Now Regrets It,* UPI, Nov. 14, 1989.

[13]*Pornography Jury Convicts Teacher,* N.Y. TIMES, Oct. 10, 1992, at 6 (discussing the conviction of Larry Bateman, former Phillips Exeter drama teacher).

Somewhere in the middle of the spectrum are the hard cases that are said to make bad law.[14] There may be something to the argument that management does have an interest in the health of its employees who elect to smoke or maintain morbid obesity, especially if they are covered under an employer-paid insurance policy. While a common law court is likely to side with management on both issues (based on the response of arbitrators in grievances involving unilaterally imposed smoking regulations on the job[15] and their rulings in weight cases)[16] we believe that arbitrators would rule the other way. There may likewise be validity to the argument that a public sector employer has an interest in whether its police and fire fighters are following the "straight and narrow" and not associating with organized crime figures or drug dealers, or if its elementary teachers appear in *Screw Magazine*. In both cases management is likely to prevail when interests are subjected to a balancing test, although decisions the other way are not uncommon.

More difficult are the cases where management concerns itself with the off-duty criminal activities of its employees (drug offenses, shoplifting, domestic violence, or sex offenses). Once an employee places management on notice of instances of physical violence, a company should not be compelled by a court or arbitrator to take a chance on that employee knowing that repeat behavior may result in tort liability for negligent retention. Clearly, some crimes, by their very nature, imply an impairment in the employee's judgment, stability, reliability, or social capabilities in performing the job, notwith-

---

[14]Northern Sec. Co. v. United States, 193 U.S. 197 (1904) (Holmes, J.) ("hard cases make bad law").

[15]*See, e.g.,* Johns Manville Sales Corp. v. Machinists Local 1609, 621 F.2d 756, 104 LRRM 2985 (5th Cir. 1980); Union Sanitary Dist., 79 LA 193 (1982) (Koven, Arb.) (holding that total ban against smoking unreasonable); Nicolet Indus., 79-2 Lab. Arb. Awards (CCH) ¶8398 (1978) (Rock, Arb.) (holding that smoke-free rule would result in termination of long-term addicted employees); Schien Body & Equip. Co., 69 LA 930 (1977) (Roberts, Arb.) (holding that health could not be improved if employees could smoke on breaks and at lunch and if nonsmokers still exposed to smokers).

[16]Man Roland Inc., 52 LA 175, 180 (1991) (Speroff, Arb.) (reversing transfer of obese employee where "[c]ompany did not prove a direct or significant correlation existed between the grievant's corpulence and the number and/or types of sustained injuries he experienced"); American Airlines, Inc. & Flight Attendants (APFA), No. SS-345-89 (1990) (Sinicropi, Arb.) (unpubl.); United Airlines, Inc. & Flight Attendants (APFA), No. 64-08-1-130-90 (1990) (Sinicropi, Arb.) (unpubl.).

standing mitigating factors. The easy cases, for example, include off-duty child abuse by a nursery-school teacher; armed robbery by a plant guard; marijuana use by an air traffic controller; marijuana dealing by an airline pilot. In this respect management should be permitted to resort to expert testimony to demonstrate to a trier of fact that an employee's off-duty conduct will affect its customers. Further, we see no infirmity when triers take judicial-type notice that some misconduct, by its very nature, impacts the organization. At the same time, it is possible that some crimes may make the employee better suited to perform his job, such as a high-school guidance counselor who is convicted of off-duty vehicular homicide while alcohol impaired.[17] In the words of one court, "the teacher who committed an indiscretion, paid the penalty, and now seeks to discourage his students from committing similar acts may well be a more effective supporter of legal and moral standards than the one who has never been found to violate those standards."[18]

Cases involving speech are particularly troublesome (except to academic communities), such as when a private university, attempting to diversify its student body, disciplines a professor for writing and expressing views outside the classroom that "on average, blacks are significantly less intelligent than whites."[19] A local school board, with a large minority student body, may likewise become apprehensive when its faculty, even though unidentified, starts wearing white robes with peaked hoods while attending political rallies in Louisiana.[20] Should management be compelled to take a wait and see posture to determine if religious and racial hatred and intolerance (undeniably the message of the Klan) will spill over to the classroom? Must management wait for actual complaints by its student body or declining enrollments or headlines in the *Chicago Tribune* before *any* discipline can be imposed? Are the rules different in New Orleans, Louisiana, than in Nowhere, Iowa? There are, of course, always more

---

[17]West Monona Community Sch. Dist., 93 LA 414 (1989) (Hill, Arb.) (sustaining discharge of guidance counselor/coach for off-duty vehicular homicide conviction while testing positive for cocaine and alcohol).
[18]Board of Educ. of Long Beach Unified Sch. Dist. v. Jack M., 566 P.2d 602, 606 n.4 (Cal. 1977) (citations omitted) (holding 16-year teacher, arrested for homosexual solicitation, not per se unfit to teach).
[19]*White Professor Wins Court Ruling*, N.Y. TIMES, Sept. 5, 1991, at A20.
[20]*Klan Challenges Law Against Hoods*, N.Y. TIMES, Apr. 15, 1990, at 12.

questions than answers in the lifestyle and privacy area ("it's a maze"),[21] especially when management's regulations impact what, in the public sector, otherwise would be First Amendment rights. The solution, as suggested by Arthur Ross,[22] is not found by comparing the intrinsic culpability of different employees or even the nature of the offense, although both present a good starting point for an analysis of the problem by employers, courts, and arbitrators. Whatever the perspective of the decision maker, the better rule remains: Absent an objective evidentiary nexus between the off-duty conduct and on-the-job performance, any inquiry or regulation impacting lifestyles should be effected with caution.

---

[21]It's a maze, this garden, it's a maze of paths
   Meant to lead a man astray
   Take a left, and then, turning left again's
   How a soul can find the way.
LUCY SIMON & MARSHA NORMAN, *It's a Maze, on* THE SECRET GARDEN (Columbia Records, 1991).
   [22]*See* A. Ross, *Discussion, The Criminal Law and Industrial Discipline Labor Arbitration—Perspectives and Problems, in* PROC. OF THE 17TH ANN. MEETING, NAT'L ACADEMY OF ARBITRATORS (1964).

Table of Court Cases

Index

About the Authors

Marvin F. Hill, Jr., is currently Professor of Industrial Relations at the College of Business Administration and Adjunct Professor of Law, Northern Illinois University, and an Iowa attorney. A member of the National Academy of Arbitrators, Hill is actively engaged in arbitration and mediation in the public and private sectors. He has contributed articles to many journals, including *The Arbitration Journal, Labor Law Journal, Indiana Law Review, DePaul Law Review,* and *Oklahoma Law Review.* He has also co-authored (with Anthony V. Sinicropi) three other books, *Management Rights: A Legal and Arbitral Analysis, Evidence in Arbitration,* and *Remedies in Arbitration,* all published by The Bureau of National Affairs, Inc. (BNA).

James A. Wright, currently an attorney in private practice in Peoria, Illinois, is a member of the Illinois Bar Association. Wright has contributed articles to *Northern Illinois University Law Review, Missouri Law Review, The Proceedings of the Forty-Fifth Annual Meeting, National Academy of Arbitrators,* published by The Bureau of National Affairs, Inc. (BNA), and the *Illinois Bar Journal.* Wright is also a member of the Industrial Relations Research Association, the American Bar Association's Section of Labor and Employment Law, and of its committee on Labor Arbitration and the Law of Collective Bargaining Agreements.